IRRESPONSIBLE FREAKS, HIGHBALL GUZZLERS

UNABASHED GRAFTERS

A Bob Edwards Chrestomathy

IRRESPONSIBLE FREAKS, HIGHBALL GUZZLERS & UNABASHED GRAFTERS

A Bob Edwards Chrestomathy

In which are collected extractions from the Calgary Eye Opener, Wetaskiwin Free Lance, The Channel *(Boulogne-sur-Mer, Fr.) & other* estimable broadsides helmed by the late R. C. Edwards, M.L.A.

FACT, GOSSIP & FICTION
FOR
READERS OF THE ENGLISH LANGUAGE

"Flashes of merriment that were wont to set the table on a roar."
—Shakespeare.

Prepared & Selected,
with Introductory Essay, by James Martin

PREFACE BY ALLAN FOTHERINGHAM

Brindle & Glass Publishing Ltd.
Est. 2000
Calgary, Canada
"Stock Guaranteed to be Always Fresh"

Library and Archives Canada Cataloguing in Publication
Edwards, Bob, 1865-1922.
Irresponsible freaks, highball guzzlers & unabashed grafters : a Bob
Edwards chrestomathy... / prepared & selected, with introductory essay, by
James Martin ; preface by Allan Fotheringham.

ISBN 0-9732481-5-7

I. Martin, James, 1970- II. Title.

PS8459.D8A16 2004   C818'.5209   C2004-904867-8

Cover images: Upper: Shedden Collection: *Eye Opener*, May 16, 1908. Lower: MacEwan/Foran
Collection, *Eye Opener*, May 20, 1911.
Interior images: Please see list of images on page 258
Cover and interior design: Ruth Linka

The editor and publishers would like to extend grateful thanks to Ian Doig, Tine Modeweg-Hansen,
Fiona Foran, Bonnie Shedden, and the staffs of the British Library, Calgary Public Library,
Glenbow Archives, Library and Archives Canada, McLennan Library at McGill University.
Rats to the Bibliothèque nationale de France. This book would simply not be possible without the
toil and scholarship of Dr. Hugh Dempsey and Dr. Grant MacEwan. Dr. Dempsey's *The Best of Bob
Edwards* (Hurtig Publishers, 1975) and *The Wit & Wisdom of Bob Edwards* (Hurtig Publishers, 1976)
were, and remain, essential in keeping Bob Edwards's memory—and most crucially, his words—alive
in an amnesic world. Similarly, the late Dr. Grant MacEwan's *Eye Opener Bob* remains an invaluable
resource and inspiration. Thank you, sirs, for your tireless efforts.

Canada Council   Conseil des Arts
for the Arts   du Canada

Brindle & Glass acknowledges the support of the Canada Council for the Arts
and the Alberta Foundation for the Arts for our publishing program.

Brindle & Glass Publishing
www.brindleandglass.com

Brindle & Glass is committed to protecting the environment and to the responsible use of natural
resources. This book is printed on 100% post-consumer recycled and ancient forest-friendly paper.
For more information please visit www.oldgrowthfree.com.

1   2   3   4   5   07   06   05   04

PRINTED AND BOUND IN CANADA

This volume preserves Bob Edwards's original spelling, some of which may strike the contemporary reader as eccentric or just plain wrong. "Fyle" for "file," that kind of thing. We mention this only so you don't go thinking you've discovered a typo. We need no such attitude, friend. You may also find it unusual that a Scottish-educated man, writing in Canada, would often employ "American spelling." We think so, too. While we're at it, we should probably mention something about how Bob Edwards was way ahead of his time in terms of environmental awareness. Meaning: he recycled jokes left & right. In this spirit, we have intentionally duplicated eleven entries. The discovery of all eleven is a task ideally suited to bored children on rainy days.

Something else to know: all dated references to the *Wetaskiwin Breeze* or *Wetaskiwin Free Lance* do, in fact, refer to reprints of same appearing in the *Calgary Daily Herald*. Finally: all unspecified references point to the *Eye Opener*. If, say, you see a lonely "April 20, 1912," your brain should amend it to read, "*Eye Opener*, April 20, 1912."
It's okay to say this aloud.

The editor dedicates this volume to Dr. R. M. Shaw, a Bob fan from way back.

CONTENTS

Preface *by Allan Fotheringham* ix

Introduction *by James Martin* 1

Foreword *by Bob Edwards* 9

Chapter One: Aeolian Harps Struck by Lightning 11
    In which the reluctant politico slings a nasty pen before succumbing to the hustings.

Chapter Two: The Outcast's Prayer 43
    In which your esteemed editor & bottle-washer questions holy authority,
    parses scripture, & forgets his flask in the pews.

Chapter Three: Jopplebunky, Frukkledumky, Chucklesnorter, Jinks 61
    In which your crackerjack reporter provides all the local news that's fit to fabricate.

Chapter Four: Rushing The Growler 88
    In which your in-house boozological artist implores, "Don't do as I do. Do as I tell you."

Chapter Five: Nemeses... 120
    In which the editor of the great Christian organ throws mud, holds a grudge, has a change of
    heart — & defends himself against charges of being a libeller, a character thief, a coward, a
    liar, a drunkard, a dope-fiend & a degenerate.

Chapter Six: A Lovely Little Tablet of Corrosive Sublimate 150
    In which the editor of the E.O. himself (applause) furthers the legend of …
    the editor of the E.O. himself (wild applause)

Chapter Seven: Gloating Over Pictures of the Hootchee-Kootchee 169
    In which your uncle rails against sexual predators, police brutality, land-sharks,
    movie-house chatterboxes, & other big issues of the day.

Chapter Eight: The Builder of Bum Jokes 182
    In which the village weekly editor gives away dogs, cooks cats, & likens the Kaiser to a skunk.

Chapter Nine: Letters from a Badly Made Son 203
    Being the collected correspondence of Albert "Bertie" Buzzard-Cholomondeley,
    remittance man & gopher rancher.

Chapter Ten: The Most Unfortunate of Men 221
    In which your uncle regales the masses with the picaresque exploits of Peter J. McGonigle,
    hard-luck editor of the Midnapore Gazette.

Hindword *by Bob Edwards* 251

Dramatis Personae 252

A Bob Edwards Chronology 254

Endnotes 256

List of Illustrations 258

About the Editor 260

PREFACE

> Now I know what a statesman is: he is a dead politician and what this
> country needs is more of them.

The scourge of Ottawa is *Frank*, the little mag printed on toilet paper that fascinates the chattering classes—read only by only the politicians and the journalists in the town that fun forgot, all of them pleading and praying that they are not in it that edition.

It of course is patterned on London's *Private Eye*, wherein all the hacks on Fleet Street send in the dirt and insider info—who is sleeping with whom, who is sucking up to the editor—all the stuff that is talked about in the pub but no one will print.

Alas, they all are 102 years behind the original, when someone invented a paper that frightened into catatonic rage the Establishment. At one stage, Bob Edwards's *Calgary Eye Opener* was denied the mails. The CPR—which made Western Canada— banned it from its trains.

> Probably the saddest thing about Ottawa is the number of fourth-rate
> intellects applied to first-rate problems.

Robert Chambers Edwards was born in Edinburgh, educated at a private school and Glasgow University, and continued his studies in Berlin, Paris and Rome. Before he was thirty, he had seen most of Europe, had edited a small journal on the Riviera, and ended up in Calgary and the long bar of the Alberta Hotel.

For twenty years after 1902, the *Eye Opener* frightened the bejeezus out of Calgary, which reaching a peak circulation of all of 35,000. It could—and did—make or break politicians. R. B. Bennett blamed his 1904 federal defeat on Edwards. The mayor of Calgary declined to run for re-election when the *Eye Opener* opposed him.

> Some fellow made the remark the other day that there was small differ-
> ence between the Liberal and Conservative parties. There is all the dif-
> ference in the world. One is in and the other is out.

On October 6, 1908, three weeks before a federal election, Daniel McGillicuddy's rival *Calgary News* launched a personal attack on Edwards in a two-column despatch on the front page.

It called the *Eye Opener* "a disreputable sheet, the mission of which has been blackmail and the contents of which are slander and smut." Edwards was a "ruffian, a moral leper" and a "skunk whose literary fulminations cannot but create the impression that he was born in a brothel and bred on a dungpile."

Further? Edwards was "a 'four-flusher,' a 'tin horn' and a welsher on poker debts." In future issues it was promised that "I intend to show that he is a libeller, a character thief, a coward, a liar, a drunkard, a dope dealer and a degenerate." Great stuff! We love it. Edwards sued for libel, got a nominal hundred bucks, and McGillicuddy sold his paper and sunk like a rock.

Perhaps whiskey really does improve with age, when it gets a chance.

The only fight Edwards could never win was against the bottle. "Every man has his favourite bird," he wrote. "Ours is the bat." When the *Eye Opener* failed to publish for several weeks, everybody in town knew he was drunk. A lifetime bachelor, Bob Edwards at age fifty-three married a twenty-four-year-old girl from Glasgow. It was not successful, as he was too set in his ways and would or could not modify his drinking ways.

The *Eye Opener* has no defence to offer for the booze traffic. It is a bad business; none worse. We've been there. Nobody can tell us anything about it that we don't already know and our frank opinion is that the complete abolition of strong drink would solve the problem of the world's happiness.

True to his strange dilemma, with his active support—and his tremendous power—the necessary legislation was passed and, in 1916, Alberta became a dry province. As Hugh Dempsey described him, this "Robin Hood of the pen" was sympathetic to the plight of prostitutes, pushed for more relaxed divorce laws, spoke against sweatshops and fought Sunday "blue" laws. He threatened to print the name of a Calgary dentist who was molesting young women. He exposed real estate firms that were selling fraudulent properties. He revealed that the second-worst dive in Calgary was never raided by the cops because it was owned by a local millionaire.

The *Eye Opener* wants to know why the Grits are so anxious for another term of power. There is nothing left to steal. Everything is cleaned up. What, then, can be their object?

He sat for only one session of the legislature, speaking only once: his maiden speech, in which he condemned the damning effects of the illegal liquor traffic and Prohibition, which he now opposed. It was a subject he knew well.

In a short time—undoubtedly because of boredom—Bob Edwards died in 1922, at age fifty-eight. Rudeness is a great tradition in literature, and the better for it. One would be glad to be thrown into the class of Rabelais, Swift, Shaw, Twain. As Knowlton Nash characterized him, Edwards reflected the approach of Lincoln Steffens and H. L. Mencken rather than that of Walter Winchell and Matt Drudge. He was a muckraker who found lots of muck to rake.

There still is.

—Allan Fotheringham
Toronto, May 31, 2004

Getting Over the Big Pants
Or: Why You Should Read Bob Edwards (1860–1922) Today

An Appreciation, With Digressions

Let's unpack the ten-dollar word straight off.

Chrestomathy.

Which is to say: "Chrestomathy?!"

Which is to say: "Whuh?"

Why not call a *collection of writings* by Robert "Bob" Chambers Edwards ... uh, a "collection," maybe? Compendium? Reader? Greatest Hits? Honest to Pete, there's a host of synonyms that don't necessitate constant spellchecks.

Ergo, whence chrestomathy?

~~It sounds neato.~~

~~I wants to looky more smarter than me is.~~

To make a point.

Aaaaaaaand we'll get to that point soon enough. But right now, since we're waxing catechistic, let's go full-steam with the Joe Friday routine. Then we'll talk answers.

When discussing Bob Edwards, why nick a word closely associated with *an entirely different writer*? And by "closely" I mean "inextricably." And by "another writer," I mean "H. L. Mencken."[1] Almost a generation removed, the two gents' careers overlapped by less than twenty-five years, and there's no evidence of cross-pollination—so what does a Scottish ex-pat writing in the relative wilds of nascent Western Canada (BE) have to do with a Baltimore logophile (HLM)?

Heaps, really. Both men were tip-top stylists trading in snappy copy. Both predominantly worked in ephemeral (or, in today's parlance, recyclable) mediums. Both gleefully spelunked the depths of the human condition, surfacing with sententious observations.[2] (Knowlton Nash, for one, hypothesized[3] that Edwards would side with

---

[1] *A Mencken Chrestomathy* (New York: Knopf, 1949), billed as "his own selection of his choicest writings," stands as the definitive Mencken volume—enough so, at least, that editor Terry Teachout revived the term for *A Second Mencken Chrestomathy* (New York: Knopf, 1995).

[2] With a difference. Although Edwards's "A woman's best female friend will tell you more to her disadvantage in a minute than you can learn from her worst enemy in a month" (*Bob Edwards' Summer Annual*, 1922) philosophically mirrors Mencken's definition of a misogynist—"A man who hates women as much as women hate one another"—the former swaddles its black heart in softer diction. The distinction is important. Some of Edwards's opinions, de rigeur for his time, may now be outmoded; ditto Mencken but, as Daniel Raeburn noted ("In Memoriam: HLM," *The Baffler* no. 16), the Sage of Baltimore "was also an asshole."

[3] In *Twenty-two Provocative Canadians* (Calgary: Bayeux Arts, 1999), Kerry Longpre and Margaret Dickson, eds.

Mencken's assessment that "journalists represent the human character in complete disintegration.") Drawcansirs on the page, both men were extraordinarily generous in private. Not ideological kin by any stretch, one can nevertheless find parallels, if only in their freethinking resistance of the brass collar, between Edwards's lower-case-conservatism-slash-proto-Progressivism and Mencken's Tory anarchism. Other overlaps abound: loved the sauce, loathed Prohibition, took youngish brides at relatively advanced ages, enjoyed cigars.

Feh. It doesn't much matter how (dis)similar Edwards and Mencken are, anyway. Which brings us to that point mentioned earlier (whew!), and the reason behind this whole logodaedaly stunt: far from forgotten, Mencken is not only still read today, he's read with an *élan vital*. Bob Edwards, by contrast, is a high-profile invisible man. He deserves better.

Mencken's broader cachet may have cratered[4] in recent years, but his thumbprint is all over an exciting subset of contemporary American literature. *The Baffler*, *McSweeney's*, *Acme Novelty Library*: the anxiety of Mencken's influence—not in terms of politics per se, and certainly not emulous of Mencken's more stomach-churning opinions,[5] but manifested through fussy attention to precise diction, merry gadzookery, and delicate graphic design[6]—hangs heavy o'er the lot of them. Even indie alt-country record labels[7] are in on the action, telegraphing their own iconoclastic leanings by flying Mencken's freak flag. Heartwarming stuff, this, to see the smart kids cherrypicking literary history, and having a blast doing it.

Meanwhile, north of the 49th, we have our very own literary rapscallion, and a mighty good one at that. Yet Bob Edwards is, at best, a well-preserved museum piece. His name lives on, sure: witness Alberta Theatre Project's annual Bob Edwards Award and Luncheon, and Bob Edwards Junior High—even CBC Radio One's morning show (the Calgary Eyeopener) shoots a knowing wink in Edwards's direction. His name lives on. Exactly: his *name*. Too bad nobody's *reading* Edwards.

Not that people can be faulted for not reading him anymore. The present volume excepted, Bob Edwards's words have been out of print for nigh on three decades. Unless you're inclined to scare up a copy of Hugh Dempsey's *The Best of Bob Edwards* (1975) or *The Wit and Wisdom of Bob Edwards* (1976), or trudge

[4] In terms of academic interest, at least, Mencken isn't exactly MLA conference fodder. For likely reasons, see the following note.

[5] For all his literary muscle, Mencken had racist leanings. And sexist. And anti-Semitic. (Raeburn's "asshole" assessment errs on the side of generosity.) I by no means wish to suggest that HLM's contemporary acolytes (discussed herein) adhere to such beliefs.

[6] As if flagrant parading of Menckenian phrases such as "boob jubilee" weren't giveaways, Raeburn (in the aforementioned "In Memoriam: HLM"), renders explicit Mencken's influence on the new literati. He should know, too; Raeburn is *The Baffler*'s typographer and was the braintrust behind likeminded publication *The Imp*.

[7] Well, at least one. I'm thinking of the Bloodshot Records ad bearing the Mencken aphorism, "There comes a time when every man feels the urge to spit on his hands, hoist the black flag, and start slitting throats."

through metres of microfilmed back issues of the *Calgary Eye Opener*, it's a safe bet you're not reading Edwards. Geez, even a recent book billing itself as "in the spirit of Bob Edwards"[8] was frustratingly light on the man's *actual words*, instead favouring cursorily retro-fitted Mendelson Joe profiles and the like.

After working on European tourist rags for a spell, Bob Edwards moved[9] to Wyoming in 1882, then onto Canada shortly thereafter. His *Wetaskiwin Free Lance* debuted on the Alberta newspaper scene in 1897. He followed it with the *Wetaskiwin Breeze* and *Alberta Sun*, before locking into what would become his final, longest-lasting, and certainly most popular title. At its height, the *Calgary Eye Opener* boasted a circulation over 34,000[10] and later spawned a successful series of *Bob Edwards' Summer Annuals*. To say Edwards and his *Eye Opener* had a loyal following is to teeter on understatement. Even decades after his death, there was enough interest to inspire no less than four hour-long, primetime TV mini-movies.[11] Yes, there was a time when "Bob Edwards" meant more than nineteen points[12] in Scrabble. Today: unthinkable.

It shouldn't be this way. (Downright criminal, even.) After all, people still *like* the old-school lit-humourists. Really, they *do*. Not just Mencken, either. Stephen Leacock, whose career is oft dangled[13] as what "could've been" had Edwards 86'd the booze, is *still read*. Bill Nye, the Wyoming funnyboy (not the ditto-named "science guy") who served as literary rolemodel[14] for Edwards, is *still read*. William Cowper Brann, the Texan lit-loudmouth shot in the back by an irate reader, is *still read*.[15] Dig? And I won't even get into Mark Twain, the patron saint of all such two-fisted, hard-drinking North American laffmongers. (P.S. He's *still read*.)

Bob Edwards could, and should, be read today.

I don't mean to flatter myself, but I'm a bit of an expert at Not Reading Bob Edwards. So, since he loved to write himself into the narrative, indulge me in a personal aside. Think of it as ...

---

[8] The aforementioned *Twenty-two Provocative Canadians*—fine for what it was, but a tease nonetheless.

[9] Readers seeking a fuller portrait are advised to consult Grant MacEwan's *Eye Opener Bob*, available in a handsome reissue from Brindle & Glass.

[10] *Eye Opener*, April 20, 1912.

[11] "The Eye Opener Man" (a.k.a. "Gadfly West") aired January 11, 1959 on *General Motors Theatre*, followed on February 12, 1961 by "The Eye Opener Man and Robert Burns" (co-starring Timothy Findley!). *Playdate* aired two more sequels: "The Eye Opener Man and the Wages of Zinn" (March 14, 1962) and "Grubstake for the Eye Opener Man" (May 18, 1964). The teleplays were written by Leslie McFarlane, and starred Mavor Moore as Bob. Moore reprised the role for the January 3, 1964 episode of *Telescope*.

[12] Yeah, yeah: names don't count. I'm trying to build drama here.

[13] In *Lawyers and Laymen of Western Canada* (Toronto: Ryerson Press, 1939), Roy St. George Stubbs supersizes this idea, supposing that Edwards narrowly avoided "his name echoing down the corridors of history linked with the names of such masters of satire as Rabelais, Tobias Smollett and Jonathan Swift."

[14] In *As the World Wags On* (Toronto: Ryerson Press, 1950), Arthur R. Ford claims that Edwards personally confessed this influence to him.

[15] Gotta cop to an illative leap: Leacock, Nye, Brann are all still in print, and some even appear on undergrad syllabi—but neither point, particularly the latter, ensures they're "being read."

4

"How I Learned To Stop Being A Maroon and Love The Bob."

Five years ago: I knew Bob Edwards by name only, and that name was synonymous

The Big Pants. Get over them.

with "someone I don't care to read." It was a lack of interest I'd cultivated for most of my reading life. As a kid, the family basement bookshelves—an elephants' graveyard of volumes retired from service—warranted regular exploration, yielding a spectrum of sublimity ranging from F. Netter's medical illustrations to Thurber. That's where I first encountered Bob Edwards, via a hand-me-down copy of Grant MacEwan's biography, *Eye Opener Bob.*[16]

That book went unread (by me, at least) for years. Whenever I came close to, y'know, *actually cracking it*, I shrank from the cover's Ponderosa typeface, my synapses conjuring vast webs of negative associations. Epochs described as "gay" and/or "gaslit." Barbershop quartets. Products billed as "olde-fashioned" and other faux folksy (fauxy?) affectations. Mother Tucker's menus. Waxed handlebar moustaches. Un-fun field trips during which some petticoated history buff claims chewing pine bark is "just as good as gum." Player pianos. Sleeve garters. Be-derbied "ragtime professors." The list goes on, on, on.

My sweeping derision, already ample, became boundless when I stumbled upon the "classic" photo of Bob Edwards. It's the one *everyone* uses: a middle-aged Bob reclining in a chair. Cigar in right hand. Left thumb hooked into pocket. Necktie askew. And, most crucially: *extremely large trousers* yanked up to *just below the man-teats*. Oh! those big pants. Damn! those big pants.

The big pants tore it. Nope, this Bob Edwards character was not for me. Back on the shelf with you, sir, right between *Blood Red the Sun* and the 1973 Guinness Book.

In short: I'd never read a word Bob Edwards had written.

[16] In case you missed it earlier: *Eye Opener Bob*, handsome companion volume, Brindle & Glass, et cet.

Didn't know what I was missing.

Dumb kid.

It wasn't until researching *Calgary: Secrets of the City* (Vancouver: Arsenal Pulp Press, 1999) that I finally came 'round. Thinking, with shamefully typical arrogance, "There *must* be *something interesting* about Bob Edwards that I can use in my book," I took the unprecedented step of *reading some of his stuff.* Then: more. And: yet more. Followed by: more still. I borrowed Dempsey's two Edwards books from the Calgary Public Library so often I finally resorted to haunting used bookstores until I found copies.

Is there a word that means "I can't believe this guy was writing such gold a hundred years ago"? (Something clunky and German, maybe?) Let's just go with "wow." Bob Edwards revealed himself the sun in my orrery of oh-so-late-20th-C. pop-cult obsessions. To my great surprise, this old big-pants-wearer was one hep cat, and presciently so. As a literal iconoclast, Edwards set the stage, and packed a lunch, for idol-smashers like Lenny Bruce and Bill Hicks. (What, after all, was Edwards's "What a number of people there are in Calgary who abhor one another. Good God! And yet everybody, but us, attends church,"[17] if not a philosophical forerunner of Bruce's "Every day people are straying away from the church and going back to God"?[18]) In turns of language fireworks—i.e., to twist a Bukowski line, of banging the typewriter like it was a percussion instrument—Edwards could easily go the distance against a Lester Bangs. (The only diff being where the latter railed against Lou Reed, the former targeted the Kaiser and the CPR). As for Edwards's pitch-perfect send-ups of journalistic convention (see Chapter 3), there was only one reasonable conclusion: the *Calgary Eye Opener* was the *Onion* of the 1910s.

I could, and shall, go on. I love how Edwards blurred the boundaries between fact/fiction—caring not a whit for reader confusion—by interspersing real with fake, and sometimes even combining the two. (His accounts of the fictional Peter J. McGonigle, collected in Chapter 10, are a great example of Edwards's delight in obfuscation.) I love how he freely indulged in self-promotion[19] and mythmaking[20] (see Chapter 6). I love how he turned newspaper tropes upside-down to craft his bleak micro-narratives of urban desperation, doing for the gossip column what Edgar Lee Masters did for the verse epitaph. I love how his unique bi-cultural perspective (as a Scot transplant in Alberta) created such hilarious veracity in his fictions about British remittance men (see Chapter 9), wringing yuks out of ignorant well-

[17] *Wetaskiwin Free Lance*, as reprinted in the *Calgary Daily Herald*, March 6, 1899.
[18] *The Essential Lenny Bruce* (New York: Ballantine Books, 1967), edited by John Cohen.
[19] A point I don't feel I adequately stressed in *Calgary: The Unknown City* (Vancouver: Arsenal Pulp, 2001, $18.95 Cdn.).
[20] Although he copped a quote from *Hamlet* (Act V, Scene I) for the title page of his *Summer Annual* series, Edwards' self-presentation bore more than a whiff of the Falstaffian.

to-dos and scheming ne'er-do-wells alike. I love that Edwards could nurse a bitter, entertaining grudge for *years* (see Chapter 5), sometimes succumbing to rapprochement (as in the case of his feud with R. B. Bennett), sometimes stopping just shy of foxtrotting on his opponent's grave (as with Dan McGillicuddy). I love how he could work himself into a serious lather over a book-printing scandal in one issue[21]—then, in another, riff on the stupidity of other people's names.[22]

Bob Edwards has a P.R. problem. "He was drunk," grouse the Monday-morning lit-critics as they rally 'round the water-cooler. "He'd write one opinion one day and write the opposite the next day."[23] "Codswallop!" I sez. (Also: baloney! bushwa! bollocks!) I mean, well, *yeah*, the guy *was* a totally self-destructive pisstank, but he was refreshingly honest, and entertaining, about it. (If you want to play the macho-gonzo-onslaught card, that scourge of undergrad writing programmes everywhere, compare the booze-soaked self-mythologizing of Chapters 4 and 6 to Hunter Thompson's *Vegas* excesses. Once again, Bob was ahead of the curve in terms of selling that particular sizzle.) More interesting, however, was *how* his views changed[24] over the years—not overnight, as the naysayers claim, but over *time* and with difficulty. (See Chapter 4 for Edwards's complicated relationship to Prohibition.) What his critics deem reprehensibly labile, I see as thoughtfully fluid. Chalk up another in the "love" column.

Any study of Edwards's work is complicated by his apparent disdain for the banausic side of running a newspaper (he was notoriously slack about keeping back issues of his various titles; many are believed lost forever), with financial and boozological concerns further contributing to an already erratic publishing schedule. Establishing a timeline of his life is no easier, especially since most biographical details originated with Edwards himself—and he was, after all, the chap who sneered, "Some men spoil a good story by sticking to the facts."[25]

While preparing this volume I had difficulty reconciling Edwards's claims of having apprenticed on a French Riviera tourist rag (titled either *The Channel* or *The Traveller*, depending on what you read) with the dates listed on extant copies of same. Was this guy some kind of pre-teen wunderkind, or was funny business afoot? Taking a cue from the unrelenting journos of *www.thesmokinggun.com* (motto: "Paving the paper trail"), I dug up Edwards's birth certificate. Yep. Turns out he lied about his birthday, shaving four years off his age. This not only cleared the fog, it added a much-welcome meta-level to my already sizable appreciation:

---

[21] *Eye Opener*, June 13, 1908, among others.
[22] *Eye Opener*, January 27, 1912. "Blessed be the Roberts," indeed.
[23] Actual quote, uttered by an actual user of the Glenbow Archives!
[24] To best reflect such evolutions of thought, the entries in this volume have been ordered chronologically, on a chapter-by-chapter basis.
[25] *Eye Opener*, January 25, 1919.

Bob's D.O.B. fudgery plants him squarely in the nifty tradition of Old West reinvention,[26] suggesting he saw his Scottish exodus as the opportunity for a new life in a new world. (And c'mon—compared to the polyonymous antics of fellow self-mythologizers, his transgression is paltry.) Love it to bits!

(As for the *Channel / Traveller* mystery: taking into account the revelation about his birthday, it's most possible Edwards was behind both publications—but the only known copy of *The Traveller*, a brittle specimen held by the Bibliothèque nationale de France, is hard/impossible to access. The book you now hold, however, *does* include never-before-reprinted selections from *The Channel*. Three cheers, and all that.)

But before we commence the tearful hugging, a clarification: I ain't no Bob apologist. Not every word/sentence/article out of Edwards's pen was a keeper, a common byproduct of writing to deadline. (Even to an apparently moveable deadline of his own self-employed making.) There's also the matter of, ahem, questionable material. On the sexist/racist front, I'm happy to report Edwards was no Mencken.[27] (N.B. Don't judge Bob on the posthumous, Minnesota-based incarnation of the *Calgary Eye Opener*.[28] He had nothing to do with that crud.) But, as much as Edwards was ahead of his time, he was also a man *of* his time … and it occasionally[29] showed. Hey, he never claimed to be perfect.

Even during his lifetime, Edwards was dogged by—and perhaps secretly shared— notions that if only he got his act together, if only he gave whiskey the big kiss-off, he could write Something Really Important. Even the first posthumous issue of the *Eye Opener* (November 25, 1922), entirely devoted to memories of Edwards, includes the backhanded eulogy, "It is unfortunate that his written humor was all in the ephemeral form of current periodical writing, and contained so little which can be preserved." And that came courtesy of longtime Edwards pal W. M. Davidson!

---

[26] It's a helluva club. Frederick Philip Grove (Felix Paul Greve), CanLit chronicler of marsh-settlers and psychic ants, revamped everything except his initials. Chief Buffalo Child Long Lance (Sylvester Long) and Grey Owl (Archie Belaney) spun bestselling memoirs from phony-baloney Native lineages. Will James (Joseph Ernest Nephtali Dufault) was the most apple-pie American cow-scribe ever produced by St-Nazaire D'Acton, Quebec. And I shan't even broach relative newcomer Adolf Hungry Wolf (né Gutohrlein), because he could kick my rump.

[27] Nor a Leacock, for that matter.

[28] Legal and financial specifics are unknown, but shortly after Edwards's death, his widow struck a deal with Harvey Fawcett to publish a new *Calgary Eye Opener* in Minneapolis. (Fawcett would later make pop-culture history when he converted the neo-EO's sister mag, *Captain Billy's Whiz Bang*, into a superhero comic—thus begetting Shazam! and, by catchphrase association, Gomer Pyle.) The titular "Calgary" lingered despite the relocation, but this new publication was the *Eye Opener* in little more than name. With the exception of a few reprinted chestnuts from the writer inexplicably rechristened "Old Bob" ("the grand old man of British-Canadian fun"!), the digest-sized mag traded in sexual double-entendres, pickaninny vernacular, and racist illustrations. I mention this strange offshoot only because it threatens to overshadow its namesake: famed Scrooge McDuck cartoonist Carl Barks cut his teeth at the Minnesota *Eye Opener*, making back-issues coveted collectors items. The *Calgary Eye Opener* Mk. II ran until the early 1940s. For more on this era, consult Geoffrey Blum's *The Unexpurgated Carl Barks* (Hamilton Comics, 1997).

[29] E.g., the infamous comic-strip (*Eye Opener*, September 21, 1918) depicting immigrating Mennonites as "slackers" and "shirkers." Such stuff may warrant inclusion in a book, just not this one.

True, Edwards's more topical writings haven't aged well (as such, they've been used very sparingly in this volume). And to be fair, Davidson goes on to say "the editor of the *Eye Opener* was a genius," but …

I'm going to haul out "codswallop" again.

Let's be done with this notion of Bob Edwards as a wasted talent, a Leacock who never was, the little engine that could but didn't fuggin' feel like it. That's hooey, plain and simple, but let's not belabour the point. Now it's time for the writing (including—plug! plug!—never-before-republished correspondence, speeches, and comics[30]) to do its thing.

Like Bob Edwards himself once said, upon reporting the death of a piano tuner renowned for his barnyard impersonations: "Not lost, but gone before."[31]

—James Martin
Montréal, July 31, 2004

[30] Dictated by Edwards and drawn by Donald McRitchie, George Fraser, and Charles H. Forrester.
[31] *Eye Opener*, April 10, 1920.

FOREWORD

For fear the infuriated public may think that the idea of getting out this Annual originated with myself, I wish it distinctly understood that the crime was instigated by my fool friends.

These friendly goofs took the position that the world having become bolshevik, craved a form of mental pabulum which was simple, crude and easy of comprehension. Difficult stuff like Carlyle's *French Revolution*, Haeckel's *Riddle of the Universe* and Wesley Rowell's *Life of John L. Sullivan*, so the goofs claimed, had had their day as selling propositions, and there now was a great opening for something really punk.

This line of argument, while disconcerting to a proud man, contained enough elements of truth to make me fall for it. So here you are!

Most of the contents of this parvum opus have already appeared in the *Calgary Eye Opener* during the bygone years, but this should not make much difference, because there are a devil of a lot of people who never saw nor heard of this remarkable western family journal. Universal enlightenment, one must regretfully admit, is a good deal of a myth.

In order to properly attune your mind, dear sir or madam, to a full appreciation of this brand of literature, it is of the highest and most vital importance that you throw a few stiff jolts under your belt before starting in. In other words, have a smile "on your own" first, in case you fail to get a smile out of the book.[1]

R.C. Edwards

---

[1] *Bob Edwards' Summer Annual,* 1920.

CHAPTER ONE
Aeolian Harps Struck by Lightning

In which the reluctant politico slings a nasty pen
before succumbing to the hustings

"The irresponsible freaks, highball guzzlers and unabashed grafters who have been ruling the roost in Ottawa for so long are at last within measurable distance of their finish. The soup vats are ready."
—*Eye Opener*, January 2, 1903

Be it known that queer pairings abound in Bob Edwards's political makeup. To wit— Non-partisanship boasts & extreme axe-grinding: they giggle like old school chums!

Keen excogitation & knee-jerk response: exchange Christmas cards every year!

Anti-elitism & anti-Egalitarism: more than passing acquaintances, if you decode the sexual insinuation being hereby insinuated!

Born of the Gilded Age, Edwards's small-p populism[1] cast a suspicious eye on all levels of government, his obsession with "graft" veering toward pathological. Readers seeking herein a delineation of Edwards's shifting views on rural-urban economic integration ... are advised to look elsewhere.[2] But those seeking juvenile mudslinging—or scuttlebutt about the Minister of the Interior's adulterous dalliances, or primordial Edmonton bashing—will find their spirits duly elevated in the pleasing manner of faeces-crusted swine. Oh! and how! Those seeking Edwards's own 1921 campaign missives: equally fortunate!

---

[1] Max Foran ("Bob Edwards & Social Reform," *Alberta Historical Review*, Summer 1973, vol. 21, no. 3) suggests Edwards to be a sort of proto-Progressivist, albeit clearer of eye and less given to evangelical fervor than his ideological progeny.
[2] But, if you insist: the August 24, 1912 *Eye Opener* is a good place to start.

Wetaskiwin—A ridiculous rumor was afloat last week that Mr. Simpson, our M.L.A. (much lamented absentee) was coming up our way on a visit. It beats everything how preposterous rumors of this kind get started. The next thing we hear will be the Prince of Wales coming over to give a fete champetre at the Hobbema Agency. (*Wetaskiwin Free Lance*, January 27, 1898)

It is an extremely cold day in Calgary when there is no election on, one just ended, or one just pending. When I was there, they were filling in the time by taking a vote of the people as to whether liquor licenses should be granted to a couple of restaurants. The local lady temperance advocates objected to the granting of these additional licenses because their men-folk already had an elegant sufficiency of facilities for getting sloppy; the churches opposed it on the broader grounds of morality; and the hotel proprietors objected to it on coffee grounds—that is to say, they were not going to see their bar receipts affected by interlopers if they could help it. Thus Susan B. Anthony, Dr. Parkhurst and Steve Brodie, by joining hands, won the day by a majority of 13 in a poll of 323. Selah! (*Wetaskiwin Breeze*, March 13, 1901)

In Scotland we used to get spoonfed on the Shorter Catechism, but out here, in order to enable the children to make headway in the battle of life, they have to be taught the GRAFTER Catechism. If they don't study this deeply they cannot expect to hold their own when they reach manhood. Here, for example, is an extract from the Grafter Catechism as taught in Macleod:

Q: Why is it that Colin Genge can walk around the town with his hands in his pockets, doing nothing, and getting $7.00 a day for being inspector of a great public work like the Macleod Court House when he knows as much about building and architecture as an elephant knows about algebra?

A: He is president of the Macleod Liberal Association.

Q: How is it that Dr. Forbes gets something like $160 a month for attending the N.W.M.P. (having replaced Dr. Kennedy without notice) and acting as Dominion health officer?

A: He is a member of the executive of the Macleod Liberal Association.

Q: How is it that Malcolm Mackenzie can hold about 50,000 acres of coal lands that are unsurveyed under fictitious or borrowed names against men with money?

A: He is president of the Southern Alberta Liberal Association.

Q: Why did Thomas Scott get the contract for repairing the Custom House, after it was partially destroyed by fire, on a bid of $1,300 when Lambert's bid for the same work was $750?

A: He was a member of the Macleod Liberal Association.

Q: How is it that Grady got the con-

It is one thing to win a bet on an election and another thing to get the money.[1]

tract (on an appalling profit basis) for supplying hay, groceries and general supplies to the N.W.M.P.?

A: He was the most prominent member of the Liberal executive. Being the whole push he had a strong pull.

And so on and so on to the last page of the Grafter Catechism. (January 2, 1903)

The long eight months sitting of parliament seems to have impoverished quite a number of Liberal members from Ontario and Quebec. They are clamoring for another short session, not with a view to enacting any new laws or any nonsense of that kind, but with the view, frankly expressed, of getting their little old fee of $1,500. Why not send 'em all a cheque and be done with it? A short session of the nature indicated, assembled purely on reimbursement lines and nothing else is scarcely consonant with the dignity of Canada as a nation. (January 2, 1903)

We read in *A Book of Curious Facts* that a pair of hogs will in ten years have a progeny of 6,634,838 pigs. And yet Mike Moran and Peter McDermott, two talented citizens who are too fly for their own good, have each been married for a longer period than that and have only two children apiece. According to the above, they ought to have 6,634,838. (July 25, 1903)

"Of course, I understand," said a member of the British parliamentary party visi-

Aylesworth Election Act --- Loaded Dice.
Cliff, de barkeep: " Well, that settles it.   You're both stuck ! "

tors to a gentleman in Ontario, "that the winning party at your elections is the one that gets out the most voters."

"Not at all, not at all. It's the one that puts in the most votes." (October 24, 1903)

The difference between American and English politics is shown by Mr. Chamberlain having the gout. Over in the States a man who expected to appeal to the masses and to suggest extra taxes on their grub-pile wouldn't dare to have the gout.

It is lucky that only the finer kinds of wines like Burgundy, Maderia or Old Port, give a man the gout. If whiskey had this effect, half of Canada would be down with gout right now. (October 24, 1903)

If we can only keep up slinging a nasty pen and terrifying the government into hysterics, we may yet be offered a job on

Most of the government's troubles come from trying to uphold the blunders it makes.[2]

the railway commission or sent at a salary of $50 a day and expenses to examine into the prune crop in Oklahoma for the information of the Agricultural Department. (January 9, 1904)

Raw grafts lead to reform. Why not have the reform first? (June 25, 1904)

The cabinet minister lay dying, dying of fatty degeneration of the gall. A grave-eyed clergyman took his hand and softly said—

"My friend, your hour is fast approaching. Now is the time to repent."

"But I have nothing to repent, old cockle. I have been a successful man and die rich. What more do you want?"

"But your sins—"

"Oh, they're all right. My sins were protected by technicalities in such a way that they were not sins at all. They couldn't get the best of your Uncle Dudley."

"Great Scott, man, at this awful moment have you no desire to repent and enter the kingdom of heaven, to dwell with the angels by the great white throne for all eternity!"

"Well, I dunno. They tell me there is a big Conservative majority up there."

"So there is, so there is."

"In that case I think I'll join my party in hell. It will be more home-like. Goodbye, I don't suppose I'll see you there. Be good. Take care of yourself. You'll find a box of cigars over there. I'll be smoking myself shortly. Goodbye.

Oh—ah—um—oh—gimme breath—I guess the croaking act is on—I'm going—sure pop—tell finance minister—settle—bar bill—Russell House—goodbye, old chap—wow!—the cheese is off."

The nurse pulled down the blinds and the clergyman went out into the hall to tell the sobbing crowd that the lamented statesman had passed away peacefully, buoyed with the hope of a blessed immortality and murmuring with his dying breath a prayer for his beloved country. (June 25, 1904)

At the polling of a popular vote on some bylaws last Monday, Judge Travis distinguished himself by voting three times. (July 2, 1904)

Numerous letters from the north continue to pour in warmly endorsing Edmonton as the future capital.

Point Barrow, latitude 72, August 2, 1904

Dear Sir—

At a meeting of the Board of whalers held here last night in Trader Johnson's store—Jacob McGuffy, captain of the Calamity Jane, chairman—a resolution was passed thoroughly endorsing the proposition to make Edmonton the capital of the new province. It was the sense of the meeting that such a step might have the desired effect of opening up vast fields of ice here for settlement by a good class of walruses. If you need a new corporation seal we shall be happy to send

Why is it that all the rogues manage to get into the other political party?[3]

you down a live one. Hoping that the mortality from delirium tremens is on the decrease in your burg, I am

Yours respectfully,

Peter Markham,

Secretary,

Point Barrow Board of Whalers

Dunvegan, Peace River

Nov. 12, 1904

Sec'y, Edmonton Board of Trade

Dear Sir—

We, the white settlers in this picturesque country, beg to send our congratulations to Edmonton on the prospect of her becoming the capital of the new province. It will be of supreme benefit to all four of us. We have hardly done a thing up here since you so kindly forwarded us that bewildering army of Edmonton Route Klondykers six years ago. Their bleached bones have mostly all been buried by this time. You fellows made a big killing on that occasion, in more senses than one. Among a number of comic cuts pasted on the wall of our store is the Bulletin's celebrated "map" of the Edmonton Trail to the Klondyke. It is a never-failing source of amusement during the long evenings. You certainly deserve to have the capital for your cheek.

Yours respectfully,

Rufus McGonigle

J. B. Thornton

Abe Slupsky

Fort Resolution, Great Slave Lake

Oct. 5, 1904

Sec'y, Edmonton Board of Trade

Dear Sir—

Over a bottle of Florida water last night the Hudson Bay factor and myself decided that Edmonton was the proper place for the new capital. If Calgary is the selection it will take us three days longer to procure a consignment of Florida water, Peppermint, Jamaica ginger, Painkiller and Red Ink. The other white settler on the lake, Jimmy Simpson, would agree to our decision were he here. He owes us a big Florida water bill.

Yours truly,

Owney Geoghegan,

Director of Chores, Fr. Resolution

(February 4, 1905)

The secret of Clifford Sifton's mysterious disappearance and inexplicable absence from his duties in the House is slowly leaking out from within the inner circles of Ottawa society.

The absence of the right honorable gentleman, it would appear, has been

Probably the saddest thing about Ottawa is the number of
fourth rate intellects applied to first rate problems.[4]

due not so much to reasons of ill health as to one of those misdemeanors which are so happily featured in Smollett's works, and to which Moses made special reference on one of his justly celebrated tablets of stone.

That people should make a fuss over a little thing like this is all the more astonishing in view of the depressing fact that precisely similar jocularities are occurring every day (and night) under the very noses of husbands in every town or every country on the face of the globe. Calgary is well up with the band wagon. Sometimes you get caught and sometimes you don't.

The fact that Clifford is a staunch Methodist may be an explanation but it's no excuse. What puzzles us is that he got caught at all, for he don't drink. (February 25, 1905)

Clifford Sifton has resigned, ostensibly over the school question. This implies a conscience on the part of Clifford. The idea of Clifford resigning on the ground of conscientious scruples is laughable to the extreme. What has really made him resign is the trouble he has gotten himself into over a married woman in Ottawa. It is a Sir Charles Dilke case over again.

Now then, take a long breath and prepare for the little telegraphic despatch announcing that Clifford is about to take a trip to Europe for his health.

The story of Sifton's escapade, wherein he seems to have been ministering to the Interior in great shape, reads like some of the spicier cantos in *Don Juan*. The outraged husband is Walter Mackay, son of the late millionaire, William Mackay, the old lumber king of Ottawa. It appears that Mackay started for Montreal one night, but for some reason turned back and spent the evening at the club instead. Returning to his residence about two o'clock in the morning, he tried to open the front door with his latchkey, but the latch was fixed on the inside so that he could not get in. So away he went round to the back door of the house to see if he could get in that way.

Approaching his back door, what was his surprise to see it cautiously opened from the inside and a big, tall man issuing therefrom. "Burglar!" thought Mackay, and quickly seized hold of the mysterious unknown. It was pretty dark at the time, and the two of them tussled and rolled all over the backyard. Finally, to Mackay's astonishment, a ray from the moon revealed the sinister feature of the minister of the Interior.

"Hello, Sifton! What are you doing here this time of night?"

"Oh," quoth Clifford, panting, "your wife was in trouble over some legal matters and sent for me to discuss them."

"Well, that's strange," said the husband, scratching his nose dubiously. "I suppose it's all right, though."

Next day, however, Mackay put on his thinking cap, and rather foolishly aired the story downtown, telling all his friends about it. Their ill-concealed

Governments of the world are learning among other things that the people want to eat with considerable regularity.[5]

amusement showed him but too plainly that they had for some time been alive to what he, husbandlike, had been blind. Then the row began.

A private conference was held at the Mackay home, among those present as consiliators being Father Whalen, Archbishop Duhamel and Sir Wilfrid Laurier. Father Whalen next day took the lady to her former home in Quebec. Sifton just about this juncture left for the West, this stirring incident having taken place shortly before the elections. Ye Gods, and we didn't know about it!

By the time he returned the scandal had become the property of the politicians and of the inner circles of society, though no newspaper dared breath a word.

What between the uproar in his own family and the demands for reparation on the part of the husband, Clifford thought it was up to him to duck his nut. He left for parts unknown, and remained away from his seat in parliament, neglecting his duties and pretending he was in a sanitarium somewhere for his health. His health must have been all right about this juncture, if we know anything about this line of business.

Sifton returned to Ottawa a discredited man and handed in his resignation. That is the whole story. For the benefit of his dupes, the public, it was arranged that he should retire with dignity under the benign wing of the school question. This, in sporting parlance, is a stall. In connection with it, we rise to remark—"Rats!"

That is the plain, unvarnished tale. Not unlike one of Balzac's droll stories, eh? There are one or two other versions, one in particular which is far racier than the foregoing, but we prefer to confine ourselves to what we know to have actually happened.

In the meantime, we understand, hubby has filed a suit for divorce. The governor general, we presume, could not stand for his most important minister being co-respondent in a divorce case, though certain of the other cabinet ministers are not a whit more virtuous than Cliff. We are ruled over by a fine gang at Ottawa. (March 4, 1905)

It is discouraging to learn that several respectable, honest-minded persons in this town were highly indignant last week over the *Eye Opener*'s frank exposure of the toodledyumpty-ido pranks of the ex-minister of the Interior, the representative of the North-West in the cabinet. They are apparently of the opinion that there is nothing particularly undesirable about having our destinies, the destinies of the Territories and indeed of the whole interior of Canada, placed at the mercy of a wily reprobate who has debauched the wife of his friend, wrecked a home and dishonored himself in the eyes of right-thinking people. If they think it is all right, then their moral code needs a thorough overhauling.

It is furthermore right and proper that the common people of our land should

All that country has to do to improve the Government at Ottawa is to change it.[6]

know these things. The public should be told all about the type of men whom the fortunes of politics have placed in charge of the affairs of this nation, and, as their virtues—if they have any—are extolled, so should their vices—if flagrant and dangerous to society—be exposed.

We have no apology to offer, nor retraction to make. (March 11, 1905)

It is very odd that the appointment of Lougheed to a more conspicuous position in the Senate should have been almost immediately followed by a resolution in the House to abolish the Senate altogether. Sir Wilfrid, however, did the next best thing. He said he wouldn't object to the adoption of the United States principle of fixing the tenure of office enjoyed by senators. It is six years over in the States. If the office were elective, it would take a man very good at figures to count the number of votes Lougheed wouldn't get. (May 5, 1906)

In Okotoks, where no village official has ever yet been accused of graft, the inhabi-

Senator Blockheed

tants are wondering whether they are better than other people or only duller. (June 16, 1906)

The functions of parliament nowadays would seem to be confined to investigating graft scandals. The members have little or no time even for incidental legislation. At Ottawa the time is all taken up with squabbles and resultless debates on alleged land grafts, insurance scandals, fake immigration companies, illegal timber grants, Arctic grub-wine-cigarette polar expedition expenditures and so forth and so forth. No legislation beyond the enactment of a Sunday observance law which makes it permissible to breath of the Sabbath between certain hours. (June 16, 1906)

They are getting very toney up in Edmonton, with their fair and inauguration festivities in sight. Many of the smart young ladies have taken to wearing openwork shoes to display pretty hosiery, a charming idea. It is now in order for the men of Edmonton to start wearing open-

Ho hum! It's a dull world. Can't somebody start a scandal or something?[7]

work hats for the purpose of displaying the wheels revolving in their heads. (August 25, 1906)

Should the weather prove unfavorable to outdoor amusement, the visitors are earnestly recommended to make a study of the mayor and the Calgary Douma. Before doing so, however, it would be advisable to pay a series of lightning visits to the booze foundries in order to mitigate the shock attending a sudden contact with Brains. The local butcher shops likewise supply brains, but these are worth the price 15¢ a pound; and the purchaser does not have to pack home an alderman. There never was, and never will be, anywhere else on God's green earth, such an outfit to be found running at large. They are the limit. The whole outfit is best described as a fierce proposition. The mayor, who will go down to history as the promoter of the magnificent reception recently tendered by the city to the governor general, and who is the leading authority on prunes, has evidently succeeded in filling the members of his Douma up to the neck with the commodity with which his name is so closely identified. The manufacturers will not fail to notice this prevailing characteristic among our city fathers. The taxpayers of the city who thoroughly recognize the overwhelming business ability and broad reach of their aldermen think it grossly unfair that these men in their efforts to guide the destinies of the city's business should be precluded from

securing the millions that would inevitable flow into them if they would only attend to their own damned business, and will, before the end of the year, reward them for their disinterested labors in the city's interests by translating them to the higher plane of private citizenship, if an infuriated populace does not run them out of town in the meantime.

Anybody who knows the Calgary aldermen would never kick about the czar killing off his Douma. It might make a good precedent. (September 22, 1906)

Graft is that portion of the money taken by a public official to which his constituents tumble. It becomes graft only when discovered. Otherwise the fattening of the bank account is merely the result of good business investments. (February 9, 1907)

The way some of those political grafters quietly heel themselves against a rainy day reminds one of the custom prevalent amongst dogs of burying bones in the backyard. (March 23, 1907)

Sample debate in the Canadian House of Commons:

Mr. John Herron (Alberta) moved the following resolution: That the circumstances attendant upon the murder of his mother-in-law by John T. Peterkins, inspector of swamp lands in Ungava, and subsequent disgraceful distribution of her body amongst the wolves of that

Canadians want to be good friends with the Americans, but not to be a good square meal for them.[8]

country, and the continued retention of said official in office without investigations, reflects discredit upon the government and should receive the disapproval of this House.

Mr. Bourassa asked if the government intended to take any steps to remove from office John T. Peterkins, inspector of swamp lands in Ungava, who had recently become notorious through strangling his mother-in-law in her shack, cutting up her body into small chunks, filling them with assafoetida and strychnine, and setting them out as bait for wolves, on which there was a bounty of $1 a head. By these shocking means Peterkins had collected $145 from the government.

Hon. Frank Oliver: The honorable member has been misinformed as usual. It seems a pity that honorable members do not obtain more exact information on which to base their charges against the government. The number of pelts paid for by the government in this district was only 85, of which number Peterkins had a claim against 53. This money has not yet been paid over to the claimants, but the government sees no reason why Peterkins' claim should not be settled along with the rest. The territory of Ungava has for years been terrorized by large and ferocious bands of wolves, and the department considers that Mr. Peterkins has done the state no small service in ridding his district of the number of wild animals indicated.

Mr. Bourassa: Will the right honor-
able the minister of the interior inform the House whether or not the government proposes to retain Peterkins in the public service with this awful charge hanging over his head.

Hon. Frank Oliver: I cannot see whereof consists the "awful charge." No complaint has reached the department that Mr. Peterkins neglected the swamp lands of Ungava while sporadically engaged in trapping wolves. If it can be shown that the swamp lands were in any way neglected or allowed to fall into decay through lack of inspection, then the department may take steps to make further investigation into the matter. (Cheers.)

W. F. Mclean: That is not the point. The charge has been made that this government official, Peterkins, strangled his mother-in-law and fed her to the wolves. Surely such a monstrous piece of business should be looked into.

Sir Wilfred Laurier: I must protest against the time of the House being frittered away in this manner. Mr. Peterkins' record as a swamp inspector is unrivalled in the annals of swamp lore. The Ungava swamps have thriven as they never throve before, under his inspection, and it does credit to his nobility of disposition that he devoted his leisure moments to the eradication of wild animals which had become a menace to the country. (Loud cheers.)

Mr. Bourassa: The right honorable the premier begs the question. It has been proven beyond the shadow of a doubt that this man murdered his mother-in-

A clever politician is one who is able to cover up his tracks.
Otherwise he is just a dam grafter.[9]

law and threw her in sections to the wolves. What is the government going to do about it? Surely I am entitled to an answer to my question.

Hon. Frank Oliver: The department lays down no hard and fast rules as to what kind of bait shall be used in the case of wild animals on whose pelts a bounty is paid by the government. Ordinary meat is liable to be in a frozen condition at this time of the year, and poison administered through the medium of frozen meat takes longer to work on the vitals of a wolf. Even frozen hard it takes quite a while to melt after being swallowed, and the animal may stray for miles before the strychnine gets in its fine work, thus rendering impotent the work of the man who is out for the pelt. Fresh meat, when obtainable, is the most efficacious form of bait. Old trappers of the Hudson's Bay are unanimous in this opinion. Mr. Peterkins is one of the most zealous servants in the employ of the government and I certainly see no reason for his removal, as suggested by my honorable friend. I might mention that Ungava is a great lone land, and it is sometimes hard to find a competent man to remain there for any lengthy period in the government service. However, I am happy to be in a position to inform the House that Mr. Peterkins is about to take himself another wife and will shortly marry into a prominent Esquimaux family.

M. S. McCarthy: Out of bait again?

W. F. Maclean: Wants some more fresh meat probably.

The Speaker: Order, order.

In concluding the debate, the premier asked the government members to vote down this frivolous resolution, as it involved an attack upon the government.

Upon a division being taken, Mr. Herron's resolution was defeated by a vote of ninety to forty-one.

The House then went into Committee of Ways and Means. (March 23, 1907)

We understand—ha ha!—that—haw haw!—R. J. Stuart—ah-yaw-haw—ha ha ha!—is going to run—oh oh ha ha—for alderman—ha ha ha ha ha ha!—Ha ha ha ha ha ha—ha ha ha ha ha ha ha ha ha! (June 13, 1907)

R. J. Stuart is again a candidate. Ward 4 has our sympathy in this hour of its affliction. (June 13, 1907)

The Provincial parliament will assemble at Edmonton on the 15th. This solitary annual attraction should draw the usual number of visitors to the capital, unless the novelty has worn off. Calgary sits serenely and by virtue of its manifold attractions smiles indulgently at this lone event in the Uncle Tom-East Lynne beleaguered city up north. Dear Edmonton, will that hold you for a while? We are not sore. We do not need the parliament. There will be an occasional visitor straggling in without it. Have a drink on the House. (January 4, 1908)

One is forced to the conclusion that there is too much politics in politics.[10]

22

The attention of Providence having been called to the infamous condition of Canadian politics, it was some time ago decided to send Moses down to take a hand in the game and, if possible, introduce a little purity by way of a novel experiment.

Moses, it will be remembered, was at one time leader of the Opposition in his own country, and, like that other lawgiver of glorious, pious and immortal memory, R. B. Bennett, succeeded in having only two of his candidates, Messrs. Joshua and Caleb, representing his party in the House.

The local House in Egypt was even then strongly Conservative, the Israelite party being in an almost hopeless minority—Joshua and Caleb, like Hiebert and Robertson, vying for the leadership. Moses, however, had an excellent record as a legislator, having brought down no less than ten measures which are still on the statute book.

On his arrival at Ottawa, where he brought letters of introduction to Sir Frederick Borden, Charles Hyman and

Portrait of Stuart without his dress suit.

Clifford Sifton, Moses registered at the Russell House and was at once taken up by the more prominent members of the Liberal party. Sir Wilfrid assured him that he would speedily find him a constituency. He was fortunate, also, in being endorsed by Emerson, who invited him to spend a weekend at St. Lawrence Hall, and, altogether, "a pleasant time was had."

The electoral district of Midnapore, Alberta, happened to be open owing to the retirement of the sitting member, Peter J. McGonigle, who had been ordered by his physicians to take a post-alcoholic course at the Calgary Boozorium. Moses was declared elected to that constituency by acclamation.

In introducing the new member to his constituency, Mr. McGonigle, the retiring member who, we understand, is slated for a position in the excise department as inspector of bonded warehouses, in a voice broken with emotion and booze, took occasion to refer to his own record as representative of the growing and thriving district of

Politics, you will observe, is the science of guessing right.[11]

Midnapore. During his regime a new wing had been added to Ed Johnson's hotel and a new set of bar fixtures installed. It was now the finest bar west of the Great Lakes. He might refer to several other local improvements, but would not weary his hearers with matters of lesser importance. The *Midnapore Gazette* would soon be on a paying basis, and the new member might always rely on its loyal support. Some of his hearers had, no doubt, already heard of Moses, who was a contemporary of Sir Richard Cartwright and the Hon. R. W. Scott. Although not a native of Canada, Moses' record would stand inspection. He was of good birth, being connected with a very good old Egyptian family, the Pharaohs of Bullrush Park. Should he fall in line with the existing conditions which have made the Liberal party what it is today, he predicted for him a bright future.

The party then adjourned to Mr. Johnson's hostelry, where a sumptuous banquet, consisting of pig's cheek and cabbage and unlimited lush, was partaken of with hearty relish.

Moses, M.P., left at midnight on the Okotoks Flyer for Ottawa, taking his seat with him and arriving at the capital in time to take part in the debate on the timber limits.

Having listened attentively to Mr. Ames for about three days the member for Midnapore began to see things in a somewhat different light. He learned from private and authentic sources that most of the members had bought their

From now on until October 26th the busy man will be stopped in the street

forty or fifty times a day by the man who knows all about those timber limits.

way into parliament with money and subsequently reimbursed themselves by huge steals of public property. He found that the whole system was permeated with graft from the heads of departments down to the meanest little stinker with a government job, each with his mitt out in proportion to the size of his position.

So incensed did the member for Midnapore become over these enormities that, to the amazement of his leader, who had already arranged as to who should catch the Speaker's eye, he arose in his place on the fourth day and delivered an address of Canada. In trumpet tones he inveighed against the criminal enormities which had been perpetrated by their rulers against the people of Canada. He raked his own party fore and aft. He went after the Siftons and the Burrows, and denounced Turriff in most scathing language, saying, amid loud

Politicians these days are being divided into two classes—appointed and disappointed.[12]

applause from the Opposition that he was a Turriff for revenue only. He expressed unfeigned astonishment at the indecency which permitted the spoliation of the public domain without remonstrance from the men who could prevent it. There were lots more respectable people in certain districts of hell than were to be found in the parliaments of Canada.

At this point ex-Honorable J. A. Calder of Saskatchewan, who was an interested listener in the Distinguished Strangers' Gallery, abruptly left the chamber.

The speech of Moses, M.P., caused the greatest possible excitement in every quarter of the House, which shortly afterwards adjourned.

A heated discussion took place in the corridor among the premier, Clifford Sifton, and the member for Midnapore, Sir Wilfrid expostulating with Moses on his unheard of impudence. The member for Midnapore was heard to reply:

"I meant every word I said. You are surrounded by a lot of cold-blooded grafters and if you don't know it, you ought to know it. It's your business to know. You go around with a sunny smile while your lieutenants are rifling the pockets of the people."

"But you must not forget," said Sir Wilfrid, somewhat staggered at being spoken to thus frankly, "that Canada now occupies a foremost position amongst the daughters of the Empire."

"Empire be damned!" cried the infuri-

ated member. "This kind of twaddle makes me sick. Canada is known throughout the civilized world today as the crookedest, most immoral, psalm-singing, hypocritical, grating country on the face of the globe. You are the man to blame for this condition of affairs. If you, Sir Wilfrid, were half as honest as you pretend to be, you could put a stop to this business in ten minutes and you would have the people of Canada at your back in doing so."

"But what would I get in that event?" put in Clifford Sifton.

"You would get it in the neck," said Moses, "if this gentleman here was attending to the business of the people who put him there. But he is what he always was, an easy mark for every plausible Grit grafter that knew his way about. You grafters have grafters under you, and these grafters in turn have grafters under them, and so on away down the line until the whole system is one grand honeycomb of graft from start to finish."

"Tut, tut," ejaculated Sir Wilfrid, "I don't know of any such thing."

"That's the hell of it," retorted Moses. "You're not supposed to see anything. Your role is to hold the attention of the audience and keep them in good humor while the other fellows are going through their pockets."

"You can't prove anything of that kind against us," said Clifford, rather red in the face.

"I know enough about you," said

Political success is like a flea—now you see it, now you don't.[13]

Moses, looking Sifton squarely in the face, "to know that you are pretty clever at covering up your tracks, but your own record convicts you. You know how you were fixed when you left Winnipeg in '96 and today you own mansions in Ottawa, summer palaces at Brockville, steam yachts, newspapers, timber lands, coal lands, mineral lands, as well as a wad of the long green that a greyhound couldn't jump over. You live in the style of a Russian grand duke and you scatter money abroad to minister to your own pleasure. Your only available source of income has been your salary as minister of the interior and private member. What I should like to know is, where did you get it?"

"I don't know that Mr. Sifton is as rich as you think he is," said Sir Wilfrid mildly.

"Oh, there's a heap of things you don't know," responded Moses, "and that is where you are going to get left some day. You are the only man in Canada who doesn't seem to know anything about Sir Frederick Borden, Emmerson, Hyman and several other scallywags whom I might mention, but you'll find out all about it some day to your cost."

" I don't know that that's any of your business anyhow," said Sifton warmly.

"Touched a raw spot there, eh?" replied Moses, giving Sifton a grim smile. "It may not be my business, but it's the people's business, and the day will come when you'll find out that the people of this country decline to accept as their rulers men who are a disgrace to their country which supports them. For my part, I'm going back home. You can work out your own destruction. If hell is any worse than this place, it must be a daisy."

Moses, M.P., before leaving Ottawa, placed his resignation in the hands of the Speaker and left for heaven on the westbound express. (September 5, 1908)

The *Eye Opener* wants to know why the Grits are so anxious for another term of power. There is nothing left to steal. Everything is cleaned up. What, then, can be their object? (May 2, 1908)

R. L. Borden does not let a little thing like a rainstorm interfere with his campaign speechifying. That is the advantage of having two suits of clothes. (August 12, 1911)

Yes, the plug was pulled out. That curious soughing noise you hear is doubtless the late Grit government going down the pipe. (October 28, 1911)

After nine years steady hammering the *Eye Opener* has at last the satisfaction of seeing the Liberal Government broken into fragments.

A pitiful spectacle indeed!

Our heart goes out to the bunch. It does for a fact.

Wiped out.

Annihilated.

Bartender! Bartender! Come hither!

With this happy change comes a

Some day there will be an investigation of the high cost of investigations.[14]

change in the *Eye Opener*. In the hour of victory we can well afford to be magnanimous. It is the small souls who gloat. Although the Grit bunch, both Dominion and Provincial, have tried hard to put us out of business, we feel no rancor whatever and are ready to forgive our enemies on the pleasant theory that all is fair in love and war. Life is too short to harbor animosities and we shall now proceed to forget all about the obstacles which were hurled in our path from time to time and which, pray believe us, took some climbing over. They were clumb over, however. (October 28, 1911)

There is neither rhyme nor reason in trying to make a heroic figure out of Laurier in his hour of defeat. Laurier may be a picturesque enough figure, but hanged if we can see anything heroic about a politician who has been turned down by the voters of the country. The situation is quite commonplace. It is occurring all the time all over the world where there is popular franchise. One bunch of politicians who have got gay by too long tenure of power get chucked out and another bunch get chucked in. The latter last long enough to get fat and gay and then they get chucked out too and the other bunch get chucked back again. That is all there is to it.

SIR WILFRID RETIRING GRACE-
FULLY INTO PRIVATE LIFE
AFTER THE ELECTON.

Political parties, like many individuals we know, cannot stand prosperity. After a party has been in power for a number of years it becomes stodgy and self-complacent and its members in office by a continuous absorption of flattery from fawning lightweights at home, get to imagine that they are devilish important, devilish important. Drunken with a sense of power and immunity, the more unscrupulous ones become careless and corrupt. The canker of graft takes hold and spreads, immorality is added to corruption, scandals creep forth, an alert opposition press gets busy and the electors do the rest.

In the recent election the Liberal government got canned because the people of Canada had a very shrewd suspicion that their own premier was trying to sell them out. They were willing to stand for a lot from Sir Wilfrid, but they couldn't stand for that!

That a proper amount of B.S. will raise a man above his fellows by causing them to think him wondrous wise, might be illustrated by the following yarn:

There were three pigs in a poke. The overcrowding was scandalous. Each accounted for the evil in a different manner.

The first pig said, "This overcrowding

Apropos Liberal and Conservative parties: of two evils it is best to choose neither.[15]

is disastrous; it is because we are in a poke."

The second pig said, "This overcrowding is disastrous; it is because we are pigs."

The third pig spoke as follows, "The overcrowding is undoubtedly appalling, but you are both mistaken as to the conditions that have caused it. It is not due to our being in a poke; neither is it due to our being pigs. The evil is the direct and inevitable outcome of certain spasmodic variations in the Law of Economic Utility."

The other two pigs were much impressed, and without more ado elected the third pig leader among them. Still the overcrowding remained as bad as ever. (October 28, 1911)

And so Chief Mackie is going to close up the dives at Nose Creek and gambling joints in town, and make Calgary the cleanest city in the whole of the dominion. Well, well, if that isn't just fine! By the way, when do the municipal elections come off? In a month? As soon as that? Well, well, well, what a curious coincidence!" (October 28, 1911)

At an election meeting, one of the speakers was tormented by an interrupter who was constantly jumping up and hurling insinuations. Finally, the speaker turned on him.

"You, sir," he shouted, pointing a bony finger, "remind me of an aeolian harp that has just been struck by lightning. I will tell you why. An aeolian harp is a lyre. And a lyre that has been struck by lightning is a blasted lyre. And that's what you are!" (February 10, 1912)

What has become of all those swollen-up old stiffs that used to cut such a wide swath throughout this fair country of ours? Where are those high and mighty political pomposities to whom the people were wont to kowtow not so very long ago? Are Fielding, Paterson and Lemiux still alive? And Sir Frederick—dear old Sir Frederick? Frank Oliver, too—where in thunder does Frank (always the best of the bunch) keep himself? The only one we have heard tell of recently is old Aylesworth. When last seen, he had a whisk broom in his hand and was on his way to dust off the Newmarket canal. They are now a bunch of dead ones. Requiescat in porco. (September 7, 1912)

Politics has not ceased to make strange bedfellows, or, at least, the politicians of both parties continue to share the same bunk. You know the kind of bunk we mean. (October 5, 1912)

An eastern despatch informs a startled world that Harry Corby, of "Corby's Whiskey," has been made a member of the Canadian Senate. If Corby only made better whiskey the appointment wouldn't be so bad, but we never fancied "Corby." It tastes too coppery. If Mr. Corby would rectify this he no doubt would make a fair

Much that is labeled "financial success" is plain graft.[16]

senator as senators go. (October 19, 1912)

When Premier Sifton and Malcolm Mackenzie dine with King George, we trust they will have tact enough to praise the Queen's cooking. (November 2, 1912)

Once again we venture in the most humble manner to give Premier Borden the quiet tip that his political longevity will be placed in jeopardy if he does not get busy and do something real and tangible for the West. The first thing he had better do, is to so adjust the tariff as to make possible a substantial reduction in the cost of agricultural machinery. The second thing he had better do, is to get after the railway commission and insist on something being done towards removing the burden of excessive freight rates in Western Canada. (May 17, 1913)

History is but a record of the systematic institutional plunder of the people by a shrewd and selfish few. (March 18, 1916)

We have forgotten what we were going to write this paragraph about, but have an idea that it was something about proportional representation. However, let it go. (May 27, 1916)

Laurier, the long-haired demagogue, has never forgiven English-speaking Canada for defeating him at the polls in 1911. He is determined to become Premier again or bust. Let him bust. (December 15, 1917)

The reason the *Eye Opener* does not publish a list of the blunders made by the Unionist Government is because it is only a four-page paper. (September 21, 1918)

One of the most extraordinary hallucinations with which the average Canadian is afflicted is the supposed efficacy of a trip to Ottawa to get something done. Our asylums are full of otherwise sane men who have harbored this hallucination and made their silly little trips to Ottawa. It would be amusing, were it not so sad. Did you ever make the trip? No? The *Eye Opener* extends its congratulations. (March 15, 1919)

We are told that "Vox Populi" is to dominate at the peace conference. Doubtless "Constant Reader" and "Old Subscriber" are also sticking around in an advisory capacity. (March 15, 1919)

A father, wishing to satisfy himself as to the future prospects of his son, decided to make the following test. "Now," he said, "I will put here, where he will see them the first thing when he comes in, a Bible, some money, and a bottle of whiskey. If he takes the Bible he will be a preacher, if he takes the money he will be a business man, and if he takes the whiskey he will be no good."

Politics is a good game, but a mighty poor business.[17]

Having thus decided on the plan, he arranged the articles and concealed himself to await the son and watch results. Presently in came the boy, saw the money and put it in his pocket, took up the bottle of whiskey and drank it, put the Bible under his arm and walked out whistling.

"My gracious!" exclaimed the father. "He will be a member of parliament!" (August 14, 1920)

Did you ever hear Nellie McClung when in good form? If not, you have missed the treat of your life. Woe betide the poor fish who interpolates a silly question. He gets his so quick that his head swims for about a week. We once went to hear this lady speak in the Grand Theatre, full of amused tolerance not unmixed with prejudice. After she got through all we could gasp to the friend alongside was, "She wins." (August 14, 1920)

Premier Dury, of Ontario, has had one hundred and fifty loads of straw placed around the parliament buildings at Toronto with a view of having the members feel at home. (*Summer Annual,* 1920)

As for our own success at the polls—well, now, what the devil are we going to say about that? That we deeply and gratefully appreciate the kindness shown on every side, goes without saying. (Business of placing hand on heart and making low bow.) No speeches were made on our behalf; no meetings held. The only appeal to the electorate was the silent one of a clean sheet covering twenty years. To this might be added the kindly feeling of personal friendship towards ourself on the part of the citizens generally, who had us doped out as "a good old scout." It was a combination impossible to beat.

Up in Edmonton, when the time arrives to go there, we shall reciprocate by exercising diligence in performing the duties of an accredited representative. Perhaps an independent member may not be able to cut much swath, but if he knows enough to take his duties seriously and not be content with the role of innocent bystander, he can at least exercise some influence by participating intelligently in the proceedings of the House and keeping his eye on the indicator.

In order to try and find out what kind of speeches my constituents expect me to make in the House, I sent out some questionnaires the other day to a lot of people in different walks of life. Quite a number of sample speeches have come pouring in, samples of what they claim to be looking for. It will be very difficult to please 'em all, since no two of the specimen addresses are in any way alike. For instance, a gentleman living over in Hillhurst writes to say that he will be greatly disappointed if our first speech does not run something like this:

"Mr. Speaker, in speaking to the resolution placed in my name with the clerk of the House praying for a generous, liberal and elaborate recrudescence of lager beer in the Province of Alberta, I take this

Without the periodical scandals at Ottawa lots of decent people in the West would never hear of that place.[18]

opportunity of introducing an amend-ment to the Weights and Measures Act which will authorize three pints to the quart. (Cheers.) Allaying the unrest of the people is as nothing compared to allaying their thirst (Loud cheers.) And I think, Mr. Speaker, that God in his mercy would not be averse to seeing a spirited beer policy carried out by the govern-ment (Hear, hear!) at their earliest possi-ble convenience. I might remind the House that in Great Britain … "

But why continue? He goes on like this for ten pages. Must be bughouse.

We can only say that the variety of samples sent in are rather bewildering. One gentleman's oration is one long elo-quent suggestion that the sessions of the House be held in the Macdonald Hotel to save car fare. He cites several reasons, with which the availability of booze is not unconnected. This speech is not such a bad one, but hopelessly impracticable and could not be delivered in the House without causing a disturbance. Guess we had better invent our own speeches. (August 20, 1921)

We offer no apology for being so long getting out the *Eye Opener*. Running an election on one's own behalf and finally getting elected in sensational style, has a rather unsettling effect. Our alleged mind refused to concentrate on desk-work and so off we hiked to the moun-tains with the genial wife. There we remained for several weeks cogitating on the topsy-turveydom of the world in general. (August 20, 1921)

This is the first appearance of the genial *Eye Opener* since the eventful Election. It was some Election.

Three months ago, the editor of this paper had no more notion of becoming a member of the Alberta Legislature than had Mr. Greenfield of becoming premier of the province or Mr. Brownlee of becoming attorney-general or Alec Ross minister of public works. Fate—or Destiny—was obviously off on a wild spree, tossing some men aside, destroying others and pitchforking sundry extremely astonished individuals into the seats of the mighty where they now lie sprawled, gasping and blinking their eyes and won-dering whether it was a cyclone or just a mere earthquake. (August 20, 1921)

Some fellow made the remark the other day that there was small difference between the Liberal and the Conservative parties. There is all the difference in the world. One is in and the other is out. (July 29, 1922)

One of the consoling things about public life is that no matter what kind of a spec-tacular ass a man may make of himself in public matters, he will always receive a stack of letters commending his course. (*Summer Annual*, 1922)

When a man quits turning around to look at a pretty girl he is old enough, almost, for the Senate.[19]

Perhaps a shorter definition of graft and one that would fit in the vocabulary of politicians is: "A good thing that you are not in on." (*Summer Annual*, 1923)

--·-----·--

NO FADS, FANCIES,
PREJUDICES, OR FREAK STUFF, SAYS Mr. EDWARDS

During the last dozen days leading up to Alberta's 1921 provincial election, the *Morning Albertan* (now the *Calgary Sun*) obligingly printed salvos from all[1] the independent Legislative candidates. Save for two 120-second speeches delivered before the Great War Veterans Association,[2] the *Albertan* stumping constituted Edwards's entire campaign. (Lest it offer an unfair edge, the *Eye Opener* was on self-ordained hiatus during the campaign. The July 16 issue, which he promised would deliver a "FINAL WALLOP," failed to materialize.) Worked just fine, too: when the polls closed on July 18, Edwards placed a close second (to Alex Ross) in a field of twenty candidates, handily winning his seat.

Edwards's campaign addresses are noteworthy for effect as much as content. His *Albertan* writings find him largely trading on twenty-plus years of accumulated P.R., aw-shucksing through all his old faves (farmers, labor, returned soldiers, beer.) (That said, he conjures the occasional masterstroke, such as the brilliant "R. C. Edwards (X)" device.) And the people ate it up. As Robert Pearson, a fellow independent candidate who shared space in the *Albertan*, cheerily conceded, "I don't imagine anyone read beyond Bob's article."[3]

--·-----·--

[1] This egalitarian gesture was clearly skewed by *Albertan* editor W. M. Davidson's friendship with Edwards, who was the only candidate to grab ink in all twelve issues, his well-scrubbed mug consistently cinching top-of-the-page pole-position.
[2] *Eye Opener*, November 25, 1922.
[3] Pearson, Robert. "Bob Edwards and I." *Alberta Folklore Quarterly*, vol. 1, no. 1. March 1945.

Many a great man's reputation for wit is due to his having been interviewed by a bright reporter.[20]

Last Saturday night the five Conservative candidates commenced operations by holding a political meeting at the Al Azhar temple. These candidates evidently knew their business. They had taken the wise precaution of heralding Mr. Bennett far and wide as the orator of the evening, thus drawing a crowd. Wise guys, these.

The beauty about my own candidature is there won't be any public meetings held on my behalf at all. As a matter of fact, I am the only one of the twenty odd candidates—or rather the twenty or more candidates, because there is nothing particularly odd about any of them—who really does not intend to make speeches during the campaign. My views on every imaginable topic under the sun are already perfectly well known to all.

I have been discussing and handling public questions for a very, very long time in this province, and you must admit that I have never stalled or four-flushed on any of them.

Indeed, I think I can safely lay claim to the distinction of having delivered the longest address of any one man in this community by means of the fact that I have been addressing Calgary audiences steadily for a period extending over twenty years. On this page, each morning, I shall make an abbreviated talk to the electors, until my own paper comes out on the 16th for the FINAL WALLOP.

Perhaps I may be permitted to add, as an afterthought, that I am running simply as a normal man, free from fads, fan-cies, prejudices or freak stuff of any kind. (*Morning Albertan*, July 4, 1921)

The *Herald* quite properly considers it to be the duty of every candidate in the provincial elections to declare where he stands—whether a supporter of the Stewart government or opposed to it.

The genial *Herald* is apparently alarmed at the growing strength of at least one independent candidate, whose name modesty forbids me to mention.

Be that as it may, I have already declared myself an independent supporter of the Stewart government (*Eye Opener* issue of June 25), coupled with the frank statement that I disapproved very strongly of the taxation burdens imposed by the provincial government on the city of Calgary. If elected, I should try to have these removed altogether or at least modified to some fifty-fifty arrangement.

There are no doubt a number of kinks of a similar nature that would be straightened out by a friendly independent, where a hard and fast party member would hesitate to butt in. Of course, no government pays much attention to roars and yelps emanating from the opposition.

An unattached, or cross-bench, independent member is a sorry looking object in any assembly. He is treated by the government as a hostile, and regarded by everybody else as a stray. He gets nowhere, and his carping criticisms fall like water on a duck's back so far as the ministers are concerned. A lonely maverick he, resembling nothing so much as a

Probably the saddest thing about Ottawa is the number of fourth rate intellects applied to first rate problems.[21]

man taking a lone drink in a crowded bar.

I do not propose to be that kind of an independent member. Not on your life! If elected, I shall give cordial support to the Stewart government in all its good works. My independence shall be exercised, however, fearlessly and to the limit, whenever my better judgment whispers that the honorable course for me to pursue is to take a negative attitude. But I won't be mean about it.

No mistaken ideas of loyalty to friends shall lead me into wrong paths, if I ever enter that chamber. Going in clean, I should like to come out clean. (*Morning Albertan*, July 5, 1921)

It is perhaps not on my plate to suggest how people should cast their votes at this election—outside of voting for me, which is quite a permissible suggestion—but I do think that casting a vote for one of the Labor candidates is almost a matter of duty.

Without representation in the house Labor will be inarticulate. Spasmodic deputations up to Edmonton don't amount to a row of beans. Labor must have a trusted spokesman in the legislature, a man of horse sense, a reasonable man, one who never forgets what he is there for.

I do not mean to imply that without representation the Labor party would suffer at the hands of the Stewart government; not for a moment. But in every piece of labor legislation introduced, there are one hundred and one details

which require scrutiny, comment and suggestion from somebody of understanding and of specialised knowledge; duly elected for that purpose.

It may look as if I were making a bid to catch one of the odd two labor votes. Lemme tell you something you probably don't know:

At the very first election held in Calgary after we became a province (the famous Bennett-Cushing election) I was the choice for nomination as Labor candidate of the local Typographical union and of two other local unions—I just forget which ones they were. The late Mr. Brocklebank was another contestant for this nomination; also Fred Bagley. The convention was held in a building a few doors to the west of the present Empress movie theater on Eighth Avenue East. Mr. Macdonald, who was rather a high type of man, but whom we have not seen since, won the pot and was awarded the nomination. I must have made a bum speech. Cushing won that election by a short head from "R. B."

I mention this to show that even in those far-off days I was regarded as a good friend by organized labor.

I don't know much about Mr. Parkyn but both Alex Ross and Fred White have, with credit to themselves, earned their spurs in responsible elective positions. Here is where my suggesting stops.

Ogden shops, the mills, the breweries and the various industries humming and buzzing all around us, are entitled to an adequate representation in the legis-

The devil knew what he was doing when he invented politics, all right.[22]

lature. Do not forget this when you step behind the cheese cloth curtain and take up the little blunt pencil on polling day. And don't overlook yours truly. (*Morning Albertan*, July 7, 1921)

One thing very evident is that the electors of Calgary riding cannot be bothered attending political meetings. They positively decline to allow themselves to be bored by the speechifying and blethering of candidates, who tell them nothing they don't already know and who tell it batty at that.

The other evening, for example, the Conservative candidates held three political meetings at points across the river. The audience at the first of these whirlwind rallies consisted of five persons, there being six on the platform, counting candidates and the chairman, making a grand total of 11; at the second, 18 were in the hall, 12 individuals composing the audience; at the third, there was no audience at all, not a living soul, not even the janitor.

They have since arranged to have R. B. Bennett help them out. If left to themselves, nobody would go and listen to them for a moment.

Nor are the Liberal candidates doing much better. Their meetings, also, are very sparsely attended. It is not that the people are not interested in the forthcoming election, but that they are not interested in the candidates. At least, not to any appalling extent.

On the other hand, per contra, as it were, through the courtesy of my old friend, Editor Davidson, I am enabled to have a little chat on this page with over 20,000 men and women at the breakfast table every blessed morning. This privilege is likewise extended to my three co-independents and although none of us say anything especially sparkling, the public does not have to read it unless they like. There is nothing compulsory about it.

Heckling a speaker at a public meeting seldom produces results, either, especially when he is asked if he is in favor of something or other. He is sure to yell back, "Why, sure!"

"Are you in favor of government control of cockroaches in our kitchens?"

"Why, sure!"

"Would you favor a benevolent bottled beer policy as a cure for morose members of the community?"

"Why, sure!"

Of course, you noted the answers given by the five Liberal candidates night before last at a poorly attended meeting at Hillhurst, when asked to give their views on prohibition? Bob Marshall, Mrs. Langford and George Webster (through his able representative, Bruce Robinson) gave direct and honest answers; the two lawyer candidates, Selwood and Ford, scented danger and stalled, saying that they would need further time for consideration. Indeed, Mr. Selwood wanted the question submitted in writing and said he would answer it at a later date.

Oh, these lawyers!

A little push will generally last longer than a political pull. (Hear, hear!)[23]

The really grave question of the hour is one which every thoughtful elector should ask him (or her) self during a quiet moment of sober reflection. The question is this:

If not the Stewart government—What?

The alternative is H. W. Wood and his excited cohorts. Is it not so?

Why, sure!

So watch your step on the 18th. (*Morning Albertan*, July 8, 1921)

Who ho! The farmer bogey.

In anticipation of a preponderance of farmer members getting elected, it were perhaps as well that a few bright, wised-up, good-humored men from the cities should be elected also, if only to help with the chores.

Although the farmers are striking while the iron is hot and making the most of their Medicine Hat triumph, yet they are not opposing the Stewart government in the ordinary sense, and are certainly not doing so from any feeling of dissatisfaction with past legislation.

Far from it. They greatly enjoy seeing the cities taxed heavily by the province. It is so much the less for themselves to cough up.

Their leader, H. W. Wood, is more disposed than otherwise to be in accord with Premier Stewart's policies and has no desire to either replace or embarrass him. Indeed, his original idea, when the elections were first announced, was simply to secure strong and capable farmer representation in the house, say about twenty seats. Mr. Wood sensed that the time was not yet ripe—that the farmers themselves were not quite ripe—for assuming administrative office.

But the excitement and mental exaltation accruing from that preposterous Medicine Hat victory, which had nothing to do with provincial politics at all, carried the U.F.A. locals off their feet all over the country, and there quickly went up the cry: "Go forth, ye merry sodbusters, and smite 'em hip and thigh!" This order is seemingly being carried out with tremendous eclat.

Happily, Calgary is spared this furious onslaught, thus preserving intact many a bottle blushing unseen on the genial hip of homo aridus.

Do not run away with the idea that these farmers are opposing government candidates for the same set of reason as those adduced, for example, by Mr. Bennett. Not so. Staring them in the face is the glittering, glorious , dazzling chance to attain power at one fell swoop. Who can blame them for throwing wide open the door in response to opportunity's knock? Never again will such a chance present itself. That is all. They have not the slightest animus, one way or another, against the Stewart administration. Mr. Farmer is thinking of Mr. Farmer first, last and all the time. Nothing else matters.

Should this powerful organized body succeed in overturning the Stewart government it will be a tragedy in one sense and a comedy in another.

In trying to get up in the world, politicians use newspaper men as step ladders.[24]

By the way, to do the farmer candidates justice, you never hear of them denouncing Stewart's railway policy. Why not? Because he is sufficiently fair-minded to realize that Premier Stewart inherited and did not create the railroad situation. Taking over the job, he naturally had to carry on. But perhaps the farmer doesn't know anything about it, and cares less.

And, by the way, balancing these few dry remarks with something frivolous, did you hear about the couple of newlyweds who spent their honeymoon seeing the Carp-Demp fight? Well, they picked up many valuable pointers.

See you Monday. (*Morning Albertan*, July 9, 1921)

Third and last week!

The twenty competitors are now rounding into the stretch, headed for the judges' stand and putting in their best licks.

This election is singularly free from animosities, for the gratifying reason that the contenders are all more or less acquainted with one another and can discover no grounds for saying mean things. Friendliness and mutual respect characterize the attitude of the gallant twenty. The questions of the hour which seem to interest Calgary electors most are not the broader ones, such as the everlasting railway policy and the eternal natural resources, nor yet the immortal mess of pottage, but rather certain intimate questions which affect the pocketbook through taxation and others which touch upon lifelong habits and natural desires.

What does the average man in Calgary care about the bonded indebtedness of a railroad running up to Fort McMurray; when the thing he wants most at the moment is a glass of cool beer?

Tut, tut!

In addition to the possession of brains capable of coping with ordinary problems of development, the representative of an urban riding like Calgary ought to be one who will get right down to earth and bend an eye upon the economic condition of the citizens in their daily routine of life; most of whom are earning fair money, which is taken away from them in living expenses and taxes as fast as they make it.

While ruminating over the rasping little hardships, injustices and inequalities observable on every hand, a true-blood representative will apply to himself the good old rule: "Put yourself in his place." This gives one the correct viewpoint. It is in such attitude of mind alone that one can tackle the problem of unemployment with determination, diligence and sincerity; and it is only by getting close to the homes—to the very kitchen door—that one can realize the urgent need of lifting some of the burdens from the shoulders of the breadwinner.

An elected representative should not be above interesting himself in the task of making life more tolerable for ordinary folk, because there are more ordinary folk than any other kind.

Politics, you will observe, is the science of guessing right.[25]

Perhaps we are all getting just a wee bit tired of listening to so much chatter about the "solution of problems." Everything is a problem nowadays. Whenever a politician disagrees with something, or something disagrees with the politician, he calls it a problem. It has become quite a habit, for example, to speak of the liquor question as a problem. Given the chance and a free hand, I would undertake to settle the liquor question for keeps to the satisfaction of at least two-thirds of the adult population of this province, within a given period of six months or the year at the outside it is certainly no "problem" as far as I am concerned.

I feel just as strongly on the subject of hard liquor as the most ardent prohibitionist. Indeed, it was admittedly my newspaper that helped more than any other agency to put over prohibition on the occasion of the first plebiscite six years ago. Women's organizations all over the province gave me full credit at the time, and for a while I was quite a feller. A regular fair-haired laddie, in fact. They really ought to reciprocate now, by giving some consideration to my suggestions with respect to a beer compromise. They may be glad to do so some day.

The bit of work of which I have most reason to feel proud is the part I was privileged to play some years ago in the agitation for a system of rural hospitals, under government auspices, throughout the province. This stunt was duly pulled off, to use a colloquialism, and the results have indeed proved a blessing to the women and children on the prairies. Mrs. W. M. Davidson was the good angel of this movement, at least one of 'em.

I have always been more a doer of things than a talker. This is a Scotch trait. (*Morning Albertan*, July 11, 1921)

Tomorrow night there is to be a meeting of the returned soldiers at Paget hall. A list of questions, already published, will then be answered by the Calgary candidates for the provincial legislature.

This is the only meeting of the campaign which I propose to attend. I owe this much to the Calgary branch of the G.W.V.A. for having done me the honor of electing me by acclamation a patron of the association every year since its inception. I fear they rather overrated the small services I tried to render the boys from time to time, but it was up to me to make some effort to offset my inability, through age, to do my bit overseas. My appearance on the platform tomorrow night will be solely for the purpose of showing my appreciation for their oft-expressed goodwill toward myself, for I am no speechifier.

What upsets me more than anything else in this campaign is the way a candidate has to keep on talking about himself. It seems it has to be done. In my paper I can use the editorial "we" and it does not sound so bad, but this constant reiteration of the word "I" is quite as tiresome to me as it must be to you. We'll have to let it go at that.

Politics is a good game, but a mighty poor business.[26]

More about myself: I was born in Edinburgh, Scotland, about a hundred year ago, and was educated at St. Andrews, Fife. The latter place is where they breed golfers. It is famous for its schools and university. Of course lads educated there never by any chance learn anything—no such nonsense as that—and come away more deeply steeped in ignorance than when they started, but they become perfectly miraculous golfers. The present captain of the Royal and Ancient Golf club at St. Andrews is Field Marshal Lord Haig. He also was a schoolboy there at a private school called Clifton Bank, which I myself attended for three years. How he ever became a field marshal after attending that school, God only knows.

My residence in Alberta covers a period of some twenty years. They have been very happy years, relieved by just enough rough stuff to make it interesting. I can truthfully claim to have participated actively in practically all the important movements for the advancement of the province of Alberta.

In the old days I agitated until I was black in the face for provincial autonomy and although it was bound to come anyhow, through increase in population and natural development, I always like to think that some of us old codgers helped hurry it along.

Now that the young province is vigorous and healthy and going strong, I should like to be given an opportunity to promote the general welfare in a larger way, at the seat of government.

Try me out. (*Morning Albertan,* July 12, 1921)

Did it ever occur to you that most people attend political meetings for the purpose, or at least with the expectation, of being entertained?

If this is not so, will you kindly explain why it is that the attendance is so slim at meetings where only the candidates themselves are billed to speak? It is painfully evident that at least ten of the candidates realize their lack of platform magnetism, because did not the Conservative candidates early in the game scream for help from "R. B. " and have not the Liberals sent in hot haste for Duncan Marshall?

Being headliners of national repute, these two gentlemen naturally draw packed houses, much after the fashion of Forbes Robertson and Martin Harvey. It seems to be human nature for an audience to regard a public speaker's effort as an intriguing species of stage performance. When the speaker acquits himself brilliantly by dint of personal charm, fluency, plausibility and general all-around gift of the gab, then the people acclaim him as a wonderful chap, a veritable corker.

The fact that he may have been turning loose a stormy blether of preposterous nonsense does not enter into the case at all. The audience drift home through the night, wagging their heads delightedly and murmuring, "Great stuff! Great stuff!"

In the case of the twenty candidates

It is a mighty poor politician who cannot promise his friends and supporters anything they want.[27]

now running in the Calgary riding, I think it will be admitted that, judged one by one, they are rather clever chaps in their respective spheres. Nineteen of them are, anyway. The fact of their failing to stack up as helltooters on the platform should not be allowed to militate against their chances, because a goodly proportion of these same candidates have already proved to their fellow citizens that they can be sound, capable and honest when called upon to fill positions of difficulty and responsibility.

Although the gift of oratory undoubtedly comes in handy during a political campaign, it is a positive detriment nowadays in legislative assemblies. Longwinded speeches are taboo. Short addresses and businesslike exchanges of ideas across the floor of the house, with the object of getting the work done expeditiously, is the new order of things. It is well. A directors' meeting in Big Business is invariably short and to the point. Speaking to the reporters' gallery is played out and the day of the parliamentary grandstander has passed.

The clock has struck the hour of my arrival on the scene. (*Morning Albertan*, July 13, 1921)

--- ··· ---

I am writing this in a bit of a hurry, just before skipping over to the big soldiers' meeting at Paget hall, where we candidates will answer a set of questions.

One often wonders whether there is such a thing as gratitude in political life.

Let us glance at the case of Duncan Marshall's candidature in the Olds riding, which he has represented in the legislature for years and where he makes his home as farmer and breeder of purebred cattle.

As minister of agriculture, Mr. Marshall has done more to advertise Alberta abroad than all other agencies put together. As administrator of this department, he has operated successfully, with intensive activity, in the development of scientific agriculture and the encouragement of the horse and cattle breeding industry. The enthusiasm he has thrown into his work explains his success as minister.

Mr. Marshall hies over to England on a mission of vital importance to Alberta cattle breeders, to try and get the embargo lifted. He gives expert testimony before the commission sitting in London. He moves heaven and earth to accomplish his object and then returns home to find an election going full blast and an effort being made by his fellow-farmers to oust him from his seat.

This is the shabbiest piece of business I have come across in the whole of my western experience. Double-crossing a friend in private life is considered a low-down trick, as we all know, but attempting to destroy a friend during his absence on a special mission on your behalf is infinitely worse.

Ingratitude.

Then look at the Medicine Hat federal by-election. Of course Nelson Spencer could not possibly have beaten the power-

A propos Liberal and Conservative parties: of two evils it is best to choose neither.[28]

ful U.F.A. organization, but how did the labor vote in the city come to go against him? Spencer had put in the best years of his life building up Medicine Hat and making it quite a perky little industrial center on the prairies, and he also did his duty as a soldier at the front in a manner creditable to himself and to the Hat itself where he raised his battalion.

Did this fine record help him? Not a bit of it. He lost his deposit.

Ingratitude.

Take J. K. Cornwall, of Edmonton, who for the past quarter of a century has been working his head off developing and advertising abroad the wonderful resources of the vast North Land. His untiring work has finally brought results which even he never dreamed of. And yet, whenever "Jim" runs for an elective office in a district where the beneficiaries of the industry most abound, they fail to reciprocate.

Ingratitude.

On the other hand, should Calgary return me on the 18th as one of her members, I shall do my level best, always, to reciprocate her kindness.

Gratitude. (*Morning Albertan*, July 14, 1921)

———

Vote thus: R. C. Edwards—(X).

I have just been informed that there are a lot of people in the city who do not know that R. C. Edwards (X) is identical with Bob Edwards.

This is terrible news.

I have been calling myself R. C.

Edwards (X) during this campaign under the bright delusion that it sounded more dignified than Bob. So it does in a way, but it seems that by doing so I have lost a part of my identity, cujus magna, pars Bob fuit.

This will not do at all.

R. C. Edwards (X), be it thoroughly understood, is the same Bob Edwards who has amused you with his great family journal, the *Eye Opener*, for lo! these many years. Although Bob may be the name blown in the bottle, yet for purposes of this election it is R. C. Edwards (X).

Bear in mind that R. C. Edwards (X) is the man who is in favor of solving the vexed liquor question by having another plebiscite submitted to the people, with a view to bringing back the beer. He is death on the hard stuff.

R. C. Edwards (X) is against light wines, because these can be too easily medicated and chemicalized. Adulterated "light" wines are worse in their effect than bootleg whiskey, for whereas the latter may prompt a man to climb a telephone pole and bark like a dog, the former will make him open his grandmother's grave to try and sell the old lady a block of worthless oil stock.

Candidates can talk themselves hoarse about the debt of the province, the burdensome taxation and so forth, but what the general bulk of the people want to know definitely, once and for all, is their individual attitude towards beer.

In answering questions on the subject the candidates (all but a few) purposely

Neighbourly sympathy often turns out to be nine-tenths curiosity[29]

give confusing answers and by babbling away about referendums, direct taxation and enforcement of the law, ingeniously avoid committing themselves. Those kind of candidates, if elected, will simply give the laugh later on to the large bulk of their constituents who desire an occasional glass of beer.

Why cannot a candidate be honest about it, and come out frankly and let the voters know whether he favors beer or not? A candidate who plays both ends against the middle in a dishonest attempt to curry favor with both Moderationists and Prohibitionists at one and the same time, cannot possibly prove a satisfactory representative. Fourflushing does not go in this game.

One could quite understand a candidate for office being ashamed to advocate the sale of whiskey. Whoever should favor this sort of thing is no friend of his fellow-men. Such a one might possibly be all right as member for Hootch, but certainly not as representative of an enlightened, God-fearing constituency.

The thought underlying these questions, which are put to candidates about the liquor question, does not concern whiskey at all. No one is asking for whiskey. Nobody wants it. The gradual disappearance of whiskey can be brought about by providing and making accessible to everybody a cheap form of mild stimulant, and by no other means. The only wholesome stimulant of a mild nature, is beer. No man ever went home and beat up his wife under the influence of lager.

This is a problem that calls for compromise. The science of politics consists of compromise. Without the spirit of compromise the conflicting views of good citizens can not be reconciled. In this case the compromise or golden mean is good old beer.

In tomorrow's *Albertan* I shall have something to say about the larger questions of moment to the country. There are matters of far graver importance than beer. That, after all, affects only the social life of the community. Housing of returned soldiers, employment for all, relief from burdensome taxation and many other problems cry aloud for speedy settlement. Talking about these things in academic fashion won't get us anywhere.

Men with a practical bent of mind, businesslike as well as sympathetic in their mental attitude, knowledgeable in human affairs, of broad vision, these are the type of men to elect if you want happiness and contentment in the land.

I am not publishing the *Eye Opener* tomorrow. It is all written, but in reading over the proofs I find that it contains nothing but a bewildering variety of cogent reasons why you should vote for R. C. Edwards (X) on the 18th. I could not very well charge people 10 cents for reading my own advertising, could I?

Cert'nly not.

This is not how R. C. Edwards (X) does business. (*Morning Albertan*, July 15, 1921)

A little learning is a dangerous thing, but a lot of ignorance is just as bad.[30]

This is the last working day of the campaign.

For me, yesterday was rather strenuous, and when night fell I was so tired I simply could not prepare my usual line of conversation for this column. I moved around through the heat in various parts of the city amongst friends who are generously giving me active assistance, in most cases at considerable inconvenience to themselves, with the object of trying in some way to thank them.

They all responded in the same jovial way, by waving the hand airily and saying, "That's all right, old scout, top of the poll through yours!"

My chances look very bright. One thing the people of Calgary can rely upon absolutely if they elect me, is that I won't lay down on the job. My office door will always remain wide open to those of my constituents who wish to drop in to talk things over. Something is always cropping up that needs remedying or straightening out. The ways of Edwards are democratic ways.

This may be my last opportunity of doing some real service for the city, which has been so good to me during twenty long years, and for the province, where I have put in twenty-six years of my life. When they carry me off to the boneyard I should like people to be able to say that as a man and a representative of the people, I had made good. (*Morning Albertan*, July 16, 1921)

It's as easy to recall an unkind word as to draw back a bullet after firing the gun.[31]

CHAPTER TWO
The Outcast's Prayer

In which your esteemed editor & bottle-washer questions holy authority, parses scripture, & forgets his flask in the pews.

"Endue our ministers with righteousness, Oh Lord, and make thy chosen people less bughouse."

—*Eye Opener*, March 18, 1904

Alone & adrift in an uncaring universe? May we humbly suggest Bob Edwards for the vacant post of spiritual beacon? His qualifications are truly without peer. Herewith is a fun assortment of blasphemies & oaths, presented with the intention of vivifying the flagging spirit during even the darkest of nights. And so—

☞ The secret of David's triumph over Goliath!

☞ Detailed instructions for pilfering the collection plate!

☞ Church news!

☞ Why newspapers trump the Good Book!

☞ The folly of the Sawbath!

To be sure, the serious theologian will find much to delight in. Forecast calls for lightning strikes. Yawp!

We have a scheme for raising the wind that great financiers like Goshen and Rothschild could never have thought up if they had lived a billion years. The scheme is worked on Sunday. The better the day the better the deed. All you have to do is, on the Sabbath morn as the bells are tolling and summoning you to worship, to put some cobbler's wax on the soles of your shoes and toddle forth. Take a back seat and put on an air of reverence. Towards the close of the service a man will come zig-zagging down the aisle with the plate. By the time it reaches you, who are sitting demurely on the outside seat next to the aisle, the plate should be pretty well laden with coins. Now all you have to do is to reach towards the plate as if you were about to drop in a $5 gold piece, and by an awkward movement upset the whole shooting match. The rest is easy. The coins roll in all directions, and with many apologies and expressions of sorrow, you walk hither and thither helping him gather them up. Of course half of the coins adhere to the wax on your shoes, and you can pick them off afterwards during the doxology. The worst of this brilliant scheme is that it can only be worked once in the same church. (*Wetaskiwin Free Lance*, December 1, 1898)

What a number of people there are in Calgary who abhor one another. Good God! What is the matter with them? Are they bereft of their senses or are their better selves lost in a maze of selfishness and self-absorption? There is hardly a man but what pretends to be better than his neighbor; if not financially, then mentally; if not mentally, then morally. They've got to be better somehow.

For instance we become acquainted with James Reilly, a strong personality and we get to like the man. Another man comes along and says, "You ain't on to Reilly yet, he's…" and so on. Somebody introduces us to Lougheed, and we come away impressed with that gentleman's courteous and business-like ways; a chap meets you half an hour later and says, "Say, you ain't on to Lougheed, now there's a man who will…, etc." Mention Paddy Nolan, Bennett, Sifton or any prominent man in the community and there is certain to be some member of a class, a sect, or coterie standing around who will at a moment's notice tear his character to pieces. And yet everybody, but us, attends church. (*Wetaskiwin Free Lance*, March 6, 1899)

The following libretto, set to music, is respectfully submitted to the choirs of the Wetaskiwin churches. The composer has just about completed the score. Land seekers of various nationalities are supposed to be grouped on the sidewalk as we see them every day, chattering at the top of their voices like a flock of magpies. In singing this anthem the choir must shout it out in the most discordant tones possible, each member singing independently of the others: "Oh ah slupinsky

The "unco' guid" of this town are no doubt envying us our shady character this hot weather.[1]

skoll jopplunky kerplunk sniftersky sacre nom de dieu pas moyen le terra est mauvais I don't mind if I do kachorka dvorak ski say that lod crock I bought from Young is mais ecoutez donc le quartier awl 14-41-14 est le meilleur morceau de slopmagulcher kamarachinchoo svi da I took it up last fall and the old stiff came along and breektonka rinski squak ations preez un coup gimme a little Scotch slambango good and quicksy!"

Apropos of choirs, let me enter a gentle protest against the singing of familiar old hymns, which all have known from childhood to new-fangled airs. "Sun of My Soul," "Lead, Kindly Light," "Rock of Ages" and other good old stand-bys have their own particular tunes and the congregation can join in the singing. There is no worship or religious sincerity in the offering up of strange songs of praise to the Lord through the medium of two or three cultivated singers in the choir, and inasmuch as the tunes to these fine old hymns are very plentiful, there is nothing gained from a musical point of view in putting them to new and difficult music in which none of the worshippers can join. By the way, do we all go to church to worship? If not, what do we go there for? How many people in Wetaskiwin read their Bible during the week, kneel down and say their prayers, or give the thought to the Giver of all Good during the week! (*Wetaskiwin Breeze*, June 18, 1901)

There was a discussion in Okotoks last week as to which was the most beneficial to society, the church or the press. Of course the press won hands down. A minister may do lots of good if he is hard working, conscientious, and a competent teacher of that which makes for a good square, honest, moral life; but he has not the audience that the editor of a largely circulated paper has. A minister may, and often does, do a lot of good in his constituency by simply offering to his people the example of a clean private life. So far as a newspaper is concerned it does not matter a particle to the public what kind of a man the editor is. The best reformers are always those who need most reforming. It is generally admitted that our newspaper work up north worked a great deal of good in the rectifying of things which we knew to be wrong, in exposing abuses which the public seemed helpless to kill, and in frightening crooks into keeping straight. And yet our own private life is nothing to throw a bouquet at.

Moral guidance through life may well be sought through taking to ourselves the lesson of the life of Jesus Christ, but a knowledge of life cannot be gained by reading about the go between David and Goliath or by trying to swallow the swallowing of Jonah. The only dissemination of knowledge nowadays is to be found in the modern newspaper, valuable both to the world of commerce and in the field of morals.

The Bible was written hundreds of years ago and treats of the doings of men long since dust. The modern newspaper

The pope rises at 5:30 every morning. This should give him time for at least three eye-openers before breakfast.[2]

has an issue every morning, or every week like ours, and speaks of the works of men living and breathing. Books contain fixed knowledge, such as has grown out of events. The newspaper gives us matter fresh from the field of life. It enables us to judge prospects by the daily happenings around us. Nothing is more necessary nor should command so much respect as a newspaper. Don't pay any attention to the editor. Think of the stuff he turns out.

That person is inseparably attached to the past, without interest in the present or future of world affairs, who does not appreciate the need and value of the press. In which connection we may say that the *Eye Opener* is a dollar and a half a year. (April 4, 1902)

Men are sick to death of religion in so far as it is only a statement of creed and collection of nickels. Preachers who incommode themselves to lift the fallen from the dust and the beggar from the dunghill are as scarce as hen's teeth. Clever sermons will not alone win men to Christ. (April 11, 1902)

Last Sunday we had the privilege of listening to a fine Christmas sermon by the Rev. Mr. Clark in the Calgary Presbyterian church, the text being "A little child shall lead them." Mr. Clark held a strong brief for the children and idealised the infant in beautiful language without once introducing the proverb, "the child is father to the man," which in itself was a great feat.

Had the preacher cared to drop for a moment from the heights he might have explained to us why a child howls when it is empty and a man howls when he is full. (January 2, 1903)

In reply to "New Arrival's" letter we would say that any advice we might give as to how to get on in this country is not to be relied upon. Our advice is not considered very valuable in such matters. However, we may say that the man who puts his trust in the Lord Jesus Christ and simultaneously hustles for a job is reasonably sure to assimilate sufficient booze money for his immediate thirst anyhow. (July 25, 1903)

The question often arises in our mind "Do the churches out West do a particle of good spiritually or materially, and what effect, if any, do they have?" We know full well that, in spite of all their fine churches and eloquent preachers, Calgary enjoys the same mysterious undercurrent of immorality amongst the *creme de la creme* as it ever did. And the worst offenders in this respect have been seen sitting gravely in their pews any Sunday. Furthermore, in spite of all the exhortations from the pulpit to lead better and nobler lives there is no diminution in the number of snifters, snorts, jolts and horns passed over the bar by the gentlemanly bartenders. Here in High River it is the same. Ministers could preach here till Kingdom come, or until we get provincial autonomy and not the

Remember that Jonah said to the whale, "You can't keep a good man down."[3]

slightest effect one way or another would be perceptible. Not one game less of cards would be played and the bar receipts would show no falling off. What good, then, do the churches accomplish in a practical sense? Are they merely perfunctory accessories to our alleged civilization, to enable certain people to give themselves a weekly varnish of respectability? It looks very much like it. (July 25, 1903)

We have been requested to remove from its cosy nest above the Local column the Presbyterian church notice. No charge is ever made for such notices. We still have the Methodist church notice, however. You may always safely bet that anything the Methodists get for nothing they will stay with. (Now watch their notices come out with a chug next week.) (August 8, 1903)

We propose making a great concession to the church element in the West. If they will agree to drop the word "helpful" in reference to sermons by ministers, or lectures to young people by immaculate, unctuous and self-sufficient parsons, and addresses by lady presidents of foreign missions, we will agree to cut out the expression "boozological" from these columns. That's fair enough. (August 8, 1903)

The little tinpot enforcers of a dull Sunday will now have to take a back seat until a special act applicable to the Sawbath is passed by the Dominion parliament. There is no earthly appeal from the highest judicial court in the Empire. The only higher triumph is the one before which we are all supposed to appear when we kick the bucket. Let 'em appeal to heaven by all means. (August 8, 1903)

There are always people anxious to hear how the Israelites crossed the Red Sea thousands of years ago. The craving for the latest news will always exist. (August 8, 1903)

Better healthy exercise in God's free air than moping at home reading *The Pilgrim's Progress* and talking about your neighbors. (August 8, 1903)

The orthodox idea of a properly observed Sunday is mooching about in solemn black, "the trappings and the suits of woe," in a state of complete idleness and vacuous mentality, waiting for the said clangour of the church bells summoning you to listen to a lot of platitudes about Israel. The *Eye Opener* respectfully declines to recognize this as common sense. We lived on the continent of Europe just long enough to get this sort of nonsense knocked out of our koko, and we had an old-fashioned Scotch bringing up too, with all the Sawbaths thrown in. Ever winter through a Scotch Sawbath? A funeral is a comic opera to it. (August 8, 1903)

About the only people who won't quarrel over religion are the people who haven't got any.[4]

We had a conversation last week with a gentleman closely connected with the Presbyterian church in High River and it was pathetic to see his anxiety to prove, not so much that we were in the wrong in the late unpleasantness, but that "the best people in the town" were against our contentions. On asking who "the best people in the town" might be, he declined to specify afraid probably lest we might start laughing.

Vague generalities which start with "They say" and "I have heard" and "I am told by some of the most influential people in this town" cut absolutely no ice. At least, not with us. They may with some people.

"They say" is the biggest liar in Canada or any other country. Gullible and weakminded yaps are invariably the prey of the "They say" artists. They swallow any old piece of gossip, the more mischief in it the better, when prefaced with the familiar old "They say." Inquire as to the identity of "They" and no satisfactory answer is forthcoming. This is due in most cases to fear of being compelled to make their words good by being confronted in presence of the gossipee with the original "They," if any such exist. Recourse, to this trick of piling the onus of a lot of malice on to the shoulders of a mythical "They" is lamentable sign of moral timidity.

The most insignificant chump in existence might approach the Lord Chancellor of England, provided he had the honor of his lordship's acquaintance, and throw that gentleman into a ferment of mental uneasiness by simply saying in a confidential manner:

"My Lord, of course, it's none of my business but I think it only right to let you know what they are saying about you."

"Who are saying?"

"Oh, it's what 'they' say."

"Well, what do they say."

"They say you are going batty."

"What!!! Who said that?"

"They say so in town."

"Who?"

"They."

"Whom do you mean—name 'em."

"Some of the most influential men in this town, my lord."

"And who in thunder are they?"

"They."

"Tell them to go plumb to Okotoks, Alberta, N.W.T." (August 22, 1903)

Those Doukhobor ladies round Yorkton who think it necessary to take off their clothes and march athwart the scene in order to be strictly religious will do well to keep far, far away from High River until the present moral wave has broken on the rock-bound shore. (August 22, 1903)

Being exceedingly anxious this week to propitiate the church folk and show that we are ready at all times to give them the stuff they affect to be so fond of, we present one of those Lessons for Sunday which lend sparkle to many high class newspapers. In view of the recent Jeffries-Corbett fight at Frisco last Friday we

Some people are too good to be interesting.[5]

select the subject of David and Goliath.

"And Saul armed David with his armour." The Philistines were the most bitter and implacable foes of Israel. When Saul became king, Israel's hereditary enemy was soon at war with him. In ancient times (my dear friends) it was a custom that a champion should come forth from either army and challenge anyone on the opposite side to meet him, not necessarily for the gate receipts, but to settle the issue absolutely in single combat. This saved much bloodshed. The victor was approved by God, the vanquished was disapproved.

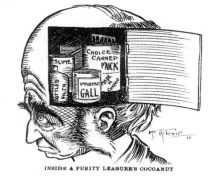

INSIDE A PURITY LEAGUER'S COCOANUT

A few years subsequent to the anointing of David, the Philistines gathered their armies to battle. Then Saul and the men of Israel lined up. Goliath came forth and began to josh and taunt and insult the Hebrews, but could not aggravate any of them into single combat till our brave Dave stepped to the front with his little sling.

Then followed the fall of vain glory and the victory of faith in God. When the giant "looked about and saw David he disdained him, for he was but a youth and ruddy and of fair countenance." He intimated to David that he would eat him up, but instead of this derision, couched no doubt in language unfit for publication in a newspaper which has been refused the mails, disturbing the balance of David's self-control he answered in words that are worth their weight in gold: "You come to me with sword and spear and shield, but I come to thee in the name of the Lord of Hosts, the God of Israel." Then the shepherd lad with the friendly sling which had stood him in stead many a time when wild beasts threatened his flocks, took a stone from his bag, and placing it in the sling, sent it on its errand of death.

It smote the Philistine in the forehead and slew him. As we read in I Samuel XVII, "And David put his hand in his bag and too hence a stone and slang it and smote the Philistine in the forehead." It is evident that David outslanged Goliath on this occasion, despite the latter's abusive vocabulary.

And where (my dear paid-up subscribers) do we discover the reason or secret of the giant's failure? Not in any defect of strength or spirit or previous prowess. He was famous far and near for courage so that the mention of his name was enough to make Israel's army quake. He looked to his pagan gods for favor and was trained to the hour. With so much at stake there was little likelihood of his throwing the fight.

What, then, was the secret of David's

No man is so religious that he considers dying a pleasure.[6]

success? Some trust in chariots and some in horse, but said the sacred writer, "we will trust in the Lord our God." David was mindful of what the Lord had helped him to do already. Out there in the open, where lions and bears were the terror of his flocks, the young man had fearlessly attacked and slain them by God's help. The lad did not claim his victory on account of his prowess or power. With him all success had been by divine favor. The main thing in David's success was his abounding belief that God could use him to humble the haughty Philistine.

Ah, my dear friends, how beautifully is the lesson worked out in our own day! The God-fearing Boers who sang hymns of praise to the Lord of Hosts before going into battle, what happened to them? They are in the soup today.

This was the same David, the chosen one of God, who later on danced in a state of nudity after a banquet before the ark of the Lord. "Leaping and dancing before the Lord," Samuel, 6.16.

This also is the same exemplary character who debauched the wife of Uriah the Hittite (Samuel 11.4) and then, to get rid of Uriah, wrote a letter to one of his generals, Joab, saying "Set ye Uriah in the forefront of the hottest battle, and retire ye from him, that he may be smited and die." (Samuel, 11.15)

Ah, my dear friends—but let us switch off to something else. (August 22, 1903)

In deference to the suggestions of our good friend *The Bee*, we shall omit men-

tion of Booze in this issue. The *Eye Opener* has to be very careful just now. So instead of prating about booze and springing ribald jests we shall this week cater to our Christian friends by handing out an item which we have been asked to publish in the interests of justice. Here it is:

Wanted for Larceny of $11,000 from the Preachers' Aid Society of the New England Annual Conference of the Methodist Episcopal Church, REV. WILLARD S. ALLEN, whose description is as follows: Age about 62 years; 5 feet 9 inches I height; 155 pounds; dark complexion, brown hair, thin on top; when last seen wore dark, thin, side whiskers; black rubber eyebrows. Rev. Willard E. Allen was Treasurer of this Society's corporation organized for the purpose of aiding and relieving sick, infirm and aged members, and in aiding widows and orphans of deceased members of the Conference. While holding that office he embezzled the above amount.

If located, arrest and hold, etc.
(Signed): WILLIAM H. PIERCE,
Superintendent of Police
Boston, August 11, 1903

We have lying on our desk, while we write, one of this reverend embezzler's photos as it appears in the circular sent to the various police officials throughout the country. He has the side whiskers all right enough and looks quite saintly.

This is really all the church news we have been able to rustle this week, but

When a minister preaches of Hell he should have an
asbestos curtain all ready to lower.[7]

shall try to do better next time. Onward, Christian soldiers! (September 5, 1903)

It has ever been a puzzle with us to know how preachers can bring themselves to talk so glibly about sin when they do not, except indirectly or at second hand, know what sin is. A course at a theological college as students; their daily life mapped out in peaceful, immaculate routine, associating only with those "already saved," carefully kept from contact with the rampage side of life, and lo! Forth they issue with a stock of crystallized phraseology and are sent out to the wooly West, ostensibly to save sinners, but really to get into pulpit practice by "trying it on the dog."

A good post-graduate course for a preacher who had finished his studies in theology would be to give him a touch of the seamy side of life for a year or two. Then he would be in a position to talk intelligently with sinners about their sins. As it is, they have not enough worldly experience to speak with authority. After the first shock of contact with the world there are many things which they would regard from a different viewpoint.

But alas! The world at large is not good enough for them. They start off as slaves of the custom and convention of their own gentle little goodly-goody sphere and remain so to the end, having accomplished little for themselves and less for anybody else. (September 5, 1903)

In view of the number of happy marriages which have gladdened High River this fall we propose boosting the good work along by a course of lectures this winter. The subjects will of course be biblical, since anything in the lecture line which is not of a political nature must, according to village ethics, be held under the auspices of a church. We have not yet secured our church, but are expecting a favorable reply from the Church of the Immaculate Shirtfront in a day or two. The subjects will be "Miriam, the Beautiful Bachelor Girl," "Rachel in Love at First Sight," "Ruth, Love in the Barley Field," and kindred subjects. Love and love-making is never prosy and general interest in the subject should be promoted by these lectures. Get your tickets early and avoid the rush. (October 24, 1903)

The church has too many glaring inconsistencies, just like civilization. They send missionaries out to China to convert the Chinks and try to get them into the kingdom of heaven, but they won't let 'em into this country. (October 24, 1903)

Theatres are full to overflowing in our cities six nights out of the week and people pay well for their seats. The churches are open one day in the week, and although a nickel will see the vilest sinner through, the attendance is light and perfunctory. Can the psychologist explain this? One may as well look disagreeable questions in the face. (October 24, 1903)

Fresh light on the Eden story. Eve was so easily tempted because she wanted some clothes.[8]

What always gives us an unpleasant jolt when we go to church is to see the nickels and dimes dropped into the plate by people who are ever ready to cough up six bits or a dollar to see a bum show. (February 13, 1904)

Your average preacher and platform orator, from the very nature of his job, must keep well up in the clouds, far above the heads of his audience. Otherwise the people would think they were not getting a run for the nickel they put in the plate.

A sinking to earth to grapple with a low-down subject like booze, in all its coarse and repulsive detail, would belittle and cheapen him in the eyes of the ice-water sacrosancts before whom he plays his part. It would queer him, sure. (July 2, 1904)

Last Sunday a prominent clergyman in

Startling phase of the Sunday Observance Act.

No, that is not a real parson. That is a mechanical dummy, fixed up with wire springs and clockwork interior to provide the necessary gesticulations. Now that the Sunday Observance Act is on tap it has been discovered that it must apply to parsons as well as to laymen. A sermon and a line of prayers are shot into a phonograph and turned on when the service is ready. The organist is also a dummy with spring attachments. Inventors are now at work on dummy congregations, so that no one will have anything to do on Sundays at all. Which is apparently the object desired. A Central Power House is being erected at Winnipeg to provide long distance services from coast to coast. Messrs. Score and Georgeson will speak their best sermons into the main phonograph.

If you must play golf on Sunday, play good golf.[9]

Calgary took occasion in his sermon to deprecate public exposure of scandals. Whether the reverend gentleman was giving the *Eye Opener* a gentle poke in the fifth rib or not we do not know. The recent exposure of a public man which has caused so much talk was an exceptional case, inasmuch as it unveiled the hypocrisy and moral obliquity of a man to whom the most important affairs of this country had been entrusted. It was an exposure distinctly pro bono publico. This paper does not handle frivolous scandals nor indulge in mischief-making to tickle the reader. Give us credit for so much anyhow. If our friend, the clergyman, only knew all the interesting local items that we DON'T put in, he would understand this and give us a white mark. Being a high-minded English gentleman himself, he is doubtless loath to believe anything bad of anyone on another's say-so. But it does not do to be too tender-hearted when dealing with dangerous political anachronisms like Sifton. These gentry are in the habit of riding roughshod themselves over the common herd and a touch of their own medicine does them no harm.

It is a good many yeas since Charles Dana received a committee of ministers in the office of the *Sun* and, after listening to a long plaint that he was handling too many things without gloves; that he was printing a good many things which were better left unprinted, turned on the gentlemen of the cloth suddenly and said:

"Whatever God Almighty permits to happen, is fit to print in a newspaper. I believe that and I'm going to keep on printing the *Sun* along those lines. Goodday." (March 18, 1905)

The Rev. Mr. Kerby's sermon last Sunday evening dealing with the farm and the glories of farm life was one of those smug and complacent word pictures to which we have long become accustomed from listening to glib tongued politicians addressing workingmen on the virtue of honest toil. We should like to hear Mr. Kerby preach a companion sermon on the same subject from the hired man's point of view. There is more humbug and nonsense written and spoken about the old homestead than about any other subject—usually by men whose experience of country life is gained at Sunday School picnics or during trips in a buckboard collecting installments on Massey-Harris notes. (November 25, 1905)

The only member of a hotel staff mentioned in the Bible is the dishwasher. Turn up II. Kings, 21:13, and you will read: "I will wipe out Jerusalem as a man in a tavern wipeth out a dish, wiping it and turning it upside down." The hotel clerk is not mentioned and the bartender is ignored altogether. (September 22, 1906)

When Lot was fleeing from Sodom and saw his wife turned into a pillar of salt, he was in a great quandary. Looking around his eye fell upon a signboard near by:

This is a dry world. Those of us who eventually wind up in hell should burn brightly.[10]

Lots for Sale.

Seizing this he fetched it over to where his saline spouse was standing and with a little ingenuity he made it read:

Lots Wife for Sale.

Then he sat down and waited for a customer, wondering the while whether it would not be as well to advertise in the *Calgary Eye Opener* also. (December 22, 1906)

What we really need is a new religion, one that will appeal not only to the well-to-do and cultured, but to the masses and the poor—to those who haven't any Sunday clothes. We can find nowhere in the Bible that the Christian religion is for the well-to-do and not for the poor and humble. On the contrary, we find that Christ taught the very opposite. Were the Savior to come to earth he would undoubtedly become head of the Salvation Army, an organization that closely and literally follows his teachings.

Perhaps the people who are dissatisfied with the Christian religion have become prejudiced by watching the week-day conduct of those who attend church and profess Christianity. For instance, the scoundrel who tried to encompass our ruin in Calgary last year, was a Methodist and a regular attender at church, so you can understand the cynicism with which we regard such people.

But do not let such people disturb you. Christ found them here when He came to earth, and they are here yet. Did He not say, "Woe unto you, hypocrites, whited sepulchres?" If people are hypocrites now the curse on them will be the greater, because now they are living in a day of light.

Heaven and hell really do exist—the writer has been in both. If a man wants to find heaven he can find it where it really is, within himself, by obeying the commandments of God.

It may be that some of the churches have wandered away from the truth, and that they may think more of pipe organs and costly buildings and basket socials and money-raising schemes than of ministering to the poor and unfortunate, but they do not learn those things from the teachings of Christ. Let us put the blame where it belongs, not on the religion, but on the people. Christ's message to the hypocrite is the same today as it was 2,000 years ago: "Ye are they of whom the prophet spoke, ye draw night unto me with your mouths, but your hearts far from me." (December 18, 1909)

The Outcast's Prayer

Almighty God, All-powerful God, we come to thee today and seek your assistance. We ask thee to rectify the great evils that exist in this old world thou hast created and to remove the cause of misery, starvation, privation, degradation, and poverty, in the land of the free and the home of the brave. Oh Lord, have mercy on the millions of workingmen that are

Eve had the best husband in the world—at that time.[11]

being butchered every day in Christian Europe, for every war is a rich man's war and a poor man's fight. In times of peace our stomachs yearn for a beefsteak. In time of war we are filled with bullets. And, Oh Lord, we ask thee to stop this useless murdering of innocent men.

Let those who declare war do the fighting. Let those Champagne Guzzling, Bleary-Eyed, Bald-Headed Plutocrats fight their own battles. It they want blood, let them shed their own blood.

Oh Lord, deliver us from the greed and graft that exists in this nation and from the parasites who neither toil nor spin, but bedeck their persons with finery until they glitter in the gloaming like a rotten dog salmon afloat in the moonlight.

Oh, wonderful God, deliver us! We are blessed with preachers who draw fat salaries. Men pray to you to send heaven on earth, and the rest of the week dare you to do it. Verily, our institutions are badly mixed, for we have Bible houses, baudy houses, barrel houses and breweries. Oh Lord, help us, for we have criminals, paupers and hordes of industrial cannibals whom we call business men, professors who draw their salary and convictions from the same source. Oh Lord, merciful God, we have thieves, theologians, Christians and confidence men; also priests, prisons, politicians, and poverty; convents, convicts, scabs and scallawags; traces of virtue and tons of vice. We have trusts and tramps, money and misery, homes and hunger; salvation and soup, and psalms sung by hypocrites

in an organized bummery who expect to pave their way to heaven by begging old pants, coats and hats and in thy name sell them to the poor, thereby spreading disease and vermin to multiply. Protect us, Oh Lord, and deliver us, for the groceries association holds us up, while poverty holds us down. Some of our butchers put embalming fluid on putrified beef, for they knew that it would not stink and the unsuspecting public would eat it without belching. Deliver us from those who make canned beef out of sick cows, mules and horses, and corpses of those who eat it, and may the price of hamburger, beef stews, waffels and holey doughnuts come down and our wages come up to meet them, and may we be permitted to fill up on those luxuries three times a day, for to be without them causes great pain in our gastric region.

The Lord will provide—that is, he will provide us with the ability to provide for ourselves. The manna-from-heaven stunt has never responded to an encore. (January 1, 1910)

How is it that biblical characters had no surnames? What were Mathew, Mark, Luke and John's other names, if they had any? Some, it is true, were distinguished by descriptive additions, like Simon the Cellarer and Peter the Painter, but the bulk to them are handed down to us by their Christian name only. Among the exceptions we notice our old college chum, Pontius Pilate, to say nothing of the McGillicuddy of that period, Judas

Were we, perhaps, not happier when we were monkeys?[12]

Iscariot. Neither Adam nor Eve seem to have had any family patronymic at all. (October 28, 1911)

A good many people do not believe in the efficacy of prayer because the Lord gives them what they deserve instead of what they ask for. (March 23, 1912)

Wetaskiwin for us has many cherished memories. It was here that we commenced our brilliant and checkered journalistic career in Canada, running the *Free Lance*, a remarkable paper, with as much eclat as was possible to be squeezed out of a burg of 200 inhabitants, all more or less busted. The paper showed a regular net profit every month of $98.00.

One thing in connection with the *Free Lance* we remember very vividly. Having been elected recorder of the local A.O.U.W., we had in our possession the key of the Presbyterian church, where the meetings of the order were held. When the day of the week wore around for us to grind out copy to send down to the printers in Calgary, our office would be almost sure to be occupied by a hilarious bunch of drunks, singing songs, and shouting and yelling. Under these circumstances we would put a flask in our pocket and quietly slip away to the church and lock ourselves in, writing all the comical stuff we could think of in the pulpit, our wits being stimulated at appropriate intervals from the flask aforesaid. One Monday morning the preacher came into the office very wrathy because at the morning service he had found an empty flask on the little shelf behind the desk where the Bible and hymn book were kept. We apologized very humbly but he was very huffy about it. (June 18, 1912)

And, Oh Lord, we do not understand why poodle dogs have private baths and are attended by maids and valets, are shampooed, manicured and kissed, fed on choice steaks and drink cream, while thousands of little children made after your own image, live off garbage cans. Christ never said, suffer little poodle dogs to come unto me; and Oh Lord, may the society women cease to give their affections to poodle dogs instead of to babies.

And, Oh Lord, we ask thee to have mercy on the blanket stiffs, such as railroaders, loggers, muckers and skinners, and may they be permitted to make at least seven dollars and six bits before they get fired, and may their mulligans be of better class and contain no more old shoes, gum-boots and scrap iron, and may their blankets rest lightly on their blistered backs and contain no insects that might discommode them.

May the farmer plant his spuds more closely to the railroad track, and his chickens roam more closely to the jungles, and we will ever be grateful to the all-powerful God.

Amen. (February 26, 1916)

John P. Quigley, the local evangelist, who

More people would go to church if it wasn't exactly the proper thing to do.[13]

fell into an open sewer and broke his flask, has fully recovered and is now able to be about. (April 8, 1916)

We hate to preach like this, but ever since some joker spread the report that the editor who is now addressing you had joined the ministry, we have felt very preachy. The law of suggestion, we presume. (March 18, 1916)

A correspondent from Olds writes to say that he went into a store there the other day to ask for an *Eye Opener* and was told that they did not sell such papers, as it would corrupt the morals of the town.

(From the fact that one of Olds' ministers of the gospel some three weeks ago, eloped with a young lady of that burg, he already having a wife and child in the States, we may be justified in presuming that the morals of Olds need no further corrupting just at present. This scandal should hold them for a while.—Ed.) (September 22, 1917)

The editor of the rag you are now reading went to church last Sabbath evening. Before entering the sacred precincts he removed a pair of rubber overshoes and set them down carefully in the vestibule. At the close of the service he found a pair of worn-out "gums" where the new overshoes should have been. It is bad enough to be a highway robber and a murderer, but the most detestable scamp of all is the scamp who will come to the house of God with an abiding impulse to steal whatever is found loose. And the crime is all the blacker when a man will steal from a Unionist editor whose poverty is one of the pathetic features of the nineteenth century, second only to the pitiable scenes in Flanders. Oh, the baseness of this bloody outrage! (December 15, 1917)

Religion is, after all, a very personal and intimate affair. How many regular churchgoers go down on their knees in the quiet of their chamber and hold communion with their God? Precious few, we take it. The church can have its eloquent preachers, swell choirs, accomplished organists and ultra-respectable vestries, but if the Sunday devotions are not merged in the daily lives of those who profess Christianity by attendance at church, then the ultimate effect is nil.

Still, one must not get into the habit of decrying the church or belittling the

Faith is a belief in something you know isn't so.[14]

efforts of those engaged in church work. The latter is uphill work indeed. Perhaps if the preachers could get a little closer to the people by participating more in their amusements, recreations and so on, it might help some. Unfortunately, the job of a preacher is something like that of a Supreme Court judge; it automatically keeps the ubiquitous hoi polloi at arms' length. Which is unfortunate, but true.

Take our own case. We have lived in this neck of the woods for twenty-five years, exactly a quarter of a century, and we do not know a single minister occupying a Calgary pulpit. Not only do we not know any of them personally, but we don't even know one of them by sight, always excepting Bishop Pinkham. This is a literal fact. How do you account for it? We know almost everybody else.

There must be something wrong. From what we hear from others, our Calgary ministers must be very likeable men. But where do they keep themselves? On Sundays a fairy waves a wand and lo! there they are standing in front of you in church as large as life, telling you all about the children of Israel. At the close of the evening service the fairy once more waves her wand, and the preacher disappears. (February 22, 1919)

Which is the worse from a moral standpoint: a man drinking a glass of beer or a preacher stuffing a kid's head full of a lot of supernatural nonsense? (April 5, 1919)

The Ford is my jitney;

I shall not want for whiskey;

It maketh me to lie down in wet waters;

It soileth my clothes;

It leadeth me into deep waters;

It leadeth me into paths of ridicule for its namesake;

It prepareth a breakdown for me in the presence of mine enemies;

Yes, though I run through the valleys, I am towed up the hills.

I fear great evil when it is with me;

Its rods and its engines discomfort me.

It anointeth my face with oil,

Its tank runneth over.

Surely to goodness, if this thing follows me all the days of my life I shall dwell in the house of Ponoka forever. (*Summer Annual*, 1920)

The craze about communicating with the spirits of the dead seems to be petering out, like other passing fads. One of Calgary's more prominent pastors, a man of culture and given to thinking out problems for himself, gave Sir Oliver Lodge and his psychic fancies an awful wallop not so very long ago. And yet one would expect support from the Church for spiritualism, the Bible being full of it. Needless to say, the pastor referred to is a Scotchman, averse to humbug in whatsoever guise it may appear.

It may seem rather a crude thing to say, but, if the truth were told, very few people

The Salvation Army is religion with its coat off.[15]

believe in the immortality of the soul or in the hereafter. What makes us think so is this, that you never hear anybody talking about it in conversation. Do you suppose for a moment, if men really believe in a future life—as almost all profess to do—that every man over fifty years of age wouldn't be making due preparation and at least occasionally referring to it in the course of chats with his friends?

But no! You never hear a word about it outside of the pulpit of a Sunday. The elderly man planning to visit Europe next year prattles about it all the time and bores his friends to death telling them of how he is going to look over the battle-scarred fields of Flanders, and makes tremendous preparations for his trip; but the same elderly man, with the prospect of the longest journey of all a few short years ahead of him, and the added prospect of an entirely new existence that is to last to all eternity, does not seemingly bother his head about it. He doesn't take it seriously and makes absolutely no preparation.

And about the Bible. The Christian world concedes that it is the greatest book in existence, a wondrous piece of sacred literature. And yet you never catch anybody reading it. Did you ever see a man in the rotunda of a hotel sitting comfortably smoking and perusing the Bible? You never did. How often have you visited a private home in Calgary and discovered a member of the family reading the Bible? Never. The only people who seem to indulge in honest perusal of the Bible are men about to be hanged. And even then, should a reprieve arrive, they will switch off to the *B. E. Summer Annual* as quickly as possible. (July 17, 1920)

Lord, let me keep a straight way in the path of honor—and a straight face in the presence of solemn asses. Let me not truckle to the high, nor bulldoze the low; let me frolic with the jack and the joker

A New Stunt

and win the game. Lead me unto Truth and Beauty—and tell me her name. Keep me sane, but not too sane. Let me not take the world or myself too seriously, and grant more people to laugh with and fewer to laugh at. (August 20, 1921)

Oh, for a prophet to appear and teach us

The man who uses religion as a cloak in this world may have more use for a smoking jacket in the next.[16]

how to have a riproaring time decently! How to raise merry hell without hurting anybody, including ourselves! We know all the rules for being good. Will someone please rise and explain how we may be good, though full of physical electricity? (September 24, 1921)

The Okotoks Methodist Ladies' Aid will give a bean supper from 6 to 8 p.m., followed by a musical program. (*Summer Annual*, 1922)

When a man mixes religion with politics the religion is apt to lose its identity.[17]

CHAPTER THREE

Jopplebunky, Frukkledumky, Chucklesnorter, Jinks

In which your crackerjack reporter provides all the local news that's fit to fabricate.

"A man can claim to have 'arrived' when his private affairs begin to interest the public."

—Bob Edwards' Summer Annual, 1922

Nothing tickles the fancy quicker, or with more queasy precision, than the misfortune of others. Merriment can be further increased by cheerily noting extreme variance between the aforementioned misfortune & one's own lot in life. (It works! Try it!)

Students of sunny misanthropy will therefore find much to enjoy in Bob Edwards's finely limned moonshine sketches of smalltown misery. Having cut his journalistic teeth peddling morbid gossip[1] to vacationing Europeans (selections from this journeyman period are printed here for the first time in 125 years!), Edwards decamped for the colonies, where he used his experience to satirize newspaper conventions of the day. In these pages, please find "send-ups" of, but not limited to—

☞ Social announcements!

☞ Theatre reviews!

☞ Household hints!

☞ Advice columns!

☞ Celebrity profiles!

☞ Apologies for the above!

Please be of the mind to remember that names & details are strictly bogus. Except when they are not.

---

[1] By his own account, Edwards published *The Channel* (1881) in Boulogne-sur-Mer, France. (Taking the word of a man who fudged his age is a leap of faith, as the paper carried no masthead.) In *Eye Opener Bob*, Grant MacEwan refers to another Edwards-edited Anglo tourist rag, *The Traveller*, but the source of this info is unknown. One wonders whether years of Bob lore somehow conflated the two titles. The only extant copy of *The Traveller*, allegedly published in Milan (!) in 1879, is held by the Bibliothèque nationale de France; access is extremely limited due to its fragile condition.

I commend the following to the notice of residents in Boulogne "of that ilk:"— James Keely, of Macclesfield, on Sunday night playfully presented a loaded revolver at the head of Matilda Royle, saying, "Must I shoot thee, Tilly?" The revolver went off, and the shot lodged in Royle's forehead. She died in half an hour. Deceased, who was to have been married next week, was 22 years of age. (*The Channel*, June 25, 1881)

Last week a dog suffering from hydrophobia was discovered at large near Wissant, having escaped from the village of Verlinethun. It was immediately pursued and shot, after having attacked and severely bitten another dog it had met on its way. (*The Channel*, June 25, 1881)

On Tuesday morning at Dunkerque a little girl two years old fell into a tub of boiling water which had just been removed from the fire. Every care was immediately bestowed on the child who expired some hours afterwards. (*The Channel*, June 25, 1881)

Messrs. Marshall and Costello, the jovial gentlemen who sit all day long playing sonatas on the keys of Liszt and Paderewsky, have informed us that they will refrain from playing on this instrument Thanksgiving day. Wherefore, if the locals from Wetaskiwin are somewhat curtailed this week, blame the day. (*Wetaskiwin Free Lance*, December 1, 1898)

What were they doing at the fire hall the night before last? About 10 o'clock yesterday having occasion to visit a friend, who had been there, we found him in bed. He sat up and asked us if he had been to a wedding or a wake. (*Wetaskiwin Free Lance*, December 1, 1898)

Ole Peterkin,
" Sundawgle,
" Tronjenier,
" Podlesen,
" Jorgval,
from Stony creek, were in town Monday and all got beastly drunk. After roaring and bellowing about the streets for a while, they hitched up and returned to their farms. (*Wetaskiwin Breeze*, March 13, 1901)

The best show of the season was that Ponoka conjuring entertainment last week. The eminent conjurer could make anything disappear he wanted to, especially booze. His gifted manager, Old Roth, also disappeared with the gate receipts while the performance was in progress. A fashionable throng was present. Mr. and Mrs. Joel Slop were present in a box, or rather a dry goods box, and seemed to enjoy the entertainment. Ms. Slop was tastefully dressed in fur lined shoes. Miss Flora Selwyn was in the paraquet wearing little else but a bland smile. Mr. Selwyn, her talented father, was becomingly attired in the suit of clothes he had taken from the corpse of the man

A feeling of superiority is the sole satisfaction some men get out of being good.[1]

he murdered last fall, who was known to be a good dresser. Those Ponoka society events are great features up north. (*Wetaskiwin Breeze*, April 18, 1901)

———

Our genial but cautious publisher writes advising us to use the word "alleged" more, as being safer in case of libel suits. We'll use it right now. J. W. Pringar of Cayley, with his alleged daughter, paid High River a visit last week. After putting his alleged horse in the barn Mr. Pringar filled up on some alleged whiskey which seemed to affect his alleged brains. It was alleged by those who saw him capering about the burg that he is under ordinary circumstances an alleged man, but few who saw him climb our flagstaff backwards will believe that he is other than a monkey. Mr. Pringar and his alleged daughter, after making extensive purchases of alleged pork sausages from George Myer, returned home the same evening, Miss P. driving. (April 4, 1902)

———

Last Wednesday being a lovely day we took a stroll out in the country and visited the charming Miss Louise Hinks. After a pleasant tête à tête with the lady we were driven home by her father, with a club. (January 16, 1903)

———

Mrs. Maybrick Preparing to Leave Aylesbury Jail.

Society Note—Miss Lottie Migglethorpe, whose hosiery is almost as remarkable as her voice, has accepted an engagement of thirty days at the Edmonton police station. When going full blast, Miss Migglethorpe can be heard for miles around and many people at the beaches think that the weird rumblings come from the Fabyan oil well. She read an interesting paper on Gordon gin at the meeting of the Leduc Y.W.C.A. last week, giving some wonderful demonstrations to illustrate her remarks. It is hardly likely that this talented lecturer will appear again in Leduc for some time. (January 30, 1903)

———

Miss Imogene McGonigle, daughter of the eminent cowman "old man McGonigle," who sold his steers last week at the top figure, gave a Soiree Musicale at the magnificent family residence which they got for a song from Bill Moran who went broke last year paying lawyers to get him acquitted of his last cattle-rustling charge. Herr von Valcheri gave a violin senato in F major and was heartily encored, responding with imitations of the farmyard. The quacking of ducks was rendered with delightful inconsciance. Miss Sadie d'Almaine contributed three songs, Massenet's "Les Larnes,"

Any man who repeats half what he hears talks too much.[2]

Schumann's "Widmung," and Reneld's "Oh, Lovely Night," with charming effect. Miss McGonigle, who apologised for her father having rather a skate on, gave two piano solos, Brahm's "Rhapsody" in G minor, and an "Etude" of Saint-Saens. Miss McGonigle intends pursuing her musical studies at the Conservatoire on the Blackfoot Reserve which is famous for imparting a certain swing to tunes ancient and modern. (August 22, 1903)

In our account of a bogus wedding which appeared in last issue we gave its supposed bridegroom a name which we thought belonged to no one in this country. It appears, as bad luck would have it, that we chanced on the name of a gentleman in the Gladys district and we hasten to express our regret for the mistake, or rather, the unhappy coincidence. (November 21, 1903)

The engagement is announced of Mr. William J. Sahara, of the hills, to Miss Marguerite Sweeney, of Medicine Hat. Mr. Sahara has lots of sand. (November 21, 1903)

The Fairies' Spring, a cantata, was produced by local talent at the Opera House last Tuesday followed by a concert made up of local talent. The music was confined to the works of British composers. Part First was sung by ladies exclusively, and Part Second—the concert—by gentlemen exclusively. As there was no electric or any other kind of light—to lighten the Gentiles, the audience sat throughout the performance in utter darkness, unable to read their programmes. Mrs. Broder, the accompanyist, found it impossible to read her music until a thoughtful gentleman hustled around and got a kerosene lamp to place by the piano. Several people were observed striking matches to look at their watches. As for the general evening's entertainment—the judgment shown in the musical selections and our opinion thereof—we would say that

_____ _____ _____

____ _____ _____

_____ __ _____ __

!!!____ ____ _____ __ __ __

_____ __

_____ ____ _____? _____

_____ _____ _____

_____ _____ __

_____ ____ __ _____

_____ _____ ___!!!__

_____ ____ ___ ____

_____ _____? _____

_____ _____ __ __

_____

_____ ____ ____ _____

_____? ____ _____ _____

_____ ____ ____ _____

_____!!!_____

_____ _____ ____

____

_____ _____? __ _____

_____ _____ _____

__ ____ _____

___!!!_____ _____ ____

If you would know what your friends say about you when you are absent,
listen to what is said about others in your presence.[3]

It is entirely their own fault when capable performers, by consenting to sing songs and play tunes concocted by unmusical composers, fail to do themselves justice. If British composers cannot turn out better stuff than what was dished up on this occasion they should confine their efforts to composing new cries for London street-vendors. A touch of Arthur Sullivan or Molloy would have helped a lot, but these composers wrote too absurdly pretty music to suit the classics walls of Hull's Opera House. The best numbers, "Trovatore" and "Farewell," were not by British composers at all, but by Verdi and Mascani respectively. Parts of the Fairies' Spring, like the curate's boiled egg, were good, and what there was of it was prettily sung especially a contralto solo by Miss Louisa Logan. Miss May Rankin fittingly wound up Part I with a well-rendered solo, "But the World Shall Claim Him Never," the words apparently referring to the gentleman who wrote the Cantata. (July 2, 1904)

The Press Association Excursion to Banff and the Glacier was an immense success and, although the private car "MacGillicuddy" was fairly bulging out at the side with cases of Scotch and Seagram and Beautiful Beer, your Uncle Robert stood steadfast and viewed the gorgeous mountain scenery with an eye undimmed by booze. We mention this supreme triumph of the cure Keelyatica jagorum as a gentle hint to all slobsters.

On this trip the Association made one fatal mistake and that was in not spending all the time at its disposal at Banff where it could have put in a delightful three days. As it was, we were on the cars most of the time and, to those who were not full of booze, the latter part of the trip became somewhat tiresome.

At Banff our convention was held. Messrs. Jamieson and Dennis, of the C.P.R. delivered sensible addresses and were the recipients of many cordial expressions of gratitude for the substantial courtesies extended to the Association by their company.

Dr. Brett, of course, was very much in evidence and was the personification of geniality, recklessly abandoning his own business to see that we had a high old time. We really should have stayed right there and kept on having a high old time.

The Doc packed us all into a lot of rigs and drove us out to Devil's Lake, where Standy and Watson have their pretty little steam launch. We were the honored and appreciative guests of these gentlemen on a delightful sail over this most picturesque of lakes, a deep blue body of water hemmed in by mighty mountains and recalling to memory the lochs of bonny Scotland. This lake swarms with trout, weighing from 20 to 50 pounds, according to what Standby and Watson think your credulity will stand.

Coming back, we were shown around the great Bankhead mine by Superintendent Stockett and were introduced to several of the gentlemen connected with the works. They all read their *Eye Opener*

A good deal of conversation should be canned and the can thrown away.[4]

every Sunday with religious attention, so they MUST be all right. We trust they will in due course prove that they are all right, by voting for our mutual friend, the Doc. What ho, Brabantio!

Glacier was a bit of a disappointment. We lost $5 at poker at the place, didn't see Marion Lake, didn't climb up to the little houses above the waterfall, didn't see the glacier at all and were defeated in five straight games of fifteen-ball pool by Doc Stewart. We should all have remained at Banff. (September 9, 1905)

The *Midnapore Gazette* is working up quite a circulation. This is one of the brightest local sheets on the south branch. Here are a few of its locals—

We understand that Mr. Shaw is seriously thinking of painting his front fence a beautiful yellow. Midnapore is the home of art.

Bob Kellock, manager of the new hotel, fell over a cow lying on the sidewalk as he was returning from church Sunday evening and the result was a skinned nose and several bruises. It is surely time this village was incorporated and a system of law and order established. Whither are we drifting?

Little Willie Fewclothes fell into Fish Creek while fishing last Thursday and was drowned. His young and blithesome life was nipped in the bud by the turgid torrents of Fish Creek. In the midst of life we are in death. His parents intended to make a parson of Willie, and he could already repeat several chapters of the bible. Much sympathy is felt for Mr. and Mrs. Fewclothes in their bereavement. See Mr. Fewclothes' ad on fourth page.

In his sermon last Sunday the Rev. Johnson referred to the tremendous strain put on the brains of editors to keep up with the times. There is hardly a night that we don't go home with our head in a whirl and our mind in a state of chaos, and yet how many people think of this when they pick up a copy of the *Gazette*? (August 25, 1906)

The following little helpful "nevers" should be framed and hung up in every library:

Never cut bread on a valuable book. It is likely to injure the binding.

Never cut the leaves of a book with carving knife until you have first wiped it clean.

Never turn leaves with your thumb knife. Use a safety razor.

Never turn leaves with your thumb. A pair of small tongs, such as come with boxes of bonbons, is the best thing to use.

Never put a hot iron on an open book, unless it is a Roycroft book, in which case the pyrography will be likely to improve its appearance.

Never throw a book at the cook unless it is a cookbook. It injures the corners and delays the dinner.

Never set a very young baby down on an open book, especially a valuable book. (August 25, 1906)

Some men drop all their money trying to pick up more.[5]

A chicken pot-pie supper and entertainment will be given next Thursday evening in the Methodist church. Tickets, 50 cents. (October 20, 1906)

Mr. and Mrs. Orville Roy Browne sent out cards this week for a reception in honor of their son, Percy, who has just returned from New York. Percy's career is of more than ordinary interest. He started life in the big city, unknown and practically penniless, being too proud to borrow from his parents. He stood off a merchant for a basket and then obtained credit for enough tinware to fill it. With this he started peddling. That is ten years ago. Today, Percy ain't worth a bean and still owes for the basket. (November 10, 1906

The following request comes to hand:

Dear Mr. *Eye Opener,*—

My mother, recognising that you have considerable wisdom, has suggested to me to write and ask your advice how to be good.

Yours truly,

Jemima P. Watkins

Be ugly, and you can't help but be good. Ed. (November 10, 1906)

Coming Events—At the Alexandra Hall, Thursday evening at 8 o'clock, Miss Leta Long, the reformed chorus girl of Black Brook fame, will give a vivid description for Men Only of her experiences in the Tower of Madison Square Garden. Prof

Why Robert Mantell Never Returned to Calgary

Bael will sing "Only A Pansy Blossom" and Tosti's "Goodbye." The Men Only are requested to bring their own refreshments. A good time is expected to be had. (March 9, 1907)

At the conflagration that destroyed a part of Mr. John Templeman's woodshed the other evening it was generally remarked that Mr. Sam Grawklehanger did all that could have been expected of any hero. He rescued a washtub and fell off the roof, and would have done more if the fire had not been put out.

Mr. James Spiffkins, our talented grocer, had the misfortune to spill a quart of coal oil over four pounds of butter the other day, and he at once thought of us and sent the butter to our house. He has our warmest thanks. The taste is rather strong, but we shall try to wriggle it down some way. (May 16, 1908)

The many friends of Hiram McCluskey will learn with pleasure that he is now tapered off down to two drinks per hour. Mr. McCluskey's iron constitution has

If there was not a sucker born every minute the other half of the world would starve to death.[6]

68

stood him in good stead during this, the hour of his affliction.

It is whispered that Mlle. Leta de Longue and Mlle. Bernice Palmerre, the latter of whom is expected down from her chateau near Edmonton, will both appear on the race track during our Dominion Fair dressed in directoire gowns. If you don't know what directoire gown is, ask a policeman. (June 13, 1908)

Society note—Mr. Thos. B. McGuigan is suffering from a severe attack of delirium tremens. (December 12, 1908)

We learn that Miss Mary E. Frobisher, of Didsbury, is engaged to be married to the well-known Calgarian, Mr. John T. Billcoe, on Nov. 20. It is apparent that Titania was not the only woman who loved a donkey. (November 18, 1911)

Mrs. P. Q. Shinkleblister, 1301 Twenty-sixth Avenue West, will receive this afternoon. She will be glad to receive anything, preferably something in the bottled goods line.

Mr. J. B. Clinktwister, 2898 Twenty-eight Avenue East, will receive the first Thursday of every month, the second Tuesday of every week, the fourth Friday before the last Saturday, and the second last Wednesday before each Monday.

Mrs. P. B. McSquatulium, Parsnip Lodge, was the hostess at a charming pink whiskey last Wednesday. Mrs. McSquatulium was gowned in a garni-ture of red curtain tassels and looked very chic. (March 9, 1912)

For the fourth time within five years, the "Who's Who" stunt has been pulled off with financial eclat in our midst. *The History of Alberta* is the latest. We don't know who got this thing up, but whoever it was must have made a pot of money. The work is in two volumes and has hundreds of biographies of the Great Men of Alberta, such as Terry McGraw and Mike McCoole, with steel engravings and all the rest of it. Getting one's pikcher in the book, along with a high sounding biography, cost $250, with a copy of the book thrown in. Great stuff, eh? We counted 582 biographies. Of course it didn't cost so much without the pikcher.

Only those who commented to cough up to those brigands got a mention in this History, or Who's Who, or whatever it is. The three Calgarians who are most widely known throughout the Dominion of Canada, to wit, P. J. Nolan, M. S. McCarthy and R. B. Bennett, are not mentioned at all. The promoters of this soft thing were wise enough to enlist the services of a prominent man of good repute to write the actual history of the Province, in order to give the thing tone and a touch of authority. They got Dr. A. O. MacRae, Ph.D., to write it and he made an excellent job of it. Indeed, this part is the only redeeming feature and is too valuable a piece of work to be thrust into a mass of wriggling biographies of eminent bounders.

People always laugh at the fool things you try to do, until they discover you are making money out of them.[7]

We venture to quote from a few of these $250 biographies. Let us take the biography of John P. Cleghorn, for instance:

"Among the most popular and progressive cleaner and presser of clothes in the city of Calgary must be mentioned John P. Cleghorn. Mr. Cleghorn has been prominently and successfully identified for many years with the pants of many of Calgary's leading citizens and is an earnest church worker. Born at an early age in St. Thomas, Ont., Mr. Cleghorn received a liberal education and came west, where he quickly showed a great avidity for booze. Having by persistence and courage and a sublime faith in his own destiny succeeded in weathering a number of exceptionally severe attacks of delirium tremens, Mr. Cleghorn pushed ahead, overcame every obstacle, and now is justly regarded throughout the length and breadth of the City of the Foothills as one of the most successful, enterprising, prominent, distinguished, phenomenal, collateral, respected, honored and public spirited exponents of the clothes-pressing at in the civilized world to-day."

(This costs Johnnie two and hundred and fifty bucks.)

The we pick out the biography of Alfred J. Renwick:

"Probably no man living today in the civilized world is held in higher esteem by the leading and prominent citizens of Calgary than Robert T. Renwick, the talented liveryman. Mr. Renwick was born south of the line, being the son of the late Peter Renwick, who was hanged at Shelby Junction in the 1893 for stealing horses from the Felury ranch. The subject of our sketch moved to Alberta in the fall of '93 with the horses which his father was hanged for stealing and has since conducted a thriving business as a conscientious horse trader, winning not only affluence, but also the kindly regard of all people with whom he has never done any business. His specialty is filing the teeth of aged horses, showing his tenderness of heart in thus alleviating the antiquity and preserving the youth of man's greatest friend. Mr. Renwick is a member of several churches and belongs to the Eagles. He is a bird. The greatest regret of his life is that he never learned to play golf. He is yet on the threshold of life and if his future success is at all commensurate with his gall, Mr. Renwick should become one of the wealthiest men in the province as he is now one of the most enterprising. We predict a bright future for Robert."

(Another 250 bucks.)

But why proceed any more? The biographies are all couched in the same strain. Each and every man written up is the most successful, the most pop'lar and the most prom'nent cit'zen that ever came over the pike. We wonder how the man that got up this book knew that we didn't have 250 bucks. Somebody must have told him. Poverty hath its recompense. What? (April 20, 1912)

Be good and you'll be happy—perhaps.[8]

Mrs. W. P. Frukkledumky will not receive again this summer. She dropped dead last Tuesday and is hardly in a position to pour tea for the talent.

At the monthly meeting of the Browning club at the charming residence of Mrs. Chucklebuster on 12th Avenue a charming paper on "Green Soap for Scalp Itches" was read by Miss Rosie Pinkleblunder. A lively discussion followed, after which refreshments were served, tea being poured by Rosie with charming eclat.

Mrs. Guzzlechuckster, of Fourteenth Avenue, gave a delightful dance one night last week to a select few. While executing the can-can diabolique at the top of the stairs, gyrating rapidly and yelling at the top of her voice, Mrs. Guzzlechuckster fell headlong to the bottom and nearly broke her neck. The guests laughed heartily at the chic episode. Coffee and ices were served and a most agreeable time was had. (May 18, 1912)

Mr. Peter McSwattie, the well known real estate agent, gave a farewell banquet to his numerous victims at the Alberta hotel Wednesday night. Mr. McSwattie, in a stirring address, beseeched them to keep cool, to be calm, assuring them that their children's grandchildren would arise a hundred years hence and call them blessed for having had the enterprise, the forethought, the courage, the backbone to see so far ahead of their generation and invest in his magnificent subdivision twelve miles from the post office. With the kindly co-operation of Mr. Seagram and Mr. J. Dewar the guests became mollified and later on accompanied Mr. McSwattie to the depot, where he caught the midnight train for the coast. Mr. McSwattie, who took his harpoons along, will open a real estate office in Victoria. (May 18, 1912)

Society Note—Mr. George J. Jinks, the popular Calgary real estate agent, is on his way home from England. At least this is the information received by Chief Cuddy from Scotland Yard. He is said to be accompanied by a rather nifty piece of goods. (August 3, 1912)

E. B. McWhirrie, the charming poker player, gave an "at home" last Wednesday evening to a number of his friends. The host was attired in a chic pair of striped pants and presided at the table in sleeves a la shirt. The decorations involved a pretty color scheme of red, white and blue discs made from celluloid and circular in shape. A delightful evening was spent. Also considerable money.

The lecture which was to have been delivered last Friday by Mr. Ferdinand Murray, the noted English publicist, on "Cockfighting in the Middle Ages," was postponed until next Monday. Mr. Murray had by some oversight miscalculated his usual number of Scotches during the afternoon and taken 40 by mistake, instead of his customary 25. Mistakes will

Happiness is the result of being poor and respectable—according to the storybooks.[9]

happen in the best regulated families.

Angus McMuckle, who used to be a plus-four golfer at St. Andrews, has fixed up his charming lawn as a putting green. Some delightful matches are being arranged, with just the proper admixture of excitement. The loser gets a punch on the nose.

Mrs. P. Buzzard-Cholomondeley, of Eighteenth Avenue, astonished her friends last week by giving birth to quadruplets. The attending physician said it reminded him of shelling peas. Mother and offspring are doing well.

Miss Eugenie Champneys has returned home from Paris, where she has been studying music under Madame Marchesi. Miss Champneys has a beautiful contralto voice and has been assured by John de Reske, Mascagni, Hammerstein and others that by carefully cultivating her voice with a hoe there is no telling but that some day she may become a prima donna in a moving picture show. (October 5, 1912)

Mrs. J. B. Junklebunker, of Hillhurst, will not receive Friday.

Mrs. P. F. Snoozer, of Crescent Heights, will not receive Friday, but will receive next Tuesday if her sore toe is better.

Mrs. John Grawklehammer, of Sunnyside, will not receive Friday. Mrs. Grawklehammer is nursing old Grawklehammer, who has been off on a big drunk.

Mrs. Bufflesnaffer, Mount Royal, will not receive Friday, though she might possibly be induced to receive Robinson Crusoe.

Mrs. G. T. Jopplebunky, the charming hostess of East Calgary, will not receive Friday. No reason assigned.

Mrs. Peter Punk will not receive Friday.

Mrs. Alex P. Muggsy will not receive Friday. Mrs. Muggsy is insistent on this. She won't receive Friday under any consideration. If anybody comes around Friday they will get chucked out. Kindly therefore note that Mrs. Muggsy will not receive Friday. Better stay away Friday. Try Saturday. (December 21, 1912)

Our Gallery of Local Celebrities—(No. 2)
J. B. McSNUFFY

J. B. McSNUFFY

J. B. McSnuffy, the popular hangman, was born in Hamilton, Ont., in 1860, coming west to seek his fortune in 1887. Mr. McSnuffy attended school in Hamilton,

At least it may be said for the industrious cockroach that it never whistles or sings as it goes about its duties in the kitchen.[10]

among his schoolmates and early chums being the present Chief of Police Smith, of that ridiculous city. Since coming west, he has (Mr. McSnuffy, not Smith) gradually worked his way from small beginnings to his present honorable position of official hangman for Western Canada, from the Great Lakes to Vancouver. All our best murderers are hanged by McSnuffy. His jovial methods on the scaffold subdue in a great measure the terrors of death and he does not consider a job a complete success unless he has sent the doomed wretch to eternity roaring with laughter at one of his merry jests. Mr. McSnuffy is the inventor of a new knot which fits snugly under the right ear, instead of the left. Many murderers seem to prefer it.

An amusing incident is related of how Mr. McSnuffy received his official appointment. It appears that a number of years ago he himself was lying under sentence of death in Winnipeg jail for strangling a negro whom he suspected of cheating him in a game of craps. Another unfortunate devil was billed to hang the same day as McSnuffy. Radcliffe, the executioner, inadvertently got drunk the night before the event and new arrangements had to be hurriedly made. Sheriff Inkster wired the Department of Justice at Ottawa and obtained the pardon of McSnuffy on condition that he hang the other fellow and accept the post of official hangman. McSnuffy fell in gladly with those proposals and his historic reply to the offer,

"You're on," has since become a classic.

Mr. McSnuffy, in addition to a giant salary, receives an honorarium of $50 for each execution, with permission to sell small pieces of the rope to curio-hunters. The suit of clothes in which the murderer is hanged is one of the perquisites of his office and Mr. McSnuffy's wardrobe is said to be second to none. His favorite recreation is trap shooting. (July 1, 1913)

Our Gallery of Local Celebrities (No. 4)
J. B. BLITHERS

J. B. BLITHERS

J. B. Blithers, one of Calgary's most popular undertakers, was born in Chatham, Ont., some fifty-two years ago, coming West to seek his fortune in the summer of '93. Mr. Blithers' rise has been steady and his splendidly fitted undertaking parlors, the finest in the West, betoken a success which has been deservedly earned. A man of culture, education and refinement, Mr. Blithers is an author of no mean merit,

If it is all the same history, it need not repeat itself any more.[11]

his "Blithers on Embalming" and "Stiffs I Have Laid Out" being regarded as standard works in corpsology.

Mr. Blithers has always been a favorite in society and his afternoon teas and musicales held in the chaste morgue at the rear of the parlors have always been very popular. Mr. Blithers takes a great pride in his profession and it is his proud boast that not over 3 per cent of his subjects have been buried alive. This is a splendid record. No wonder Mr. Blithers' customers never go anywhere else after trying him once.

Mr. Blithers employs a staff of singularly lugubrious and sympathetic-looking assistants, whose sad duty it is to be always on the verge of breaking down and giving way to sobs when any relatives of the corpse are present. An astonishing intuition enables Mr. Blithers to determine with unerring accuracy how much it will be safe to soak the relatives for the casket and funeral expenses. He nails them before their grief has petered out. Mr. Blithers seldom gets on a bat while on duty and believes in strict attention to business. His process of curling up the mouth of a corpse and giving the impression of deceased having died with a beatific smile on his face, as if he had seen angels beckoning, has been much admired. We predict a bright future for Blithers. (September 27, 1913)

The sad death is reported of Mr. Benjamin F. Blink, a promising young businessman of Calgary. It appears that Mr. Blink, who had been induced to purchase some lots out in Calgary Junction a year ago, drove out last Sunday to have a look at them for the first time. He was found dead on his property, with his throat cut from ear to ear. His pocketknife lay by his side, showing that it was a case of self-destruction. A look of intense disgust pervaded the face of deceased. Mr. Blink was an expert billiard player, being especially adept at cushion caroms. Mr. B. was married, but looked remarkably cheerful up to the time of his death. Much sympathy is expressed for Mrs. Blink and the little Blinks whom this tragedy has put on the blink. In the midst, etc. (September 27, 1913)

Mr. Peter M. Sloppington-Jopkins, the eminent geologist and Fellow of the Royal Boozographical Society of England, arrived in Calgary a few days ago and is registered at the Palliser. Mr. Sloppington-Jopkins is much interested in the oil discoveries in Alberta and is said to represent large financial interests abroad. It is whispered that he is the private emissary of the Rothschild-Baring-Seligman group.

Mr. Sloppington-Jopkins' fame as a geologist and oil expert is world-wide and far-flung, he having located the celebrated Bamboozium oil fields in the principality of Bumbugjuicio in Beloochistan, and sunk the famous Gruesome Gusher in the southeastern corner of Thibet. Mr.

History records the one race won by an easy-going tortoise, but never says a word about the many previous races won by the hare.[12]

Sloppington-Jopkins has for many years been consulting geologist for the Guggenheims and it is well known that he located Alaska for this group of financiers. In oleaginous matters he is regarded as the final authority.

Mr. Sloppington-Jopkins, who occupies a suite on the mezzanine of the Palliser, expressed himself as highly delighted with what he had seen of our city, and from what he had observed of the surrounding country from the roof of the hotel he had no hesitation in saying that we had at our doors the greatest oil field the world has ever seen. He also betrayed no little astonishment at the magnificence of the new C.P.R. hotel and was especially loud in his praises of the bar fixtures.

In an interview Mr. Sloppington-Jopkins spoke quite freely of the objects of his visit.

"Of course," he said, as he directed the bartender to pour in a little more soda, "the main object of my visit is to look over your oil areas and report to the British Admiralty. For the last ten years or so I have been consulting boozographist to the Grog Dispensers of the British Navy, which gives me a semi-official standing with the Admiralty. Jackie Fisher and I are the best of friends. Jackie and Winston and I often go golfing together. Indeed, it was after beating both of them one morning by five up and four to play that they decided, in despair, to change the fuel in the British navy from coal to oil."

"And what is your opinion, as an expert, of the Alberta oil fields?"

"Very promising, my dear sir, very promising. Oil, however, will only be discovered, where it is found. It is seldom discovered anywhere else. When I discovered the Juggernaut oil wells for the Ahkoond of Swat about 50 miles south of Khoja Saleb, everybody—especially the jolly old Ameer of Bokhara—predicted failure, but out of 47 wells drilled, 46 turned out gushers."

"How did you fall down on the 47th?"

"It wasn't I who fell down, my dear sir. It was the Ahkoond's son, Abdullah Khan. He came to visit us one day in a beastly state of intoxication and fell down the well. Whenever a member of the royalty falls down a well in that country it is the custom to close down. From there, I was ordered to Perak. I located so many oil wells in Perak that the country became riddled with holes and the natives ran me out of the country. My biggest success was undoubtedly in Patagonia, where I——"

"Would you be disposed to entertain any private invitations to locate wells in this vicinity?"

"If properly approached, I might perhaps not be altogether disinclined to do so. Of course I should have to charge a nominal fee of say $5,000 but to heavily capitalized companies this is a bagatelle. You understand, no doubt, that an oil geologist's chief duty to his client is not so much to correctly located an oil producing well as it is to prepare a Report

Nearly all men believe that honesty in moderation is the best policy.[13]

that nobody can understand, but which sounds devilish technical, don't you know."

"Certainly a great scheme."

"Isn't it, though! Why, only today I was lunching with one of your citizens at his residence in the extreme west end of the city and he chanced to remark that he would have greatly liked to float an oil company if he only had a lease. The poor chap, it appears, had been too late in applying for one at the land office. Well—ha—ha!—I had had a tip top lunch and he was a splendid fellow, so I located an anticline for the poor chap in his back yard and wrote him a strongly favorable report. As he handed me his cheque for five thou', he said it was well worth the money. Tomorrow he will go around amongst the prominent citizens and offer them 50,000 shares apiece for the use of their names on his bally directorate."

"That was very kind of you. Have another drink."

"All right, old man. You see, I always try to meet the wishes of those who are decent to me in a social way, old chap. One likes to reciprocate kindness. Tomorrow I have promised a member of the Country Club to located an anticline for him on the golf links between the third and fourth holes, but I think I shall locate it at the first tee, as I shan't have so far to walk. If Mahomet won't come to the anticline, the anticline must come to Mahomet. He wants a gusher, of course, but I can only promise him an anticline.

I really couldn't hand him a gusher for five thou'—I couldn't really."

"It must be awfully easy being a geologist."

"It is easy enough being an eminent one, but deucedly difficult being an ordinary one. Your eminent geologist never has to explain everything. The ipsi dixit, you know."

"Personally," we ventured, "I never heard of an ordinary geologist. I don't believe there are any common or garden geologists at all."

"Now I come to think of it, I don't believe there are. We are all eminent, noted and renowned. No doubt about that at all."

"I wish you would do something for me, Mr. Sloppington-Jopkins, if you wouldn't mind?"

"Name it, my dear sir, just name it!"

"Well, would you mind—but better have another drink first."

"All right, old chap."

"Would you mind locating an anticline for me in the alley back of the *Eye Opener* office? I want to get into this oil game and have no time to go spluttering all over the country hunting Claggett shales and Dakota sands and Belly River formations. All I'm getting out of this oil excitement is a bunch of ads."

A tear stood in the eye of the great geologist.

"Show me your alley," said he.

(Mem: Look out for the new Company—Ed. *E.O.*) (June 27, 1914)

What a man is when alone, is what he is.[14]

Society Note—Mr. and Mrs. James B. Buffkins of Okotoks are in the city taking in the fair. Mrs. Buffkins had her palm read by Madame Jumperine Thursday, the while Mr. Buffkins was gorging himself with hot dog on the midway. A pleasant time was had.

Society Note—Mr. Fred B. Sprawley of Edmonton, accompanied his alleged wife, registered at the King George Wednesday. (July 3, 1915)

The many friends of Peter F. Scratchley, the popular oil broker, will be glad to learn that he is rapidly recovering from a severe cold contracted while making a somewhat hasty departure, via the window, from the elegant mansion of the charming society matron, Mrs. J. T. Blinkbonny, at an early hour last Sunday morning.

The many friends of Mr. James T. Blinkbonny, the popular travelling man, will be glad to learn that he returned home from a business trip to the coast early last Sunday morning and will remain in our midst for a brief rest. Mr. B. reports business quiet at the coast.

The many friends of Miss Jennie Boggle, the charming society bud who is to be married shortly to Mr. "Johnnie" Yeast, the rising young pin-pool artist, will be glad to learn that the linen shower given in her honor proved a great success, testifying to the unbounded popularity of this talented young lady. The whiskey shower accorded the egregious

The Editor Dreams.

Mr. Yeast by his numerous friends was also a pronounced success, as well as a continuous performance. If Mr. Yeast gets out of the Neal Institute in time, the happy pair will be wedded on the 27th instant. The *Eye Opener* extends its best wishes and hopes that as they walk hand in hand down the vista of life, plucking roses and gathering posies by the way, they will always—(Cut it out!)

The many friends of T. B. McSwain, formerly of Calgary but now of Edmonton, who once wrote an unsuccessful novel called "She Had Bean Soup; or What Is She Now?" will be glad to learn that his sore toe is much better. It had been troubling him for some time. (July 3, 1915)

Last issue we put our foot in it. The little yarn we spun for the general amusement of our readers about a Mr. Hazlewood, of High River, getting very drunk at the recent Farmers' Convention and being

There is one thing in the small boy's favor
—he never pretends to like anybody he doesn't.[15]

conveyed to the Holy Cross Hospital was taken seriously by the Hospital staff. They felt very badly about it, and we wish to make them every apology for the liberty taken in making use of the name of one of the finest and oldest public institutions in Calgary. There is no such person as Hazlewood, either. The story was merely one of those josh yarns which we occasionally make up to give our readers a bit of a laugh. The Lady Superior knows that the Holy Cross has no warmer friend than the editor of this paper, who trusts he is now forgiven. (February 26, 1916)

Mrs. William Buckle, of Seventh Avenue West, was hostess at a luncheon last Wednesday in honor of her nephew, who has just been liberated from jail.

Dr. J. B. McMurder and Dr. T. M. Slaughter of Edmonton, are registered at the Palliser.

"Doc" Glube, the charming proprietor of the Bucket of Blood in Winnipeg, has been promoted to the rank of junior major in Big Nick's Battalion of Gordon Gin Highlanders. It is altogether unlikely that Archdeacon Fortin will accompany this battalion as chaplain. (February 26, 1916)

Mrs. J. B. Warburton, of Seventeenth Ave. W., was found dead in her bed last Tuesday morning with a bottle of cyanide of potassium clutched in her hand. Mrs. Warburton had been suffering from fits of despondency for some time back. A witness at the inquest informed the coroner that when the sun didn't shine deceased was miserable, and when it did she said it faded the carpets. In the midst of life we are in death.

Miss Sophie Snufflebuster, who has been enjoying a prolonged visit to the Banff Dipsomaniac Retreat, returned home last Monday. Her health is greatly improved, the purple streaks which lined her jocund countenance having almost entirely disappeared. Miss Snufflebuster's nose is now thoroughly re-established and has regained much of its pristine pulchritude. (May 27, 1916)

Last week we took a run up to Leduc, the thriving little burg south of Edmonton, where we ran a paper in the long ago. In gathering a few items of local interest we discovered that the news is almost precisely the same as in the old days. Here is our budget:

Peter Lucas sold a car load of hogs Monday. Anton Steffen, Nic Ungs, E. H. Boebel and John Hess helped haul them to town. (They always help each other haul. It involves a fair-sized bat in town.)

George Hoefer brought in his hogs Monday. Johann Singsank, Henry and Adolf Oberbrockling helped him haul.

Barney Wedever of Conjuring Creek marketed a fine lot of hogs in town Tuesday. Chug Reisberg, Anton Chucklesnorther, William Waffles and Henry Bug helped him haul.

Will Hagerman marketed 54 hogs in

Leduc Monday, averaging 315 lbs. Nic Elenz, Olaf Torgersn and Olie Petersen helped haul. Mr. Habermann and Joseph Oberbroekerling accompanied the shipment to Calgary making a total of 56 porkers. The C.P.R. helped haul.

Hans Vonlunderbosh brought in his hogs Tuesday. John and Tony Boekenstedt helped him haul. Mr. Vonlunderbosh got very drunk at the hotel and was carted home in his wagon, hauled by John and Tony Boekenstadt. (June 17, 1916)

The many friends of Martin M. Bingham will be sorry to learn that he fell down a steep flight of steps Wednesday a week ago and broke his neck. Mr. Bingham was in the act of lowering a case of Three Star Hennessey into the cellar, when his foot slipped. It is understood that the Hennessey was three-year-old and will revert to his widow. The bereaved woman is receiving many callers.

Mr. and Mrs. Guy R. Gilford, of Mount Royal, gave a dinner party to a few friends Tuesday evening. It was a very stupid affair.

"Dugout" Bridge, played in the cellar, is becoming quite the vogue in Calgary. It saves keeping a lookout on the roof. Indeed, most of our smarter social functions are now being held in the cellar.

A delightful bridge-and-supper was given Thursday evening at the charming residence of the popular and recherche hostess, Mrs. Jonas Q. Crawklesnifter. Mr. Crawklesnifter, whose delightful cellars have recently been enlarged to the dimensions of the catacombs of Rome, made an ideal host and saw that everybody got safely home in a taxi. This was one of the most successful affairs of the season.

Delmar Hodgkins, the charming Liquor Act inspector, paid one of his delightful surprise visits to the home of Syd Kimberley, Twelfth Ave. W., Wednesday night, accompanied by a party of bomb throwers. A Dugout Smoker was in progress and it was no time before the jovial participants swarmed up from below and held up their hands. Considerable damage was done the building by the high explosives. Otherwise it was a pleasant evening.

Mr. and Mrs. Alexander P. Harkness have returned from their honeymoon at Banff and taken up housekeeping in the bridegroom's heavily mortgaged residence on Fifteenth Ave. W. Mrs. Harkness will receive at her home later on, as soon as she has got fairly sick of Alexander. Which won't be long. (July 8, 1916)

Society Note—Bishop Pinkham, of the Calgary diocese, was down in Okotoks the early part of the week holding confirmation services. Superintendent Horrigan of the mounted police says he is unable to connect his lordship with the bank robbery. (November 11, 1916)

Mr. J. Dewar dropped down to Calgary from Saskatoon and remained over the holidays in large quantities.

Mr. H. Walker arrived in Calgary from

The best jokes told about a man are those he never hears.[17]

Maple Creek shortly before Christmas and is still in the city, in vast quantities.

Mr. T. S. Hennessy, the well-known star, was in the burg for the holidays, adding to the gaiety of the nation.

Mr. John de Kuyper, the popular Dutchman, is still with us.

Mr. J. P. Buchanan, the eminent Black & White artist, paid a welcome visit to Calgary during Christmastide and reports business brisk in British Columbia.

Mr. J. Burke, the favorite Hibernian, who is heavily interested in quarts mining, dropped off in Calgary and remained over the holidays. Mr. Burke, who is noted for his strength, claims to have been raised on invalid Port.

Mr. Peter Dawson arrived in town about Christmas and is still shedding gladness o'er the scene.

Mr. John Haig, who has been in the city for several weeks, has been the recipient of much flattering attention during his stay. Mr. Haig is a welcome visitor in many of our best homes. Call again, John. (January 6, 1917)

L. U. Fowler, the energetic potato expert of the Vacant Lots Garden Club, we understand, is heading a movement to have the flower beds and lawns in front of the City Hall plowed up and disked and the space used for the culture of the giddy solanum tuberosum. There is little likelihood of his scheme being adopted. (March 30, 1917)

From the *Hootch Clarion*—"Miss Annie Brock drove over to Youngstown last Sunday with Fred Gommeril, who runs the pool room. Annie may not know it, but she is taking big chances going around with this unmitigated blackguard." (March 30, 1917)

From the *Hootch Clarion*—"Miss Myra Jennings has gone east to visit friends. We always thought something would come of that picnic to the lake last summer." (March 30, 1917)

Society Note—Mr. and Mrs. Percival B. Jenkins gave a charming drunk to a few choice friends at their cosy bungalow in Elbow Park last Monday. A delightful evening was spent with cards, song and informal dancing. His guests had just about persuaded Mr. Jenkins to consent to run in South Calgary as Liberal candidate, when the booze gave out. Of course, the world came to an end right there.

Society Note—A delightful At Home was given Wednesday afternoon at the residence of Mrs. Franklyn B. Wigglemore, on Mount Royal, when a helpful paper was read by the hostess showing that Premier Sifton had been a notorious cattle rustler in the early days of the North West Territories, with a price on his head offered by the Stock Association. In a touching peroration she urged her guests to vote for Dr. Brett who was not only one of the great statesmen of the day, but had once removed the tonsils of her little boy. (May 11, 1918)

Knowing things that are not so is the worst kind of ignorance.[18]

Funeral Notes

James T. Blaney, prominent in Calgary real estate circles, died last Tuesday at his home on Fourth Ave. West. Nobody will miss Blaney. He was no good.

Death with his sickle keen never pulled a more popular stunt than when he picked off old Daniel Warrenton, of Crescent Heights, last week. Deceased had become a veritable nuisance and it was only a question of time when he would have been murdered.

The funeral of Mrs. Anne B. Palmer, of East Calgary, was held last Friday to the Union Cemetery. The casket was of finished oak with nickelplate fixings and is said to have cost $75. Asleep in Jesus.

John Moran, of Sunnyside, who was killed last Wednesday by being run over by a Ford car, was a good fellow and deserving of a more dignified death. There will be a sale of empty bottles at the Moran residence Saturday afternoon at 2 o'clock, to defray the funeral expenses.

Michael Colquhoun, who ran a livery here before the days of the automobile, dropped dead Monday afternoon at the Bank of Montreal corner. He had been waiting for a Belt Line car when the Grim Reaper overtook him. Mr. Colquhoun was one of our heaviest drinkers and owned several prize bulldogs. His imported Towser Second won first at the Edmonton Exposition. Thy Will be Done. (September 1, 1917)

The many friends of Mrs. Thos. M. Olin, of Sunnyside, will be glad to learn that she is able to be out again. It is nearly three weeks since she kicked at the cat and missed it, dislocating her knee cap. Society is all agog over her charming recovery. (September 22, 1917)

The Bert Palmer mentioned in yesterday's issue of the *Herald* as being charged in the police court with an offence under the Liquor Act, is not the Mr. Palmer of 2421 First Street West.

We are requested to state in this column that the Pete Johnson who is being held by the police for cutting his wife's throat is not Mr. P. T. Johnson, the well-known haberdasher of First Avenue West, whose new spring stock is now on view.

The mutilated body of a man which was fished out of the Bow River last Tuesday and later identified as James Swettenham, is no connection of Swettenham Brothers who run the most up-to-date pool rooms (including an English billiard table) on Eighth Avenue. Snooker pool a specialty.

Friends of Mrs. J. B. Basham, the popular milliner, have asked us to kindly inform the public that she is not the Mrs. Basham who was taken to the Ponoka Lunatic Asylum last week and lodged in a padded cell. Mrs. J. B. Basham has just got in her spring stock of hats and is prepared for a rushing business.

Miss Genevieve Gillam, the talented manicurist and sore toe specialist, is anxious it should be known that she is not the

A certain amount of ignorance is necessary to the enjoyment of our existence.[19]

Gillam woman who was recently charged with receiving two cases of stolen liquor, the property of the C.N. Railway. The latter lady is colored, while Genevieve is of the blond persuasion and charges only 35 cents for trimming the nails. Her parlor is in the David block. Three taps at the door will secure admission.

Hank Borden, who was hanged at Lethbridge last week for a most atrocious murder, is no relation to Sir Robert Borden, premier of Canada. Sir Robert expects the present session to be a short one.

Cappie Smart, Calgary's amiable fire chief, desires us to state that the Capt. Anton von Smart, shot in Winnipeg last week for a German spy, was no relative of his. Cappie has been chief for twenty years and is still going strong. A statue has been erected in his honor in Dundee, Scotland, the home of his birth. It faces the John Jameson distillery and is connected up with a private suction pipe running from the big vat. (March 30, 1918)

It is not considered comme il faut for a woman to come down to breakfast in her night gown and her hair done up in back numbers of the *Eye Opener*. It shows lack of breeding.

When making a call at a private house do not keep harping on the good old days when one could get a shot of booze. It is exceedingly bad form.

Should you accidentally upset a cup of coffee on the tablecloth, do not stare at it in consternation and exclaim "This is a hell of a note!" Laugh it off pleasantly and apologize to the hostess.

When shown the family album by the daughter of the house, do not start laughing immoderately when you come to the picture of her pa and ma taken on their wedding day.

If asked to a whist drive given by a ladies' club, make it a point to go sober. It is almost impossible to remember the cards when a bit off.

When attending a dinner party it is considered bad form to slip from the parlor a few minutes before the gong and secrete yourself under the table, later on arching your back suddenly while the guests are lapping up their soup, thus tipping over everything in sight. Most hostesses hate this sort of thing.

Never discuss a man with his wife in presence of company. When a woman's husband is under discussion, she isn't in a position to say what she really thinks.

At a church wedding it is considered the correct thing for the bridegroom and his best man to show up perfectly sober. There is nothing so disconcerting to a bride as to see her husband trip on something at the altar and plunge headlong into the stomach of the officiating clergyman. (June 15, 1918)

Society Note—Hon. Crothers, Minister of Labor, has accepted an alluring offer to go into vaudeville, and will appear at

Many a train of thought gathers no freight.[20]

Pantages very shortly in monologue. His contract calls for a 15-minute humourous talk on his administration of the Labor department. It should elicit considerable laughter. (October 19, 1918)

Society Note—Mayor Brown, of Medicine Hat, is to attend the Industrial Research Conference next week in Edmonton. He will find that the only research that interests them up there is whiskey. When they don't find it the first time, they research.(January 25, 1919)

From the _Hootch Clarion_:

Mrs. John T. Bugge sold her hogs last week and has purchased a sprightly new spring hat. Mrs. Bugge got the top price for her hogs and is looking quite chic.

Some scoundrel stole our hat last week while we were engaged in a game of pool. This is a dastardly outrage.

There is a splendid opening for an up-to-date barber shop in this burg. The present tonsorial artist is intoxicated half the time.

The village council at their last meeting voted the sum of $4 from the treasury to fix up a hog wallow on main street. The poor hogs will miss the spot, but such is life. (May 12, 1919)

It is unlikely that T. B. Mulligan will run for the council as announced in the press. Mr. Mulligan does not get out of jail until Dec. 20, too late to file his nomination papers.

Mrs. Jonathan Wilder gave an at home Thursday to a few friends whose aid she was enlisting on behalf of her husband, who is out as a candidate in the provincial elections. There was no booze and the function was a miserable frost. Mr. Wilder has no more chance than a snowball in hell.

George B. McCoole, who has been running around with a bottle soliciting votes for his aldermanic campaign, called at this office and wanted his picture in the paper. If McCoole will bring up another bottle and not take it away as he did the other one, we will give the matter our prayerful consideration. (November 22, 1919)

Society Note—Another aldermanic candidate looms on the scene in the person of the Rev. W. Rufus, who is running on an uplift platform. Mr. Rufus is a trifle austere, inasmuch as he objects to drinking, smoking, dancing, theatres, card playing, horseracing and laughing. Otherwise he is all right. He is sure to be elected. Someone ought to teach Mr. Rufus how to shoot craps, to keep him from going crazy. (November 22, 1919)

Society Note—Mr. Percy Redingot, who was recently caught in flagrante deplunko with a careless dame, has gone east for his health. Mr. Redinot has been suffering from his lungs for some time past, but there is nothing the matter with his gall.

Society Note—A delightful tea boozant

An educated fool is more foolish than an ignorant one.[21]

was given by Mrs. Scufflechopper at her charming residence on Seventeenth Avenue West. The absence of any signs of tea did not detract from the enjoyment of this recherche function and the guests were kept delightfully busy telling each other that they could take a drink or leave it alone. How they all got home, God knows. (December 6, 1919)

Obituary Note—John M. Crawley, of Seventeenth Avenue, one of our best-beloved Rotarians, was found dead in his bedroom early Wednesday morning, hanged to the bedpost by his suspenders. At the inquest the coroner's jury decided that Mr. Crawley, whose sad demise has cast a gloom over the community, met his death by coming home full and mistaking himself for his pants. Not lost, but gone before. (April 10, 1920)

Miss Lottie McGlory, the debonair blond sport who took the part of Nell Gwynne, Charles the Second's extra-special, on the main float in the H.B.C. Parade, was entertained at a blow-out Wednesday night by the Sons of Bonnie Scotland. Miss McGlory, who is known amongst her friends as "the Arid Belt" because she is always dry, certainly cleaned up on the

booze on this occasion. (May 15, 1920)

Algernon Sweeney, one of our most prominent pin-pool exponents fell into an open sewer late Thursday night and broke his leg. We are requested by his family to state that Mr. Sweeney was not under the influence of liquor at the time the sad accident occurred.

The Bon Ton Literary Society held their first meeting of the season last Friday evening, the subject up for discussion being "Did Shakespeare or Bacon found the *Winnipeg Free Press*?" The question was decided in favor of Bacon, on the ground that the paper was on the hog.

Society will feel the loss of John T. Snooke, the popular piano tuner, who passed away at the general hospital last Wednesday. Deep sympathy is felt for Mrs. Snooke, who desires us to state that she will not receive Tuesday. The late Mr. Snooke was noted in society circles for his clever imitations of farmyard noises, his rendering of the quacking of a duck

More "Party" Politics

Some people might just as well be crazy for all the sense they have.[22]

being a notable performances. Not lost, but gone before. (July 17, 1920)

Fashion Notes—A chic wrapper, the latest creation of Lucille, which is worn without corsets or anything else for that matter, is now much in vogue at whiskey socials in the afternoon. Ladies on a bat can sprawl comfortably all over the place in these charming wrappers and indulge in high kicking to their hearts' content. No jamboree is complete without one. (*Summer Annual*, 1920)

Poor old John McSwalligan, beloved by many friends and old-timers, is the latest victim of the flu. Before passing away, Mr. McSwalligan divulged to his broken-hearted family a secret cache in the house where ten gallons of F.O.G. were stored away. The sorrow engendered by the visitation of death was thus tempered with joy and gladness. The Lord tempers the wind to the shorn lamb. The number of people who have called to express their sympathy has been something fierce. (*Summer Annual*, 1920)

Society Note—Mr. and Mrs. Thos. B. Squirrelle gave an informal drunk at their charming residence in Elbow Park last Tuesday evening. They called it a party. It was some party. (*Summer Annual*, 1920)

Society Note—Miss Lena Bingham left on the eastbound last Thursday to visit friends in Winnipeg. Her many friends hope to see her back soon, also her front. (August 14, 1920)

Society Note—The family and relatives of Henry M. Beaglet, of Fourteenth Ave. W., are rejoicing in his death by being run over by an automobile at the Bank of Montreal corner last Saturday night. Old Beaglet had lived long enough and won't be missed. There should be a law compelling drivers of automobiles to run over men like Beaglet when they catch sight of them. It was rather a bum funeral. The corpse was not the only stiff present, there being three or four weird-looking bums, friends of deceased, who appropriately enough sang a wreckquiem at the graveside, in which the driver of the hearse lustily joined. Later in the evening they all repaired to the Plaza. (September 11, 1920)

Oliver P. Johnson, who was at the foot of the poll in the mayoralty race, received only two votes. He has since been arrested as a repeater. (December 25, 1920)

If the widow of the man who dropped dead on Ninth Avenue last week with a copy of the *Eye Opener* in his pocket will call at the office, she will receive a $25 bonus.

J. B. Engleside has returned from a visit to Lethbridge, where he attended the hanging of Basoff, the murderer. Mr. Engleside brought back with him a piece

---

Some people never change their minds because they are like a man with only one shirt.[23]

of the rope and is getting lots of free drinks showing it to his friends. (December 25, 1920)

Society Note—The many friends of Mrs. T. Tinglebutter, of Elbow Park, who recently underwent an operation for appendicitis, will be glad to learn that she is dead. She was an awful bore. (February 19, 1921)

Society Note—Mrs. John S. Lobscouse, of Baview, whose husband is running for the legislature on an anti-Ginger Ale ticket, gave an "at home" Wednesday afternoon to a charming coterie of booze artists. It is a wonder they were not all pinched. (June 25, 1921)

Miss Evangeline Golightly gave a charming musicale down at the police station Wednesday afternoon. She was screaming to beat the band and had to be given a shot of snow. (August 20, 1921)

Society Note—Mrs. Montague Macdooryboory of Seventeenth avenue west, will not receive Tuesday. Why not, goshonly knows. (*Summer Annual,* 1921)

In the latest issue of his rag, the *Clarion,* the following local items appear. Even in our most reckless moments we could not dare say the things Tompkins does. Listen to this:

Martin Burk, who runs the grocery store facing the depot, is doing a poor business. His store is the dirtiest we ever saw. How can he expect to do much?

Rev. J. M. Broadhurst preached last Sunday on charity. This is a hell of a place to discourse on the subject of charity. (August 20, 1921)

Society Note—Mrs. Thos. F. Crawley gave an afternoon tea to a number of her friends last Tuesday at her residence in the West end. It really was tea that she served, and the guests left feeling very much disgusted, declaring that they would "lay off" the Crawleys in the future. (November 19, 1921)

Society Note—Premier Meighen has decided not to extend his western tour beyond Moose Jaw. The expense of the dining car on this tour has drained the Liberal Conservative exchequer and his party are now living on crackers and cheese. This is a bum diet to speak on. Up to Tuesday it had been thought that they might have crackered and cheesed it as far as Medicine Hat, but God willed otherwise. (November 19, 1921)

Society Note—Miss Mollie Poffkins, the amiable stenographer in a well-known law office in the city, desires us to state that she is not the Miss Poffkins who was arrested last week for stealing a crosscut saw and sledge hammer from Ashdown's Hardware.

Why, cert'nly. The nicest people are always those we don't know anything about.[24]

Society Note—Mrs. J. B. Scluff, of Fourteenth Ave. W., entertained some of her neighbors informally last Monday afternoon. That is to say, she and her cook had a quarrel on the front porch.

Society Note—Miss Annie Jugglebuster has left for her home in Hamilton, Ont. What is Hamilton's loss is our gain. (*Summer Annual,* 1922)

Society Note—The debating society of the Y.M.C.A. held their usually weekly discussion late Wednesday evening in the basement of the Methodist church. The subject, "Is Square Gin or Old Tom the more Potent in a Collins?" led to rather an acrimonious debate, necessitating the calling in of Mr. Tom Peers to give a final decision. The expert recommended a series of experiments and the following morning the city was in an uproar. This sort of thing is giving Calgary a bad name. (*Summer Annual,* 1922)

James T. Postlethwaite of Hillhurst had the misfortune to break his neck last Wednesday and will be buried this (Saturday) afternoon. Deceased had suffered a sharp attack of sciatica between the shoulder blades and his wife, under the doctor's instructions, had applied alcohol lotions to the spot. It was while trying to lick it off that Mr. Postlethwaite dislocated the medulla oblongata. Not lost but gone forever. (*Summer Annual,* 1922)

S. B. Jenkins, of Edmonton, who blew his brains out last Monday after a delightful weekend at Sesba Beach, was cremated Wednesday in accordance with the wishes of the family. Thus is hell cheated of cheap fuel. Jenkins was a tough nut. (July 29, 1922)

Society Note—John M. Solly has been confined to his house in Elbow Park with delirium tremens for the past few days. His physician states that he has passed the crisis and will soon be around again shaking hands with old friends. (*Summer Annual,* 1922)

Etiquette—Entering into a heated altercation with your pastor with regard to the relative merits of rye and Scotch is considered bad form. If he prefers rye that is none of your business. (*Summer Annual,* 1923)

Society Note—Lt. Col. James Walker is in the city today having been here for the last thirty years. He will likely be here tomorrow also, and the day after.

Society Note—Rev. Jabz McSnorter, brother of Mr. J. B. McSnorter, is paying a brief visit to Murillo. Rev. McSnorter is one of the most eloquent devines in Canada. He got thrown out of a rig last Tuesday, but sustained little or no damage. He was fairly sober at the time. (*Summer Annual,* 1923)

When a man proclaims in a loud voice that he is a gentleman it's a safe bet he isn't. especially if he pronounces it "gen'leman."[25]

John F. Ballington, one of our most prominent and intelligent citizens, met with a nasty accident last Thursday night; while hastily climbing down the rain pipe from a ladies bedroom window, on one of our fashionable avenues, he lacerated his hand on a jagged piece of lead. The wounded member was dressed by his family physician and little danger is expected from blood poisoning. (*Summer Annual*, 1923)

One of Fred Adams' fine white wyandotte hens which he proposes to show at the Dominion Exhibition inadvertently swallowed four tacks last Sunday. Fred got very much excited and the hen is now laying carpets. (*Summer Annual*, 1923)

Society Notes—Mr. James Howell, the well-known professor of Arts and Sciences at Youngstown, dropped in to the *Eye Opener* office Wednesday and wished the staff a merry Xmas. He expressed himself as delighted at finding the staff, who is ourself, comparatively sober. (*Summer Annual*, 1923)

Re the Carroll shooting case, in which Miss Lottie McCullough is charged with firing three bullets into Mr. Fred Carroll, it is expected that she will plead self-defense, on the ground that he shot one into her first. (*Summer Annual*, 1923)

Illusions are the grand ideas we have about ourselves; dillusions are the silly ideas other people have about us.[26]

CHAPTER FOUR

Rushing the Growler

In which your in-house boozological artist implores,
"Don't do as I do. Do as I tell you."

"When one is driven to drink he usually has to walk back."

—*Eye Opener*, August 4th, 1906

The alert reader is forgiven for thinking redundant a chapter dedicated to the procurement & consumption of potent potables. What ho! True, the Bob Edwards oeuvre oozes the stuff,[1] with alcohol multitasking as subject matter & incidental colour (viz. virtually any page in the volume at hand), muse & mistress. Yet: study of this topic sees Edwards undergoing a tortured, fascinating evolution. And so—

☞ Behold! good-natured josh about intoxication, delivered in slurred vernacular.

☞ Marvel! how early anti-temperance rantings slowly soften into reluctant, qualified Prohibition boosterism.

☞ Fidget Uncomfortaby! at Edwards's self-effacing sweetening of his own life-long[2] alcoholism.

☞ Laugh & Weep! at the alternately scatological & affectionate sentiments found in never-before-printed correspondence twixt patient & nurse.

☞ Do More of the Same! as you cast your optics on the long-lost text of Edwards's 1922 booze musings before the Alberta Legislature.

☞ Shake a Fist Heavenward! at the realization that his greatest inspiration ultimately proved his downfall.[3] (Requiescat in boozo, indeed.)

---

[1] To the degree that, in a letter to B. F. Neary (January 22, 1957), Grant MacEwan cites *Boozological Bob* as the working title for what became *Eye Opener Bob*.

[2] Despite his best efforts, Edwards's addiction dogged him to the grave. In a letter to George Murray (August 1, 1918), he appends this postscript: "Haven't had a [drawing of a bottle and shot glass] for 3 years!!!!!!!!!!!!!!" However, in "Bob Edwards and I", friend and fellow M.L.A. Robert Pearson reports that Edwards went on a bender shortly after delivering his 1922 Legislative address. He was dead within the year.

[3] From behind a gossamer veil of euphemism, Edwards publicly admitted his drinking dictated the *Eye Opener*'s erratic schedule. Robert Pearson (*ibid.*) goes further, opining that alcohol "not only hampered his work, but greatly shortened his life." (The pair began an eighteen year friendship in 1904, when Pearson's Methodist missionary duties took him to the Banff sanitarium where Edwards was detoxing.) The official cause of death, as recorded by attending physician Dr. Neil Macphatter, was "Dilation of the heart with loss of compression" due to influenza; one suspects long-term abuse left Edwards's system less than robust.

Alcoholism is a disease which no politician or preacher on earth can handle. There are only three people who can—doctors, snake charmers and the cheerful boozers, the latter especially. (*Wetaskiwin Free Lance*, September 20, 1898)

We take this opportunity of informing numerous friends and admirers who make a point of visiting our place of business when, by some special benignity on the part of Dame Fortune, a flask has been secured by the management, that there are two flasks. One contains the real stuff. The other consists of a blend of acidulated prussic acid and concentrated lye, flavored with just enough whiskey to fool a stranger. It is almost impossible to tell the two flasks apart. Visitors, therefore, during our absence, are implored to leave our whiskey alone. (*Wetaskiwin Breeze*, March 13, 1901)

He came down the street at a swinging stride, a smile on his face and his eye clear as spring water. To the first man he met he explained without being asked, that his unusually fit appearance was the result of having quit booze altogether.

"You take my advice and quit it altogether, like me."

"How long have you let up?"

"Oh well, lemme see, since day before yesterday."

"You're doing well. Stay with it. I was just going in to flop the bartender. Come along and watch me stick him, and you can ring in on a cigar."

Half an hour later the gentleman with the swinging stride may be heard expostulating with the barkeep, "I threw shix shixes, thazright thazright, leave it to thisman. Didn't I throw shix shixes? Why, sure thing. Thazright! Gimme a little Scotch." Thus do the summer roses fade. (*Wetaskiwin Breeze*, March 25, 1901)

People should rise early these mornings and take a spin down the track before breakfast. It beats the insidious "eye-opener" at the bar hollow. To be on the safe side, I take both. The brilliant sunrise and the bracing air, with the touch of frost in the light breeze, and the wonderful mirages which fill the horizon with reflections of wooded lakes far away, are all worth rising early for. The man is not altogether bad whose spirit sometimes yearns for the poetry of the early morning, although, perhaps, he cannot become very spiritually exalted when he has a lot of chores to do. (*Wetaskiwin Breeze*, March 25, 1901)

Here is the recipe for soup *à la* green snakes, suitable for breakfast after a sociable evening. Soak your head in cold water over night. If you have any stock out in the country, put in a little of that, together with lemons, herbs, spices, vegetables and a ham bone. Add a plug of chewing tobacco. Mix with a puree of has-beans, a heaping teacupful of cayenne pepper, and

Soaking the brain in alcohol does not preserve the mind.[1]

three or four rotten eggs well beaten up. Open the window and pour the whole into the street. Then holler to the bartender for a Collins. (*Wetaskiwin Breeze*, March 25, 1901)

Booze is a bad thing when it is aboozed. Used in small quantities it is harmless enough. The difficulty lies in using it in small quantities. With those who have a constitutional tendency towards liquor one drink means two, and two means a drunk. Therefore those who, as is often the case, have hereditary tendencies in this direction should abstain altogether. The poisonous stuff will catch them napping at last.

One thing our benevolent government might do is this. They should make the inspectors do a little more to earn their salaries. It should be part of their duties to appear unexpectedly at the various hotels in their district and make a thorough test of the spirituous liquors sold over the bar. This, I gamble, would bring forth some startling revelations. Barney Cooper's first official test of bulk whiskey would read "Muriatic acid one quarter, alcohol one eight, fusel oil one eight, fish-hooks one quarter, hokey pokey one eight, strychnine one eight." Think of pouring that mixture down your epiglottis fifteen or twenty times in a day, trying to make yourself believe that you are having a good time. It is a fool's paradise.

The result? Sore heads, shattered nerves, empty pockets, and worst of all, the loss of the friendship and respect of good men and women. It is the vendor of the booze that wears the diamonds. Once in the maelstrom it is hard to get out, for there is no gainsaying that the booze-life has its fascinations. One hears bright conversations at the bar and some very pretty wit is occasionally slung around. Things are looked at from the roseate point of view. They remain roseate till the following morning, when it takes three or four fish-hook cocktails to get back to par. This is the thorn. Better to eschew the beastly stuff altogether. Don't do as I do; do as I tell you.

I do not believe in that most impracticable piece of legislative nonsense that goes by the name of Prohibition. Where Prohibition exists the people drink spirits almost exclusively, because it is easier handled by the vendors. Those who formerly drank light lager have to slop up some villainous concoction which they regard as sweet because it is stolen fruit. Make the procuring of booze as easy as possible and there will be less booze drunk. Give every responsible man who has a hotel which complies with the statute a license. The revenues will be increased without any additional drunkenness. A man has only so much to spend on booze anyhow and will spend that much if there are one or twenty bars in his town.

My advice to beginners is to leave it alone altogether, even beer and light wines. In the case of socially inclined young men, indulgence in these harmless

The undying love of an old boozer for whiskey goes to prove that familiarity doesn't always breed contempt.[2]

beverages too often degenerates into a craving for the fish-hooks. The whole traffic only breeds sorrow and ought to be side-stepped.

Temperance is corporal piety. It is the preservation of divine order in the body and diffuses through its innermost recesses a healthful spirit which has no fish-hooks in it. (*Wetaskiwin Breeze*, June 18, 1901)

Mean's Well, But ———

Let us not despair of continued prosperity. The Calgary Brewery is to have another addition put on as large as the present building. This has no special significance in connection with our coming to locate in Calgary. They were going to put it up anyway. (January 2, 1903)

We are sometimes upbraided for featuring booze and the bar in these columns. What would you have us write about? We have to write about what goes on around us and it cannot be disputed that the bar is the centre of social life in small western burgs. There is no town society in the usual acceptation of the term. It is a very extraordinary occasion when a High River young man finds himself sitting in the parlor of a private home talking to the ladies. He is never asked. There is infinitely more hospitality out in the country than there is in the town. Hence the bar becomes perforce the social centre, and there you are, preachers to the contrary notwithstanding.

The bar is indeed a social necessity in western towns. At any rate, the bar is there and the necessity too. Man is a social animal, whether he lives in a Pat Burns baronial castle or batches in a shack twenty miles from town. But the baronial castle has resources; the shack has not. It is a good place to get away from as frequently as possible. The bar is bright and cheery and always on the spot and also touches the spot. The man craving human companionship can always find some of the gang there and the throb of a human heart. He finds, too, in the bartender one who understands his wants and laughs at his jokes. Oh yes, the bar's all right. (June 11, 1903)

It has just occurred to us that the reason we become so intolerably sick after a jamboree is because, unlike most other

Set 'em up, and the crowd is with you. Go broke and you go it alone.[3]

country editors, we don't use a patent inside. (July 25, 1903)

We cannot too strongly recommend Witteman's beer, as made in Prince Albert. It seems to be having quite a vogue in the West, being greatly appreciated for its purity, body and stimulating qualities. This beverage is not slosh and reminds one more of the draft beer the pretty barmaid draws for you, in an Old Country pub. Call for it. All the bars have it, or ought to. (July 25, 1903)

A want that has been long felt by new travelling men whose daily avocation or the nature of whose business (cigar business, for example) is likely to involve them in considerable drinking at bars is a training college where they may get acclimated to the fearful and wonderful varieties of Western whiskey, before going out on the road. Such an institution is on the tapis, to be known as the Tanglefoot University and to be supplied with a staff of qualified professors. As Calgary will most likely get the Presbyterian College, it is only fair that High River should be chosen as the logical site for this new seat of boozing.

Tanglefoot University will cater specially to young men from eastern wholesale houses who are about to enter upon their career as commercial travellers. Many of these fall by the wayside and go to piece as soon as they go up against Western bars. The hard stuff has too many kinks in it for them. The curriculum as laid down in the prospectus which has just been drafted will obviate all danger. Students will be instructed in the delicate art of slopping up all night without getting sloppy, of mopping up countless drinks with customers and still securing large orders, and of talking to a lady while full as a goose without giving themselves away. Many useful hints will be given to guide them in safety through the dissipated towns strung all along the C. and E. from the bibulous cliffs of Edmonton to the delirious pandemonium of Macleod.

A special course will also be given to show that a man may go to Dr. Brett's at Banff to get boiled out, without getting on a prolonged toot and making himself worse.

Lectures on Alcoholic Hallucinations will be given once a week by one who has

The most difficult part of a drinking song is the refrain.[4]

been there, accompanied by colored illustrations of alligators, pink rats, performing elephants, gila monsters, rams with bronze medals, lizards, snakes, and reptiles of every description. Visions at the foot of the bed will be fully explained. X ray photographs of the interior of a drinking man's stomach will also be on hand to impress on the mind of the ingenuous student the necessity for letting up once in a while.

Tanglefoot University should make a hit. It will save many a good man from going strong, imparting so clearly the secret of successful boozing as to enable the incipient traveller to have a good time on the road and yet hold his job. We are willing to accept the presidency and a thoroughly qualified staff of teachers can be procured right here in High River. After we get through with them they won't need any post-graduate course. (July 25, 1903)

The *Calgary Herald* has the following quotation from a speech recently delivered before the twenty-first International Christian Endeavor convention at Denver by Rev. Dr. W. F. Wilson, of Hamilton, Ontario:

"The saloon everywhere is a curse: in London, Paris, Berlin, Glasgow, Boston, Washington, Toronto, and Denver it is the same," he continued. "It is the Gibraltar of greed, the Jericho of lust and crime, the slaughter house of character and health; it is the sewer pipe of misery and despair; a mighty tyrant, a menace to freedom, purity and prosperity; the birthplace of paupers and criminals; the very foundation head of blasphemy, brutality, and anarchy."

This pronouncement will doubtless cause a profound sensation around "Jimmy's" in London and the American Bar (off the Rue de Rivoli) in Paris. The Glasgow pubs will also feel chagrin over this aspersion on their fair whiskey. Toronto barkeepers will also throw a few fits. Oh dear dear! Those pawsons!

This type of blatherskyte is all right in the teaparty and foreign mission set. These exuberant temperance orators who (in many prominent instances, notably John B. Gough, Murphy, Small and one or two others, the most eminent of them), enthrall the audience with 'orrible tales, owe their power to theatrical gifts of anecdote and illustration; $50 or $100 a lecture. We've heard 'em all. The above mentioned orators hit the hard stuff right along during lecture tours. Gough only of an occasion, but Murphy and Small right along. Small used to be an evangelist, associated with Sam Jones, but he got hitting the rotgut so steadily that he quite evangelism and turned temperance lecturer.

We presume the above paragraph will shock our agricultural Ontario friends, but we are out for the bare truth whether they like it or not.

John B. Gough got on a "still" toot during his last tour in Britain at the St. George hotel, in St. George Square, in

The water wagon is certainly a more dangerous vehicle than the automobile. At least more people fall off it.[5]

Glasgow, and his lecture at the St. Andrew's hall was postponed till the following evening. We were employed at the City Chambers close by, a hundred steps away, and were next to all those little features. Yet the following night J. B. delivered one of the most eloquent addresses on temperance ever heard in Glasgow. We were right there, astonished beyond measure at the orator's unlimited gall.

Another man from the City Chambers, Glasgow, who was there that evening if our memory does not fail us, was W. Kelso Hunter, now in one of the government departments at Regina. He and a mutual friend, William Johnstone, of Moffat. We had a great laugh, you bet.

It is, we know, hardly fair to pick out the 'ornery specimens from amongst temperance orators and preachers, but the hypocrisy and make believe and jollying propensities of some of these smooth-tongued chicken-feeders are a little too much. A con game or race track is just as reputable.

It was the Rev. Mr. Campbell who told us that our paper had lost 25 per cent in value since we drew attention to his unfortunate gaucheries. It is to laugh—*c'est a rire.*

The *Eye Opener* columns are this week a trifle on the shy order. We do not exactly know our ground. (August 22, 1903)

The carpenters are making fine progress with the new school house, the roof being put on this week. It is the most conspicuous object on the landscape and may be seen for miles round. If they would only put a dome on it instead of a roof. It would look like St. Paul's cathedral, and there might be some grounds for placing in convenient corners, statues, busts, and marble tablets to the memory of distinguished citizens who died from booze. (October 24, 1903)

Bob MacMillan, of Gleichen, writes to ask: "When is a man rich?" The answer to this is not to be found in any of the modern encyclopedias, but we can safely hazard the guess that it is when he has about eight drinks under his belt and 75 cents left. (November 21, 1903)

Swear off. Climb into the water wagon. Life is a one-sided fight for the man who is his own worst enemy. Swear off. If you make one hundred good resolutions and only keep one you are just that much better off. But let that one be booze. The others will follow. We speak with authority. (January 9, 1904)

The Calgary Brewery has always been willing to sell beer to the trade so that it could be profitably retailed over the bar at five cents a glass, but the hotel keepers won't have it that way. It costs the Brewery eight cents to produce one gallon; the public pays fifteen cents for one glass!

As the beer is so light that you cannot "get a glad on" under fifteen or twenty glasses, the man in the street finds he is

Sometimes the humor of a man is so dry that he has to buy drinks to get anybody to listen to it.[6]

getting his money's worth only when he calls for whiskey. Surely the temperance people are not so dense as to fail to see the point thus crudely conveyed. (July 2, 1904)

Now that Bennett's temperance address is several weeks past and gone and the oratorical sky-rockets have fallen spent to earth, can anyone show the slightest jot or tittle of good that has resulted therefrom? It has had about as much practical effect as have the sermons delivered in our churches upon Calgary's morals. Raindrops on a duck's back soak in by comparison.

Although it is a fact, admitted by all experts on the subject, that drunkenness would be materially lessened, and drinking rendered fairly innocuous, by the introduction of 5-cent beer, it does not suit the dignity of your preacher and temperance orator to stoop to the discussion of such paltry detail.

Beats Oil

They could not work up the requisite pyrotechnical display of oratory over a 5-cent beer proposition. Besides, it would be positively vulgar to advocate 5-cent beer before an audience of smug respectables.

It is far safer for the orator's reputation in the community that his listeners return home exalted with high-sounding and exquisitely-worded generalities about its being every citizen's duty to his country and the empire to abstain from liquor than it is to have them walk back with a cold-blooded advocacy of 5-cent beer ringing in their ears. It is enough to make an orator throw a fit even to hint at such a plain, every-day, common-place subject for his philippics. (July 2, 1904)

A sincere worker in the temperance cause instead of hitching his wagon to a star, would hitch it to the post outside a saloon. But your modest reformer cannot get along without talking, talking, talking, amid the dramatic environment of a church or hall, with the admiring ladies in front and the organ and the hushed silence and the collection by the gentlemanly ushers and all the rest of it. (July 2, 1904)

Having changed our lodgings in Calgary recently, we distinguished ourself the other night by entering the wrong house, sober as a judge, walking upstairs and entering a lady's bedroom. Luckily the lady was not there. Descending the stairs we met the proprietress of the house and explained matters. Instead of being angry, she laughed like to kill herself.

Whiskey floats more troubles than it drowns.[7]

Which was lucky for your uncle.

We only mention this awkward little incident because it brings to recollection an extraordinary and literally true adventure that we had in London some twenty years ago. On coming up from Glasgow we had taken a room in a rather swell and exclusive private boarding home in Cecil street, off the Strand, kept by a very religious Scotch old maid, Miss Machattie. Four ladies and two gentlemen had come there also, high-toned propositions. It was a pleasant place to stop as the ladies were musical and there were always lots of visitors in the drawing room of an evening. The only thing we didn't like about it was the evening "family worship," which Miss Machatttie, Scotchlike, insisted on having before retiring to rest. However, in those days, we were pretty well used to that particular feature.

Well, one night we were coming home from the Alhambra, feeling pretty how-do-you-do-thank-you. It must have been after midnight. Those who know their London will remember that at the corner of Cecil street stood one of Attenbury's justly celebrated pawnshops. (The present Cecil Hotel, we understand, is built there now.) At this precise spot we ran into a young woman who appeared to be in distress. She said she was busted and had no place to sleep.

Note that we were young and fresh from Gleskie.

Remembering that there was a lounge in our room, we thought it would be a charitable act to smuggle the lady into the house and give her a night's sleep on it. We suggested this to her and she thought it a most brilliant idea. Those last drinks before the pubs close in London are most disastrous.

Our room was at the top of the house. Deftly opening the front door with the good old latch-key, the two of us slipped inside. The house was at rest, and a dim light burned in the hall. In order that only one pair of footsteps should be heard ascending the stairs by listening ears, we persuaded the lady to jump on our back and be carried up. This feat was most successfully accomplished.

The lady immediately rolled on the lounge, hat and all, and went to sleep. We think she had been drinking gin. The idea uppermost in our mind was to be sure and wake up about five or six o'clock and smuggle her out again. With this last thought we, too, fell asleep on the bed without undressing.

Just fresh from Gleskie!

When our wearied eyelids opened in the morning it was broad daylight. Consulting the watch we nearly took a fit on discovering that it was after nine. The tired dame was still snoring away to beat the band on the lounge. The question at once arose how to get her out of the house. Shall we ever forget sitting on the side of that bed regarding the poor girl taking her rest on the little old lounge, oblivious of the awful jackpot she had got us into?

Opening the door gently we went to the head of the stairs and listened. It was

This is a dry world. Those of us who eventually wind up in hell should burn brightly.[8]

the breakfast hour but all seemed quiet enough. Now or never. Giving the slumberer a rude shake we told her to come on quick and jump on our back again for the return trip.

With her arms twined around our neck and a pair of striped stockings sticking away out under our arms, we started down. All went well for the first flight of stairs. We weathered that landing nicely. But just—we must have walked under a ladder the day before because we arrived at the landing where the drawing room and the dining room were, a door opened, that of the dining room, and out marched Miss Machattie, followed by the four ladies and the two gentlemen. They stopped as if shot.

Behold your uncle gliding cunningly along with a strange female perched on his back, the most conspicuous thing in view being striped stockings. It makes us turn hot and cold every time we think of it.

Dropping the female unceremoniously we gave her a vigorous shove towards the stairs and told her to scoot. She scooted. As for ourself, we made for the banisters and slid down them schoolboy fashion, actually reaching the front door before the lady. The two of us tumbled over each other in our haste to reach the crowded Strand, where your uncle stood her a much-needed drink and told her to duck her nut.

That is the story. We sent for our trunk, and got it. The two gentlemen, whom subsequently we often met, were requested to seek other quarters shortly afterwards, because they had acquired a habit of simultaneously going into convulsions of laughter for no apparent reason, thus disconcerting the ladies. Funny world, this. (November 19, 1904)

———

In cities across the line, it is a common thing for the working man to vitalize himself when tired and thirsty by rushing the growler, or "chasing the can," as some bibliographers have it. This is a great institution, especially during the heat of the summer. Three or four men employed at the same job send a kid around with a tin bucket and ten cents to the nearest saloon, and back comes the kid with the vessel brimming over. On big jobs where large gangs of men are employed a kid is usually hired by the foreman to do nothing else but rush the growler for the different little groups of workers as they may require it. The men who do this are not necessarily "drinking men."

The growler is a time-honored institution amongst the laboring element over there and is not objectionable to the bosses. These hard workers who rush the can when thirsty or feeling tuckered out are not as a rule of the class that loaf around the bars. Of an evening they are more likely to be at home with their wives and children, enjoying a quiet smoke and a read of the afternoon papers.

Imagination pales before the idea of a working man in Calgary trying to rush

Daily health hint: cut out the booze.[9]

the growler. It would take his whole day's pay to get the can filled.

Yes, dear reader, we are talking to you about rushing the growler. The working man's beer cuts a decidedly more important figure in a populous community than does the clubman's Scotch and soda. In England the masses will, under protest, stand a slight increase in the price of bread, but no government unless it was contemplating suicide, ever ventured to do anything that would increase the price of beer by even the most infinitesimal fraction of a farthing. Moreover, they recognize the importance of beer as a factor in the daily life of the average Briton, by making peers of the principal brewers!

Try and assuage your thirst in Calgary on 10 cents. It is an actual fact that 10 cents won't buy a drink of ANY KIND in this town, except during the summer when the soda fountains are running. (January 28, 1905)

The Alberta Press Association is now an actuality, a thing of beauty and a joy forever. About thirty editors from Alberta proper and from West Assiniboia and British Columbia gathered in Calgary this week and formed themselves into the nucleus of what is destined to become the most important organization in the West.

Their genial presence has interfered, however, with our contemplated enlargement of this paper. We have been too busy doing the polite, showing the visitors the Fire Hall, the new churches under construction, the theatre and the magnificent city hall.

"What do you think of our city?" asked the mayor of a well-known newspaper man from the north.

"I notice great improvements since I was last here, sir. The bar at the Royal Hotel has been enlarged to almost three times its former size and the Alberta bar has been moved, improved, enlarged and decorated until it is the swellest in the Territories. These, to my mind, shows a state of enviable prosperity."

"Calgary, as you perhaps already know, is the centre of the live stock industry."

"To be sure, to be sure. And, speaking of live stock, how is the Hornby horse?"

"Oh, come off! Let's have a drink."

On Friday the business men of Calgary gave a swell luncheon to the visitors, and in the evening there was a $10-a-plate banquet served in their honor. They were also the guests of the *Herald* Friday evening at the Lyric theatre.

On Saturday they all went to Banff to be the guests of Dr. R. G. Brett, than whom newspaper men have no better friend.

The visit of the editors has not been altogether in the nature of a junket. Much important business was transacted at the convention, the proceedings of which we may give later on.

J. J. Young was appointed president of the Alberta Press Association, by acclamation. Col. G. C. Porter, editor of the

Every man has his favorite bird. Ours is the bat.[10]

Herald, was elected Secretary-Treasurer, and all communications relating to the association should be addressed to him.

Our own office was that of chairman of the reception committee, the main duty apparently being to set 'em up to the visitors as they dropped into town. (January 28, 1905)

The *Eye Opener* was all ready for publication last week when the editor was unexpectedly laid low with let us say, a very bad cold. Much of the stuff in the present issue was not up for last. In order to get out this week and appease our infuriated subscribers, we shall let it go. Some of it is somewhat chestnutty, from the local standpoint, but out-of-town infuriated subscribers won't mind that. (February 25, 1905)

Dr. Brett's immense new Sanitarium Hotel at Banff is now completed and is a corker in every respect. It is one of the handsomest, most artistic and really comfortable hotels in Canada, having charming grounds round it and a magnificent view the mountains. You can have a far more interesting time at this establishment than you can at that unspeakable C.P.R. joint where the pretentious veneer of semi-ready swelldom acts as a wet blanket on those who have come to Banff for a few days careless, easy, knock-about enjoyment. Give us Brett's every time. (June 24, 1905)

This report that whiskey drinking is declining in Calgary will cause no surprise. Most of the politicians are out of town telling the festive farmer which way to vote. (September 2, 1905)

To a newspaper man it is always a source of intense amusement to watch for the editorials which appear in a paper the morning after the editor has been at a banquet. They gave Sanford Evans, the popular retiring editor of the *Winnipeg Telegram*, a great farewell banquet the other night and, of course, the new editor, Eddie Nichols, was present, singing "For he's jolly good fellow" with the rest of the boys. Anyone familiar with life on a morning paper in the festive city of Winnipeg could have called the turn on the dear old stock editorial which had inevitably to be run on this occasion. It was on the momentous question of Seed Grain and Noxious Weeds. There was only one editorial lambasting Walter Scott, instead of the usual even half dozen. In Calgary, after a night out, an editor always sends down a lot of crap about the Sugar Beet Industry. This is an old standby and a great favorite—with the comps. In our own case, we don't get out a paper at all until the booze has completely worn off. (December 2, 1905)

The genial traveller for Seagram's whiskey concern was in Calgary this week hustling up business for the firm. He presented the newspapers and his customers

After taking a few swallows of rye a man begins to feel his oats.[11]

with a large colored picture of Joe Seagram's race horses. The *Eye Opener* was favored with one of those pictures, enclosed in a $7.50 frame, on the distinct understanding that we were to give Seagram a write-up. We shall do so.

We consider Seagram's whiskey to rank very high amongst the numerous poisons now on the market. Not that it is any worse than other whiskeys, but, being the most drank, it creates more havoc throughout the country. It has put more men in their graves than a corps of census sharps could enumerate in a year and has put thousands upon thousands of good men on the hog. Seagram's wealth is built on the folly of others and each of his race horses represents a hundred or more wretches who have died of delirium tremens brought on by mopping up an overplus of his rotgut. We have no more respect for a man in Joe Seagram's business than we have for Radcliffe or the murderers whom Radcliffe hangs. They are all in the killing business. Seagram's race horses and his wealth cut no figure in our eyes. We have helped him buy too many of his flyers and so has almost every other d——d fool of our acquaintance. (August 25, 1906)

As an illustration of the marvellous resources of this district, a well known visitor, prominent in eastern business circles, who spent a day amongst our factories and smaller foundries throughout the city, was more than surprised at what he saw. In fact, he was so overcome that towards evening, his eyes grew tired and although he used glasses of various hues (not being particular what he drank out of) his eyesight became perverted to such an extent that objects doubled up on him and he wound up by being unable to see anything at all. Indeed, the board of trade representative who called on him at his hotel during the evening reported that he was "blind." This, however, is a condition which is frequently noticeable among newcomers and is attributed by that eminent scientist, Sir Andrew March, of the Royal Boozographical Society at Banff, to the altitude.

This gentleman was interviewed in his room early the following morning by the *Eye Opener* representative, who was accompanied by an old friend, Mr. J. Collins, whom the visitor had expressed an ardent desire to meet as soon as possible. In answer to our little pleasantry as to how they were coming, he inquired, "Where am I?" On being introduced to Mr. Collins, whom he greeted with somewhat effusive cordiality, he was greatly comforted to find that he was within easy reach of all of Mr. Collins's immediate kith and kin. Indeed, he seemed much easier and was not unwilling to give his impressions of Calgary. Although he had lived for many years in Chicago he was appalled at the stupendous height of our buildings, some of which, especially the Boozonic Temple, seemed to him to be about forty-eight storeys high. He was willing to admit that this western country

A drink in the hand is worth two in the bottle.[12]

was forging ahead at an incredible pace. He was unable to understand how there were two moons here, while they had only one in Chicago. This was an infallible sign of western progress and development. The city hall compared not unfavorably with those he had dreamed about and he had never seen anything like Gillis before. He expressed his wonder and delight at all he had seen in Calgary and said he preferred it, if anything, to Chicago. (September 22, 1906)

Three men back east somewhere drank barber-shop bay rum and are dead in consequence. The average man who has had it rubbed over his face and dashed into his nostrils will believe this story without documentary evidence. (November 10, 1906)

This is February 23, skidoo, and almost all the Jan. 1 passengers on the water wagon have dropped off, like snow in the Thaw trial, Jean.

Yes, dear, we shall tell you how a man falls off the water wagon.

In the first place, a man never falls off at all. He jumps off. Excuses for this act of mature deliberations are many and ingenious.

Let us illustrate. A newspaper man, say on an evening paper, comes down to his office about nine o'clock on the morning of January 2. He has kept his good resolutions for a week. Moving about with a virtuous air among the boys, he catches

an occasional fragrant whiff of matutinal Collinses, familiar scent, delightful memory of long ago—one week. Stodgy with fried steak and poached eggs, he envies the jovial bunch who were unable to face breakfast at all, but were fain to be content with a couple of jolts.

To his desk he goes and lights a cigar. For six days he has been able to forego his usual visits to the joint across the way, where the bartender affectionately calls him "Old Sox." He smiles as he thinks how he has dreaded this breaking with a habit which he had to admit was not only doing him no good but was an expense at the end of the month.

His mind running on this channel, he ponders deeply on the situation. Why does a man take a drink? Most drinks are taken for sociability, to be sure. But, still, he could remember a few times when he had slipped out for a quiet hooker when the "story" was slow in stacking up. These were times when he had persuaded himself that he was not feeling just right, when, as a matter of a fact, he was just a little dopey—as all newspaper men will get once in a while.

Well, he must get to work and turn out some copy. There is that graft scandal to write up. But unfortunately one of the political friends of the paper is in on it. He must protect the political friend at all hazards. Now, lezzsee, wot's the best way to go about this? Hum—aw—the ingenious ideas don't come. He feels dopey, or imagines he does.

Now that he came to think of it he was

Gallons of trouble can come out of a pint flask.[13]

sure he had that same kind of "gone" feeling that had stolen through his system on those other occasions. The little bracer used to straighten him out in the old days, barely a week ago. He began to wonder if his favorite bartender was on in the morning, and found himself figuring out the shifts in the joint across the way.

He wondered—and he held his breath as he did so—if it really would be advisable to take "just one." Yes, there was no other way out of it. This stuff had to be written and time is the essence of everything in a newspaper office. One Manhattan and all would be well. Or what was the matter with a good stiff Collins? Just one. No, that might start him off on a drunk. A spot of Johnnie Dewar would touch the spot, and not nearly so dangerous as a Collins.

Sticking on his hat he walks carelessly into the outer office and asks somebody for a match. Then he strolls out. Guiltily he looks up and down the street and then dives across the road and disappears.

"Hullo, Old Sox!" cries the jovial bartender. "Been sick?"

"Oh, no, but my stomach's a little out of whack today. I think I'll have—lemme see—I think I'll—just make me a Collins, Charlie, and put lots of gin in it."

In about half an hour he moseys back to the office, feeling fit as two fiddles. He sits down to his desk and grinds out a column and a quarter on the graft scandal, pleasantly alluding to the morning newspaper which exposed it as our genial but blackguardly contemporary. After

which, being highly satisfied with himself, he tells the boys that it is his birthday—there has to be some excuse—and invites them all to step across the way and have something.

Late that night a hack is seen vanishing into that night.

Next morning, no fried steak, no poached eggs. Just a Collins, and 1907 is started on the old highway. God bless our home. (February 23, 1907)

Another idol shattered. It turns out that the cuckoo is the earliest riser of any bird, and the greenfinch next. The lark is the latest. Next thing we hear will be that the lark can't get up without a Collins. (July 13, 1907)

Jan. 1: "No thanks, old man, no more booze in mine. I'm off it for good this time, that's straight."

Jan. 2: "No siree, not on your life. What? Not at all—I don't mind going in and having a cigar with you."

Jan. 3: "Yes, I've cut out whiskey altogether. It was getting the better of me. A man can't attend to business and drink whiskey, that's one thing sure. Fred, gimme some soda with a touch of John Bull bitters in it."

Jan. 4: "Aw well, I guess a little claret won't do me any harm. Got any good claret?"

Jan. 5: "Sunday. Safe so far."

Jan. 6: "Fred, gimme a poney of beer—

Some men are hard drinkers, but others find it absurdly easy.[14]

just a poney. I was eating some salt her-ring today, etc. etc."

Jan. 7: "Say, don't put so much froth on that beer. Now shove in a little gin and make a dog's nose of it. Here's how!"

Jan. 8: "And you call this seven-year-old, eh? It's the awfulest rotgut ever I swal-lowed. However, here's looking at you."

Jan. 9: (Morning)—"Make me a Collins."

(Night)—"Say, thish tempransh bishnesh izzalldamnonsense, don't you think? What? Eh? Ain't that right? Course thaz-zright. Lezzavanother and then we'll call a hack—we'll callahack—ain't that right? Betyerlife thazzright!" (January 4, 1908)

The *Eye Opener* has no defence to offer for the booze traffic. It is a bad business; none worse. We've been there. Nobody can tell us anything about it that we don't already know and our frank opinion is that the complete abolition of strong drink would solve the problem of the world's happiness. (April 18, 1908)

The institution which is known among the medical fraternity as a Boozorium is one of the most up-to-date establish-ments of its kind in America. Like most of the stately homes of England, it stands in its own grounds, which include, in addition to the Boozorium itself, a taste-fully laid out Boozological Garden, as well as a well-stocked Boozological Museum for the use of convalescent patients. The museum feature is an excel-lent one, inasmuch as it affords the patients an opportunity of comparing the wild animals they have met during the earlier stages of their treatment with those provided by the management. The Snakery is alone well worth the price of admission, although we must confess that in our earlier days, before we got religion, we saw snakes several sizes larg-er and a great deal more active in their movements. However, everybody is not as fortunate as we were.

The Boozorium itself is excellently equipped, the furniture in some of the best rooms being nailed to the floor and the walls being tastefully decorated in padded canvas. The windows are all fitted with heavy iron bars, presumably as a precaution against burglary. Each room is supplied with a straight jacket in case the patient should desire to rest his arms. In order to screen the patients from the morbid gaze of the casual passerby, a six-teen-foot reinforced concrete wall, sur-mounted by broken bottles, has been erected and the attendants are all men who have shown their capabilities in the prize ring. (September 5, 1908)

The Visitor (cautiously)—"Does your husband periodically—er—suffer from an excess of spirituous—er—liquids?"

The Visited—"Ow's that, ma'am?"

The Visitor—"Does your husband per-mit his appetite for alcoholic beverages to cloud his intellect?"

The Visited—"I don't seem to foller you,

Perhaps whiskey really does improve with age, when it gets a chance.[15]

ma'am. Can't you say it a bit slower?"

The Visitor—"Does your husband drink regularly?"

The Visited (proudly)—"Reg'lar as clockwork, ma'am, an' twice a week. When he comes 'ome drunk I allus knows it's either a Chewsday or a Saturday." (November 21, 1908)

Curious Reader: You want to know what kind of a breakfast we tackle the morning after a bat? That's easy. A Collins, a steak and a little brown dog. What's the dog for? To eat the steak. (December 4, 1909)

Veritas, Regina: Yes, there are other animals besides camels that can go a considerable time without water. Newspapermen, for example. (December 4, 1909)

Yes, to be sure, we knew some darned idiot would turn the paper upside-down to read this part. Have a drink. (January 1, 1910)

It is a curious fact that as soon as a man has made up his mind, or has been induced by his friends, to take the jag cure, he at once proceeds to go off on a terrific bat. He makes a thorough and complete job of it, finally being packed off to the jagcureatorium in horrible shape. The advanced pupils size him up from the windows as he stumbles out of the rig, but beyond a good-natured

remark or two about the dimensions of his jag, make no comment. That is an unwritten law at those places and a very good law too. Talk about your etiquette! We have never been inside one of those institutions, but have heard all about them from those who have. Being a lifelong teetotaller—what ho! bartender. Just fill those up again. (June 4, 1910)

We held the bottle up and took
A brief and scrutinizing look
And then we put the thing away
And muttered hoarsely "Not today."
(January 27, 1912)

We are sorry, indeed it pains us, to have to lay a complaint against such a well-known hostelry as the Yale, but we are of the opinion that their Scotch contains just a trifle too much sulphuric acid and not enough bluestone. (February 10, 1912)

Bartender (calling down cellar)—"Boss, is Murphy good for a drink?"

Voice—"Has he had it?"

Bartender—"He has."

Voice—"He is." (November 2, 1912)

Health Hint—When suffering from violent toothache in a hollow tooth, fill the cavity with whiskey and hold there for thirty seconds with your head cocked to one side. Swallow whiskey and refill cavity. Repeat this experiment until you

You cannot wet your whistle with the whiskey that is past.[16]

don't give a damn whether you have a toothache or not. (August 2, 1913)

Was arrested as German spy in the bar of the Chateau Laurier this morning. Am imprisoned in wine cellar. Terrible suffering. No corkscrew. Authorities mistook my Scotch accent for German gutterals. Intend to make this a matter for international authorities. Meanwhile pray for me. (*Calgary News-Telegram*, August 29, 1914)

My dear Miss Ross,

I fear you will think I have been coming "Billy McDonell" on you. Well, I guess I have, all right, but you must forgive me. I won't do it again. If you only knew how I dread *starting* to write a letter! I keep putting it off, until the letter is never written at all. That I am sitting down now to write this one, is perhaps the most astonishing event of my life. Every other line I have to stop to pinch myself to see that it is really me. I should not be at all surprised if some day I should find myself sitting down to answer Billy McDonell's last four letters!

I saw Mrs. Johnson yesterday. She was looking fine and was in her usual high spirits, though complaining that she missed you terribly. She spoke about seeing Dr. Birch to offer you position as one of the nurses to look after the health of school children, but while I did not discourage her in this brilliant scheme, I did not encourage her, as I don't think such stupid work is in your line at all. You better stick it out in New York until times revive here. Business has gone from bad to worse in Calgary,—all over Alberta in fact. I don't know what is to become of us all. I haven't bothered publishing a paper since the December municipal elections, though I intend coming out on the 20th of this month just to show the maddened populace that I haven't been killed in the trenches. And here it might be appropriate to remark that I have been on only one (beer) bat since you left. Was all right again in three days. I haven't touched spirits (outside of a stray morning Collins) since that memorable occasion when I died and came to life again—or rather was *brought back* to life again. I shall never forget what I owe you for your great work that time. The scare has done me good. By the way, Mrs. Johnston says you wrote me three letters and sent me a bundle of papers. All I have received from you is the two brief epistles from—ahem!—Paisley. The other letter and papers must have gone astray.

The other night I was out to the movies with Angus and we have arranged to take 'em in again next week same time. Forbes-Robertson is playing at the Grand the first half of the week. I have secured a couple of damngood seats for *Hamlet* on Tuesday night. Charlie Taylor will on this occasion witness a Shakespearian performance for the first time in his life. I am quite prepared to hear him whisper in my ear during one of Hamlet's noble soliloquys—"Bull—all bull!" However, let us

Man is made of dust—which explains why some men are always dry.[17]

hope that a pleasant time will be had.

Do you know what I've got an awful good mind to do this summer? (*What?*) I've a good mind to rustle a pass from the C.P.R. and take a trip to New York to see you and Billy McDonell. We could take a scoot over to Landsdowne, which is close to Philadelphia, and pay the old sport a visit. Then you could show me over New York and show me 42nd street and the Flatiron Building. A pleasant time could etc. etc. Life, the daily life of Calgary is precisely the same as it was the day you left. The oil game has made no progress, although the Moose Mountain well is producing oil in small quantities—but not enough to break out into a rash over. Last week I invested in 100 shares in a gold-dredging scheme in British Columbia—north of Ashcroft on the old Cariboo trail. The dredge is already right in the river all ready to commence operations in the Spring. It is located in an out of the way part of the world, but the Guggenheims took millions out of the very same part of this river some 30 or 40 years ago. If I pull an odd million or two out of it myself, I shall drop you a picture postcard at once.

Local news is of such an inconsequential nature that I am driven to stating—by way of providing you with the latest intelligence—that I have five or six new records for my pianola. "Where the River Shannon Flows," "A Perfect Day," "California and You," "Crazy Bone Rag" and a few Harry Lauder songs. Of course I have played them over & over until now

I am sick of them. I have also secured a beautiful new picture for my wall,—a splendid large photo of Freddy Welsh and Charly White as they appeared toward the end of the tenth round in their ten-round go in Milwaukee. Both look pretty well done up. It is a far more interesting picture than Reuben's "Descent from the Cross" or Raphael's "Last Supper" and excites general admiration. Little Miss Hart is well. I laid her off for a month, but she pops around and attends to my correspondence two or three times a week and keeps the business end alive & up to date. Yesterday afternoon she appeared on the scene with a cousin, a frightful looking Jewess called Miss Epstein. It was a social call and in order to get rid of them I had to start playing the rottenest tunes I had on the darned old pianola. They soon faded out of the room.

I want to tell you a funny thing in connection with that bat I got on some time after you left. It was only a beer one, but it had a solid foundation of Collinses. I commenced to *wither* on a Saturday and forgot to lay in enough beer to last me over the Sunday. I had half a dozen quarts, but drank 'em up in no time after I had gone to bed. About 2 in the morning (Sunday) I woke up and hunted around for a drink. The only thing I could find was a bottle of unfermented port which Mrs. Cook, the woman who looks after my rooms, had brought me in a present some weeks before. I started mopping up the stuff, for I was awfully

Whiskey is a wonderful drink it is said. It starts for the stomach and goes for the head.[18]

thirsty, with the result that I became sick and had a vomiting spell, leaning on my elbow out of bed and removing the port from my stomach into a basin. Of course I occasionally missed the basin and saturated the edge of the sheet with a dye of bright red port. It was a bloody looking sight. Finally I grew so weak & sick that I deemed it prudent, in case of collapse, to get up & dress and go to a hospital. It was all I could do to dress, floundering about a forest of empties. When at last I had on my coat & hat I went out & slammed the door. Then I discovered I had forgotten my glasses. I at the same time discovered that I had lost my keys and I couldn't get back into the room. You remember that step ladder that stands outside my door? Well, I took that and busted in the glass panel, enabling me to reach in and open the Yale lock. I got the glasses & hied me over to the Western hospital, no one being any the wiser. On Monday morning old Mrs. Cook arrived as usual at eight o'clock and was alarmed to see the glass part of the door busted in. She peeped in and saw I wasn't there. So reaching in her arm she opened the door & went in. The rooms bore a striking resemblance to Louvain the morning after the Germans sacked it and she feared something had happened to me. Glancing towards the bed her eye lit on the bloodstained sheet and her worst fears were confirmed. A tragedy had occurred. Some evil persons had broken in to my rooms and murdered me *sure*. People in the neighbourhood tell me that poor Mrs. Cook was running around like an old hen with its head chopped off.

You seem to have quite a gay time of it with your nursing, Miss Ross. It must be an agreeable change nursing millionaires on the Hudson from nursing incorrigible old drunks in Calgary. I often walk around by the old Columbia and give Memory full sway, thinking of the time I died & came to life again! By gum, but that was a close shave! I shall always remember though I have never spoken much on the subject, that you saved my life. I believe that this episode has had a great deal to do with your kindly thoughts towards this old slayer. Jimmy Reilly occasionally drops down from Edmonton and runs up to visit. We always talk a lot about you and everything we say is very nice, I can assure you. He is always saying, "There is only one Miss Ross," and I quite agree with him.

Charlie Taylor is Transport Officer of the second biggest camp in England,— Wibley Camp, Surrey. He is doing fine. Dr. Dunlop, Dr. Birch, George Robinson & a lot of other friends are over in France. Won't it be great if I can get over amongst them? And you too? However, this is all too good to come true. I have a disagreeable hunch that it will never be.

Am still in the same old rooms and lonesome as the devil. Am thinking of investing in a dog this spring.
So long,
Bob.

Mind & send back these letters. (Personal

The ability to take a drink and let it alone takes constant practise.[19]

correspondence to Jessie McCauley Ross, February 7, 1915. Glenbow Archives, Bob Edwards Fonds, M 353)

The *Eye Opener* has always been well treated by the hotel men of Calgary, not with booze, because they never by any chance set 'em up, but with advertisements. With practically all of them we have long been on terms of personal friendship. Now that we have come out in favor of this Prohibition Bill those ads will probably be withdrawn, but our loss in revenue may perhaps be some poor devil's gain in longevity. So what of it? Tomorrow is another day.

On the other hand, it must be admitted that the hotel-keepers of the Province do not deserve harsh and drastic treatment at the hands of the Liberal Government at Edmonton. The hotelmen and wholesalers of the Province have been shaken down every election by the Attorney-General's department for fat campaign contribution. The money thus provided by the licensed victuallers practically purchased and preserved intact the power which has been continuously enjoyed by the Sifton bunch for so long. "The trade" is now being bitten by the dog it fed. (April 3, 1915)

The Bill itself is a faulty Bill, inasmuch as it does away with the consumption of beer altogether. It permits a man to send away for his booze, and it can be readily understood that a man is not going to pay freight on a lot of slop. What he sends for will be whiskey. You can bet your life on that.

The temperance cranks do not understand the game. Nor will they take advice from old stagers like ourself. We maintain, speaking as one singularly well posted on the topic, that the only solution of the problem is cheap beer. Prohibition or no Prohibition, you can no more stop a man from "rustling" a drink when he wants it than you can stop him from "rustling" the other thing when he wants it. You can guess what the other thing is—it isn't whiskey either—and get a free trip to the Panama Exposition. If beer should happen to be the only beverage available, the man rustling the drink will be quite satisfied. It is a drink.

Here is another flaw in the Bill. It says that the Act does not prohibit the consumption of liquor in one's own home provided the liquor does not exceed a fixed amount at one time. How on earth are the inspectors—we presume the country will be flooded with inspectors—to find out how much a man has in his home? Certainly no householder in Calgary or any other town in Alberta is gong to allow any inspector to raid his home and inspect the premises. Should any inspector ever poke his nose into our alleged home in a downtown block, he will get a crack over his idea-box with a length of gas pipe. This is official. (April 3, 1915)

The more we think of it, the more we are

The cup that cheers is a noisy piece of crockery.[20]

convinced away in the back of our noodle, that this Prohibition Bill is going to be defeated. As a bill it is a weird and most grotesque affair and the men supposed to be in charge of its wild career are as little children. But, as we said before, we shall support the bill on the off chance of ridding the country of this damned whiskey which has put so many of us on the bum. (May 8, 1915)

Liquor is the nation's worst enemy. It degrades family life, politics and business, causes poverty, insanity and death. It is worse than war and pestilence. It is the crime of crimes. It is the source of three-fourths the crime, and, of course, it takes three-fourths of the taxes to care for the criminals, and to license this incarnate fiend of hell is poor business. (July 3, 1915)

Whiskey is all right in its place, but its place is in hell. The liquor traffic hasn't one leg to stand on. (July 3, 1915)

A friend of ours who has not touched a thumbleful of booze in over a year, though formerly a consistent bear on the whiskey market, broke out again last week. At the bar of the Palliser, where we met him, he gravely explained that he was buying another race horse for Joseph Seagram. From the size of his jag, it ought to be a pretty good horse. (April 8, 1916)

Most people living hereabouts will admit that the editor of this great family journal ought to know considerable about booze psychology. True, we cut it all out a year ago (less one month), but have not forgotten the finer points of the game. You can take it straight from us that with strong drink suddenly eliminated from the daily routine, there must be a substitute.

An absolutely harmless substitute is now being offered and stands in danger of being rejected. And the alternative? That is easy. Send a wire to Field and back comes a bottle of blue ruin by express. You can get a fresh bottle every day, or indeed several bottles if you get some friends to wire in their own names and have them turn it over to you afterwards. Sporadic drinking over a bar will pale into insignificance compared with some of the quiet, intramural toots that will be indulged in over the Field and Golden route.

As an ex-tank of some notoriety "along these lines," we can assure the Provincial Government and temperance societies that permission to sell temperance beer is the one and only way to head off importation from British Columbia. It will not stop it altogether, of course, but it will have the desired effect of lessening it considerably. That is what they want, isn't it? Well, what are they kicking about? It will pay them in the long run to meet the average man half way and allow him his glass of non-intoxicating beer.

It is a curious but easily understood

Confound these bootleggers! They ought to be shot.
You can never find one when you want him![21]

fact that during our drinking days the one day above all others when we wanted a snort, was Sunday. The subconscious feeling that all the bars were closed and we couldn't get it, made us very dry. On one occasion we stepped around to a drugstore and bought a bottle of Peruna. You should have seen us Monday morning! Wow! (July 8, 1916)

What an awful lot of booze is offered you when it becomes generally known that you are on the water wagon! During Christmas week the temptation for us to fall off was great indeed. One idiot, who was lit up for fair, entered the *Eye Opener* office on Christmas Day waving a bottle of Scotch and blathering out, "Dewar unto others as you would others Dewar you." This sort of thing is very annoying. (January 6, 1917)

The Moral and Social League of Alberta, alias the Drys, meet at Paget Hall next week for their annual celebration of victory. No, that's wrong. We take it back. The Drys may win a victory but they cannot celebrate it. Their kind of victory destroys the means of celebration. (February 8, 1919)

The *Eye Opener* management gave a party this week because of its seventeenth anniversary. None of the guests turned up. This is what comes of being a Prohibitionist. (March 15, 1919)

On the desk in front of us we have a copy of the Aims and Objects of the Moderation League of B.C. and cannot say we altogether agree with it. It features the hard stuff too much and would permit the sale of spirits under conditions which, though intended to act as a restraint, would not in our opinion work out right at all. However, the B.C. Moderation League is entitled to its own views. (March 15, 1919)

The *Eye Opener* will never be found advocating the sale of spirits in any shape or form or under any government camouflage whatsoever. We print herewith for your information the Aims and Objects referred to and you will notice that No. 6 says:

"Permits to purchase spirits shall be issued to all persons over twenty-one years," etc.

This obviously would make whiskey accessible to everybody as of yore, and we are strongly against it. Beer is our pet idea of a happy compromise, and will remain so.

All we have been contending for so long is the establishment of cosy, respectable cafes where people can foregather during moments of leisure, have their little chat, exchange ideas, swap jokes and roast Sam Hughes—all a-seated at little tables quaffing a glass or two of real honest-to-goodness beer at 5 cents a glass. Nothing very disreputable about that, surely.

No Moderation League is going to

There is a great deal printed that you can't believe—especially on bottles.[22]

inveigle us into saying one solitary word in favor of whiskey under government or any other auspices. It is bad medicine. (March 15, 1919)

Doubtless much of the talk of the drug danger is too alarmist, but it stands to reason if people used to stimulants cannot get them they will tackle drugs and patent medicines, such as essence of ginger and the like. A man was telling us the other day that essence of ginger has an awful kick. One Sunday, some seven or eight years ago, we got on a bat all by our lonesome on a bottle of Peruna. Never shall we forget that day! Why did we take it? Oh, because the bars were closed. It took five Collinses on the Monday morning to get the taste out of our mouth. (March 15, 1919)

Catarrh, the Bane of the World Pe-ru-na, the Standard Remedy.

Catarrh is recognized all over the civilized world as a formidable disease. In the United States alone, two hundred thousand people have catarrh annually. In other countries the ratio ot victims is as great.
For many years Pe-ru-na has held the foremost place as a standard remedy for catarrh.
Persons objecting to liquid medicines can now purchase Pe-ru-na tablets.

Spring! The immemorial, the elemental urge! The lure of far hills, and strange horisons! Do you not hear the call to the long trail? Come let us go and have a drink. The bootlegger beckons on yonder lea. What ho! (May 5, 1919)

It happened in the good old days.

A train slowed up at a busy country station, and a man was seen to put his head excitedly out of the window.

"There's a woman in here fainted," he cried. "Has anyone got any whisky? Quick!"

Some one in the crowd on the platform handed him a bottle. He uncorked it frantically, put it to his lips, and took a noble pull. "Ah," he sighed, "that's better. It always did upset me to see a woman faint." (May 5, 1919)

Prohibition is the extreme of the temperance movement, the same as Anarchy is the extreme of Socialism. (May 5, 1919)

There is no use trying to be funny about Prohibition. To the wets there is nothing funny about the dry situation and the Prohibitionists never see any humor in anything. (November 1, 1919)

Counsel—Was the prisoner sober?
Witness—No, sir; he was as drunk as a judge.
The judge—You mean as drunk as a lord.
Witness—Yes, my lord. (April 10, 1920)

The first drink is the Adam of a drunk.[23]

Our views on the subject of Prohibition have undergone considerable change since the memorable days when we worked so hard in favor of it. The whole thing has proved a farce. It may be true enough that the elimination of the bar has brought good results by removing temptation from the path of wage earners with families, who had no moral right to divert their money from proper domestic channels; but in other circles, the damage wrought by so-called Prohibition has been something fierce.

We have kept hammering away at those booze parties in the home for a long time now, with no tangible results outside of an occasional knowing wink and smile from the cognoscenti. Everybody knows of the disgraceful orgies that are pulled off nightly in private homes along our quiet avenues which look so innocent, childlike and bland during the day. They form a favorite subject of cynical conversation amongst men during office hours. If the women who participate in these debauches only knew how lightly their names are bandied about amongst the men downtown, they would surely pause and do some calm reflecting for their own sakes.

We do not intend in this issue to refer at length—though many have asked us to do so—to the recent notorious "party" which wound up in one of the saddest tragedies that has yet befallen a Calgary home. Silence is the most eloquent comment on this sickening affair.

The curse of the whole thing—and most men will bear us out in this—is that perfectly decent and respectable women get lured to these parties without knowing in advance what kind of a jackpot they are getting themselves into. They don't realize until it is too late that they wouldn't be there at all, that it is no place for them. It is to be hoped that the case referred to in the preceding paragraph will be a lesson to lots of good women in this city, who quite naturally enough enjoy a bit of fun once in a while, to be might careful of the class of bogus-society hoodlums who invite them out to their parties.

God knows, we should be the last one to talk about other people drinking. Our own reputation as a booze artist used to be second to none, but such drinking as we did was always amongst men. In twenty years' residence in Calgary we have never had a drink in a private house, nor have we ever been to one of those drunken parties in the home that we hear so much about. In the hook shops across the river in the old days there was not as much drunk in two nights as there is in one night at one of these parties today. While it was part of the duty of the girls to make the men buy as much booze as possible, for the benefit of the house, they themselves rarely got under the influence of liquor. The landladies would not stand for that. One point in favor of the hook shops was that no decent women were present to be dragged down and put on the bum with bad whiskey. For which

A man when he's drunk will tell you all he knows—but what's the use?[24]

reason we take it that the much maligned old hook shop was the more respectable of the two.

The explanation of a portion of the above paragraph may perhaps be found in the fact that across the river they only gave you ponies of beer and mere thimblefuls of whiskey, and the champagne only looked like champagne—they called it "wine." The chaps who went over there usually had a good snootful before starting, so did not suffer. The uplifters could greatly improve the morals of this city if they would allow some of these institutions to reopen. It is the uplifters themselves who are responsible for the breaking down of the social fabric with respect to morals in general. No one who has the inside track of what is going on will deny this. (July 17, 1920)

Some remark we made in a previous issue was doubtless the cause of a lady jokingly asking us the other day what it felt like to have the jim-jams. We never had 'em. But we can tell her about a fellow up in Wetaskiwin when Jerry was running the Driard and kept in his backyard a collection of animals in a pen, two pet bears, a badger and some birds. This chap was standing one day in front of the hotel gazing over towards the elevator.

"What are you rubbering at," we asked.

"I'm just watching the animals."

"But they're round in the backyard."

"Not mine," he said, drawing his hand

over his eyes. (*Summer Annual,* 1922)

The latest stunt is fountain pens filled with whiskey. We have just bought a dozen and expect to do much spirited writing during the coming year. (*Summer Annual,* 1922)

No power on earth can keep a man from "rustling a bottle" if he is bent on getting it. This booze business is essentially a business of mystery. Booze is always to be had. Prohibition acts may be enforced with a direct form of penalties, distilleries may be shut down and all the whiskey in the dominion confiscated and poured into the rivers, so that not a single drop apparently remains; but do you suppose this would worry your indomitable booze artist? Not a bit of it. As a magician conjures an article from the empty air, so does a droughty boozer cause a bottle to appear from nowhere in the critical hour of over-mastering thirst.

There is just one suggestion in connection with bootlegging in Calgary which we should like to offer to the magistrate and the chief. It is this: that all bottles or flasks of whiskey sold by bootleggers (at $6 per) which are seized by the police, should be analyzed by the city chemist. Some of this stuff is made by the bootleggers themselves and is sufficiently poisonous to endanger life. Indeed, we have a shrewd suspicion that at least one very recent death in the city was directly attributable to this cause.

Try a cool beer or long Collins for your fit of pessimism.
Why be poor when you can be rich for half a dollar?[25]

We know a chap, long used to his horn, who not so long ago took a couple of drinks out of a bootleg bottle and was confined to his bed for a week. He nearly died. Another man told us of getting a bottle from a bootlegger on Ninth Avenue from which on being opened there issued a bluish gas. What would have happened to him had he taken a snort, he hated to think. It cost him six bones. (*Summer Annual,* 1923)

"With The First Barrel They Brought Down The Wets…"

Huzzah for the Lazarus act! Just when Bob Edwards's political career seemed every bit as lacklustre as his election campaign[1]—one wag characterized his early Legislature behavior as "giving every evidence of a state of mental death"[2]—he brought the House down[3] with a ripsnorting return to form. Chatty mudslinging! Impassioned reasoning! Shameless showboating! Over the course of 45 minutes,[4] Edwards defied the notion of absolute Prohibition by arguing in favour of legalizing 7% beer. Granted: he bungled the proposal submission process.[5] Granted: the amendment died a quick death.[6] Granted: so did Edwards. But still!

Mindboggling innovations in scissors/paste technology have rescued this momentous address, heretofore lost to the sands of history. What follows is a reconstruction pieced together from reports appearing in the *Morning Albertan, Calgary Herald,* and *Edmonton Journal.*[7]

[1] Consult Chapter 1 of the present volume.
[2] "Bob Edwards Asks Question [sic] Liquor Control: Calgary M.L.A. Throws Poison Dart in Direction of Government Benches," *Edmonton Journal,* February 24, 1922.
[3] According to *Calgary Herald* and *Edmonton Journal* reports, Edwards's antics met with great mirth.
[4] As per the recollection of John R. Boyle, M.L.A., in the obituary issue of the *Eye Opener* (November 25, 1922).
[5] "Strong Beer Amendment Provokes Lively Debate, and Finally Withdrawn," *Calgary Herald,* March 21, 1922.
[6] "Legislature Overwhelmingly Defeats Proposal Submitted by Edwards for Plebiscite on Sale of Real Lager," *Edmonton Bulletin,* March 24, 1922.
[7] Intriguingly, the *Albertan,* so crucial to Edwards's victory less than a year previous (perhaps nursing a vested interest in presenting R. C. Edwards as Serious Politician), made no mention of the audience's laughter— nor does it relate the shenanigans involving the home bootlegging kit. Not so the *Herald* and *Journal.*

One advantage of prohibition is that you no longer hear the pet grievance which men unload on you after the third drink.[26]

In which R. C. Edwards, M.L.A. delivers his maiden (& only) address to the Alberta Legislature

I don't know much about the Social Service League,[i] except that it is a weird band of teetotallers, who pursue their activities under the smug assumption that they are right and everybody else is wrong. I am not one of those who are laboring under the delusion that the government is allowing itself to get under the thumb of that awful body. Judging from the calibre of those placed at the head of the administrative posts of this government, and also judging from the conformation of the prime minister's jaw, I do not think that there is the slightest danger of the government ever getting under anybody's thumb. As for the Social Service League, the bitter lessons of the past few years have put no dent whatever on those people.[ii] They know it all, you can't do anything with them.[iii]

We have had Prohibition for about five years. The country is disrupted and demoralized. Trouble from one year's end to another.[iv] One of the worst results of our over-drastic form of prohibition—the saddest result of all—has been the diverting of whiskey from the barroom into the home. This introduction of whiskey into the home has started many women drinking, women who in the old days would have been horrified at the very idea of having a bottle of whiskey in the house. Young girls have followed suit, no doubt thinking it smart and fashionable to do something they know they shouldn't do. My reverend colleague here, Mr. Pearson, who knows more about these things than I do, will no doubt bear me out when I say that if Eve hadn't been forbidden the apple she probably wouldn't have bothered her head about it at all.

The drinking is done in private, in hotel bedrooms, in apartment blocks, in the house—in fact, any old place. What is known as "parties" have come into vogue and believe me, Mr. Speaker, they are some parties! Why, even in the disreputable old barroom days one neither saw nor heard of wild, reckless "parties" such as these which participate citizens of high standing in the community, women of recognized social status and perfectly good, respectable and refine young ladies. The consequences, or rather the potential consequences of this sort of thing are obviously of a dangerous character.[v]

Where do they get the whiskey? All they need is the price and the whiskey appears by magic. The first still in Calgary was found run-

Some men are good because they find it cheaper than being wicked.[27]

ning at full blast in the basement of one of our leading churches. It was only the caretaker of the church who was running the still.

A farmer at Fort Saskatchewan was fined $200 and costs for selling whiskey of his own manufacture and appealed to be allowed to go to his farm to get the money. He went and loaded up his car with liquor, sold it to the bootleggers and paid his fine.

The only wealthy people today are the bootleggers.[vi] It is highly exasperating to think that in these times of business depression, when everybody is more or less broke, with much unemployment and considerable distress and hunger in the land, that the only class of men waxing rich in the community are the bootleggers. Any hour of the day one can see the lordly bootlegger driving around in his Big Whiskey Six, as my friend Mullin calls it.

The reason why whiskey—good, bad or indifferent—finds such a ready sale, is due entirely to the inaccessibility of beer. Cheap, wholesome beer. Few men would bother much about expensive, bad whiskey if they could get access to good, cheap beer. Most normal men like a glass of beer when tired or thirsty, by way of a tonic, or stimulant, and my firm conviction is that if the government were to make beer available, the liquor law would be cheerfully obeyed by practically all who are now breaking it.[vii] The request is a simple, sane and honest one. The body of people who ask this ask it modestly, and not truculently as did the temperance faddists, in asking for prohibition.

Here is a package, containing ingredients for making several gallons of 20 percent strength beer. It is being sold by a Winnipeg house all over the country, and if the government does not put good beer before the people, these people will start bootlegging on beer.[viii] Pretty soon the rotten old moonshine whiskey will be followed by this stuff. I am going to turn it over to the government for analysis, otherwise I will have to take it down to Calgary and try it out myself.[ix]

My plan is simple and clearly defined. This plan of mine is to tighten up on the sale of whiskey, making it practically impossible to get at all except for really genuine medical purposes. I shall not offer any suggestion how this can be accomplished because any suggestions of mine would be automatically turned down.

The Rev. Mr. Bishop, no doubt, will have some plan to convert the

You may be justified in blowing your own horn, but not in going on a toot.[28]

druggists, the moonshiners and the bootleggers by inducing them to join the Methodist church.

The other part of my plan is to legalize and open up the sale of beer containing 3.5 percent weight alcohol, which is the same strength that it used to be. It is non-intoxicating. A light wholesome lager beer will provide just that small, inconsequential element of stimulating force that is needed to meet the weakness and perverseness of human nature halfway.

Were the 3.5 percent proportion of alcohol to be concentrated within the limits of a wineglass, it would be a different matter altogether, but it is spread over so much bulk that no one can drink enough of it even to become hilarious. The human paunch has its well-defined limitations. The only class of people in this country who might be expected to hold enough to produce intoxication are the country editors of weekly newspapers, because they all carry patent insides.

I need not remind the government that the G.W.V.A. has expressed by official resolution their desire to have the beer back, and the Alberta Federation of Labor, at their recent convention at Lethbridge, passed a similar resolution to this effect.

I submit that the returned solider and the federation of labor are an irresistible force to buck. All they were asking for was some elasticity in the application of the liquor law with respect to beer. They did not ask for whiskey or the return of the bar, or any nonsense of that kind. All they wanted was their beer back, and this has been refused.

Shortly after the government assumed office, the Attorney-General took a trip to Ontario and, while there, conferred with the Attorney-General of that province, the unspeakable Raney. This trip filled me with misgivings. I knew that one of Mr. Raney's pet hobbies was engaging ministers of the gospel to help enforce the Liquor Act, and, as it turned out, one of the first things our own Attorney-General did on his return was to engage a Methodist preacher to take full charge of the enforcement of the Alberta Liquor Act.

The Rev. Mr. Bishop is a gentleman of admittedly high repute in his calling, enjoying the respect of the province at large, where he is widely known, and I can only express the hope that he won't follow

All the good people don't die young. Lots of them live to a ripe old age and die poor.[29]

in the footsteps of the Rev. Spracklin, one of Mr. Raney's liquor staff in Ontario, who one on memorable occasion forced his way in the dead of night into a man's house in search of liquor and shot the poor man dead in the presence of his wife and children.

What I am most afraid of in the appointment of a Methodist parson is the strong probability of this fair province being over-run with stool pigeons. I will not labor the fact that these gentry are the scum of the earth. That is generally recognized.[x] We Britishers resent keenly living in an atmosphere of espionage, and we want no "human blood hounds" to enforce the act.[xi] In fact, only the other day the Calgary G.W.V.A. passed a resolution to expel from the association any member who acted as a stool pigeon. The significance of this is unmistakable.

The other day I had a question on the order paper asking the government when it was going to take a referendum in accordance with one of the planks in the official U.F.A. platform, published two weeks before election. This question was based on Section 16, which I will ask the house to listen to with close attention. It is quite short and is divided into two parts—although there is enough call in it to have been divided into three parts:

"Prohibition: To enact and enforce such legislation for the control of the liquor traffic as the people may sanction by referendum."

Honorable members will observe that this part held out a promise to the wets that a fresh plebiscite would be granted by a U.F.A. government if elected to power.

The next part of the self-same plank, separated from the first part by a semi-colon, reads:

"Prohibition is an internal part of the Farmers' Platform, and the U.F.A. will use its influence in that direction."

I hardly know how to describe that second part. It might perhaps be fitly described as a graceful gesture in honor and recognition of the alleged teetotal proclivities of the farmers. When I ran across this plank the other day in the library, I was reminded of the interesting discussion which took place in the house when the Game Act was up over the relative qualities of the pump gun and the double-barreled shotgun. This Section 16 was the double-barreled shotgun used by our friends during the campaign in their merry hunt for votes. With the first barrel they brought down the wets, and with

Most of our tragedies look like comedies to the neighbours.[30]

the second barrel the drys!

You can't beat that! Deadly stuff!

I ought perhaps to explain that my only reason for putting that question on the order paper was for the purpose of ascertaining whether the U.F.A. government intended to run true to its platform.

Well, I think, Mr. Speaker, that I have talked long enough. Suffice it to say that the best men in the land are finding lots of fun in being lawbreakers. They regard the Liquor Act as a huge joke.[xii] It has got so that one half of the population of Alberta is trying to get liquor, and the other half is trying to keep them from it. It is just like a game: if you get it, you win. And if you don't, you lose. You can't expect to enforce any act with half the population against it.[xiii]

[i] *Calgary Herald*, March 21, 1922
[ii] *Albertan*, March 21, 1922
[iii] *Herald*
[iv] *Edmonton Journal*, March 21, 1922
[v] *Albertan*
[vi] *Journal*
[vii] *Albertan*
[viii] *Journal*
[ix] *Herald*
[x] *Albertan*
[xi] *Journal*
[xii] *Albertan*
[xiii] *Herald*

While some of us have more ups and downs in this world than others, we'll all be on the dead level sooner or later.[31]

CHAPTER FIVE

Nemeses

In which the editor of the great Christian organ throws mud,
holds a grudge, has a change of heart—& defends himself
against charges of being a libeller, a character thief, a coward,
a liar, a drunkard, a dope-fiend & a degenerate.

P. J. NOLAN: Do you believe Mr. Edwards a ruffian?

W. H. CUSHING: I have never seen him behaving himself wrong.

NOLAN: Do you think his paper is a ruffian?

CUSHING: Some of it is pretty rough.

—transcription from Edwards v. McGillicuddy

libel trial, November 11, 1908

Has the law "let you down"? Dissatisfied with judicial decisions? Rejoice! for with the paltry investment of several years of unwavering bitterness, moral surfeition can still be yours!

Bob Edwards's literary career was shaped by two court cases—we speak, of course, of his legal tussles with the Canadian Pacific Railway (1905) & Dan McGillicuddy, editor of the *Calgary Daily News* (1908). In the following chapter, Edwards instructs by example on—

☞ Drawing legal ire through libelous baiting!

☞ Winning a court case, but harbouring ill will all the same!

☞ Salving bruised feelings by haranguing your opponent's lawyer!

☞ Having a change of heart! Or, alternately—

☞ Gloating even when, or possibly because, your opponent is dead!

Please know: The volume at hand is not responsible for any legal proceedings resulting from use, or misuse, of the instruction within its pages.

<hr>

R. B. BENNETT & THE C.P.R.

Bob Edwards was never more, shall we say, "fluid," than when discussing the topic of Richard Bedford Bennett, the Calgary lawyer who went on to become Canada's eleventh Prime Minister (1930–1935). He was much more steadfast in his continued dislike of the Canadian Pacific Railway.

As the following passages show, Edwards started out as an unrepentant Bennett booster, and extremely critical of the C.P.R.'s "irrigation scheme"[1] to transform twenty-five million acres of not-so-prime Alberta plains into viable farmland. Edwards wasted no opportunity to mock the C.P.R.'s "irrigation ditch"[2]—to the point that C.P.R. bigwig J. S. Dennis slapped him with criminal libel[3] charges. (Dennis seems to have been a reactionary hot-head. *The Daily Herald* reported him taking "a most extraordinary and childish stand"[4] by proposing a localized media blackout concerning C.P.R. dealings—because he was tired of the bad press.) The C.P.R. retained R. B. Bennett as its attorney, and so began a feud that would last for years.

Edwards won the trial, but nursed a public grudge against Bennett. (He also took great delight reporting accidents at the C.P.R. crossing in downtown Calgary.) Bennett, in turn, banned the *Eye Opener* from being sold on the trains. By 1911, however, Edwards had repealed his hard feelings[5] and reinstated himself as Bennett's number one fan. As for his views on the C.P.R. ... not so much.

There is a man whose career we shall follow with interest in the house of legislature, for the reason that from what we have observed he is destined for higher honors on the political battlefield in days to come. We allude to R. B. Bennett. Let him not, however, antagonize his opponents overmuch, as he is prone to do. The sly old politicians never do that. The soft word which turneth away wrath does not necessarily eliminate the fortiter in re feature.

Regarded from various points of view, Bennett is the best-equipped man for the fray of the whole galaxy of M.L.A.s going east from these regions. Mentally and by

[1] The skinny: the federal government plied the C.P.R. with the "fairly fit for settlement" land in order to further encourage the massive undertaking that was the transcontinental railroad. A. Mitchner's "The Bow River Scheme" chapter, in *The C.P.R. West: The Iron Road and the Making of a Nation* (Hugh Dempsey, ed., Vancouver : Douglas & McIntyre, 1984) offers a good primer on the subject.
[2] It's possible Edwards's merciless hammering was rooted in something other than issue with the project itself: Mitchner mentions the irrigation scheme had the "unqualified support" of minister of the Interior—and longtime Edwards rival—Clifford Sifton.
[3] *Calgary Daily Herald*, December 12, 1905.
[4] *ibid.*
[5] Due, it is widely believed, to the olive-branch machinations of Bennett. Consult *Eye Opener Bob* for details.

We say just as mean things about others as they do about us,
but of course that is different.[1]

study he is the peer of any one in this country and although he don't drink, he is not a bad fellow.

We don't want to keep harping on Bennett, but his platform is one which should be kept uppermost in the minds of all the members from this part of Alberta. Let them not forget it either. Alberta a province; Calgary a capital; railroad connection with the transcontinental American lines to the south; irrigation works constructed by the government;

MacJolt: "Wot I like about ole Cush is he don' drink. You hardly ever see him in a saloon."
O'Snifter: "Thaz why I like Bennett too. You seldom see him with a skate on."
MacJolt—"Thaz ri' Lezzav one on ole Cush."

and one or two other minor matters. Bennett is essentially an initiative man. In him and Rosenroll we place our trust. Let them never be confounded. (*Wetaskiwin Free Lance*, March 22, 1899)

Bennett got there. I am glad that Bennett gained the victory, if only to fool some people who tried the double cross on him. The best thing Bennett and Haultain

can now do is to take a walk together out to Irish's, bury the hatchet shake hands, laugh the thing over, and work together. Both men are genial roosters admire each other's ability and ambition, and would be very efficient legislators if they once clasped hands.

Which they won't. (*Wetaskiwin Breeze*, April 18, 1901)

That most colossal of all fakes, Mlle. Rheo, the palmist, has been sewing up the easy propositions of Calgary in room 37 of the Alberta Hotel. We enjoy seeing Calgary, a town of imperfectly educated and sparsely travelled suckers, getting tangled up in this sort of sideshow-of-an-up-country-fair business, because it may impress upon their minds once for all that they are nothing but common or garden chumps. Any smooth guy, man or woman, can strike Calgary any given moment and make a killing. The Rheo feature was up in Edmonton. She made her fare. We wish her well in her travels because she is a smart young woman, pleasant spoken, and possessed of the true old Chicago South Clark street method of jollying the sloppifactors out of one dollar a head. Even R. B. Bennett

We are scared to indulge in any josh this issue for fear somebody might take offense and bring a libel suit. These are parlous times.[2]

and Jerry Boyce, neither of them particularly celebrated as suckers, fell into the meshes. This is the worst fake at present operating in the Territories.

We asked Rheo to strike a horoscope on the *Eye Opener*. She quietly declined, and we backed out of number 37 and fainted in the arms of French Johnnie who was waiting outside. (March 4, 1902)

Who do you suppose we met in Calgary on Wednesday? Dr. Brett and the ever-genial R. B. Bennett. They were both in great form. They exchanged a little friendly badinage with us about our *Eye Opener* and then passed on. Ships that pass in the night. Good men these, their turn is coming. (March 14, 1902)

During the Oliver-Bennett campaign we listened to an eloquent speech by Bennett in Robertson's hall, Edmonton, in which with a wave of his hand, he drew attention to the great waterway at their door by which they had a route already made for shipping merchandise and grain down to Prince Albert and saving the roundabout railway journey. He was laughed at for this. In private conversations afterwards the old timers said that Bennett very evidently didn't know what he was talking about. Yet—

—Here we have, only last week, the council, the board of trade, and the press of Edmonton going off on an excursion down the Saskatchewan on a thirty foot gasoline launch to ascertain whether the river is such as to admit the establishment of a line of steamers for the conveyance of freight and passengers up and down the river.

Bennett apparently did know what he was talking about. Only, the Edmontonians resented having a self-evident proposition rammed down their throats by a stranger—as Bennett practically was to them then. R. B. certainly talks a good deal when he gets started, but his worst enemies will concede that he usually knows very clearly what he is talking about when he does talk. (July 25, 1903)

R. B. Bennett recently assured a friend of ours that he had no intention whatever of running for parliament at the next general election. Bennett should call in a specialist who can tell him how to say what he means without putting it the other way. We could understand him not wishing to run for the Skupshtina, but the Canadian parliament is fairly respectable. (July 25, 1903)

Last Wednesday in Calgary about 4 or 5 o'clock in the afternoon, a High River gentleman despatched a telegram to a merchant in High River on important business. The following morning, Thursday, this gentleman came down himself by train arriving in High River about 9:30. The telegram he had sent from Calgary the previous day reached High River several hours AFTER he him-

He who never does wrong never does much anyway.[3]

124

Hon. John Moseley, last Wednesday night, listening to Bennett's heart-rending description of the political situation.

self had arrived here the following day. People who carp at the slowness of the C.P.R. should in future remember this remarkable feat of one of her passenger trains beating electricity by nearly a day and a night. It surely must have been that famous windsplitter, Old 32, that did the trick. (August 8, 1903)

"No sir," said the imperturbable Bennett, tilting himself back in his chair, "I have never entered a hall or public place without being vociferously cheered. It is most embarrassing. Other great men, sometimes manage to slip in unobserved, but the crowd always appears to be on the alert when I enter. I have often been asked to explain why this is so. The explanation is easy. Do you suppose Napoleon or Bismarck or the Pope could appear before a crowd without being instantly recognized? Their faces, or at least, the pictures of their faces, are familiar to everybody. People begin when they are mere children to see pictures of Napoleon and Bismarck and the Pope and they never forget those remarkable

faces, so full of character and individuality. It is the same with me. If you were to ask almost anybody what four great men's personalities were most familiar to him he would instantly say they were those of Napoleon, Bismarck, the Pope and Bennett. Is it any wonder then that I am immediately accorded an ovation wherever intelligent people abound? The Pope and myself are alas! the only two really great men left, though we differ in this much, that His Holiness has much of his reputation yet to make. Now I am afraid your two minutes are up. I am a very busy man, my dear sir, a very busy man! Goodbye!" (July 2, 1904)

R. B. would be a very clever fellow if he did not know it. (June 17, 1905)

Bennett need not give himself the slightest uneasiness. Although Bennett is not "one of the boys," he possesses those finer and sterner qualities which the boys admire, and which they recognize as essential in the man who is to represent them in the serious affairs of provincial legislature. (October 7, 1905)

To succeed in one's profession and wrest reluctant admiration from one's fellows, is of itself a proof of merit. Some decry Bennett for being the C.P.R.'s solicitor. Great Scott! Did it never occur to them that a man has to be a corker, a stemwinder, an ace full on kings, to be employed as the skilled western adviser

Lazy men bump against a lot of criticism, but they usually live long and contented lives.[4]

and legal watchdog of this most exacting corporation. (October 7, 1905)

R. B. is too jealous of his own reputation as a public man to do aught while in the employ of the C.P.R. that might harm the welfare or retard the development of this section of Alberta. If he sees a better hope for Alberta through the entrance of the Jim Hill lines, he won't stand in the way. Of this we feel confident. (October 7, 1905)

R. B. Bennett has been relieving his feelings by telling his friends that he will run the editor of the *Eye Opener* out of town.

He will like hell. (November 25, 1905)

Dennis and Bennett, who have been at their wits' end since the election, both being somewhat uneasy about their jobs with the company, have been taking every opportunity of saying in public that we "tried to hold up the C.P.R." A hold-up usually implies money and these men have purposely been conveying the impression that we tried to hold the C.P.R. up for money, while carefully confining themselves to the expression "hold-up." Of course, nothing of the kind ever occurred, and they know it. The fact is, Dennis and Bennett are not quite accountable for what they say these days. Their pride has had an awful jolt. (November 25, 1905)

Hot air will carry a balloon up a long way, but it wont keep it there.

The proposal of leading Calgary Conservatives to erect a statue of the late R. B. Bennett on some high point overlooking the scene of his former triumphs, is meeting with some opposition. We are not wholly of opinion that the matter is of vital importance, but it would be high-flown insolence on the part of the City Council, which is of Conservative complexion, to lay aside any of the people's money to provide a Bennett statue. The ratepayers would never stand for such effrontery.

Let all the Conservatives of Alberta be invited to join in the projected apotheosis of Bennett and contribute liberally towards a nice bronze statue which will ever act as a reminder to them never again to be led around by a ring in the nose under the spell of oratorical froth, which, when blown off, discloses very small beer indeed. (November 25, 1905)

Were it not for the lazy men in the world lots of labor-saving devices would never have been invented.[5]

In his Calgary speech Duncan Marshall took occasion, while alluding to our Open Letter to Bennett, to warn us to look out for the knife. His warning was timely. The knife has been thrust at our gizzard lately with an unpleasantly ticklish effect, but the chuckleheaded local Mafia will have to try again. (November 25, 1905)

"It's funny," said R. B. Bennett one day, "but nobody ever seems to be glad to see me."

"And haven't you ever found out the cause of your unpopularity?" inquired his candid friend, who, being from New Brunswick also was permitted to take liberties.

"No, I can't discover it."

"Well, well, it's right under your very nose." (March 24, 1906)

Not a life was lost or a buggy smashed at the C.P.R. crossing last week. (March 24, 1906)

Calgary luck is still on the ascendant. No tragedy at the crossing. This is fool's luck. (April 7, 1906)

No astrologer has had the nerve to tackle our Crossing at First Street West with a line of predictions. (May 5, 1906)

The government should step in and examine the C.P.R. bridge across the St. Mary's River between Macleod and Lethbridge before a trainload of passengers crashes through it to a horrible death. We understand that this St. Mary's river trestle bridge was condemned over a year ago, yet the C.P.R. still "take chances." They are great on the dividents. Engineers, brakeys, conductors, travelers and all who have been over it once (especially in daylight) dread to cross this notoriously rotten old bridge. It is liable to collapse at any moment while a train is passing over. The C.P.R. are framing up for themselves a sensational lawsuit, in which the charge of manslaughter is apt to cut a disagreeably big figure.

Travelling men going to Lethbridge

C.P.R. Crossing at First Street West.
A Fore cast.

When a sociable man has a minute to spare he goes and bothers some man who is busy.[6]

from Calgary usually double round by Medicine Hat and up to Lethbridge and back again to Medicine Hat, rather than risk their lives by going over this bridge. The C.P.R. dare not run trains over it by daylight for fear the passengers will see their danger. One traveller who happened to go over the bridge recently, in daylight, says that all the wealth of the Indies would not tempt him to cross it again. (May 5, 1906)

The very first thing Lougheed does after receiving his pompous-sounding, but empty, appointment, is to join with some other C.P.R. fatheads and decry the entrance of the Hill railroads into the west. And the west shouting for increased transportation facilities! Dear, dear! Lougheed's mythico-historical relationship to Lord Strathcona is a great asset, to be sure. (May 5, 1906)

And the C.P.R. hotel—ah! the C.P.R. hotel. It is a distinct—we had almost said a novel—pleasure to be able to say something nice about a C.P.R. institution. (August 4, 1906)

That gigantic illuminated sign over the C.P.R. land offices at the depot, proclaiming "C.P.R. Irrigated Lands," has caused many an intending settler to return to where he came from or to continue his journey on to British Columbia. It is, we repeat, the most damnable knock that Central and Southern Alberta has to con-

tend with. (October 20, 1906)

The illuminated C.P.R. irrigation sign, of which we have been complaining so loudly, is now dark. Messrs. Bicycle & Davidson wish it distinctly understood that it is not being kept unlit out of deference to the clamors of the *Eye Opener*, but simply because they have been notified by the Calgary Water Power Company that the river is so low that there is not enough water to generate the electricity. This still further complicates matters. If they haven't enough water to provide electricity for an illuminated sign, where in thunder are they going to get the water to irrigate their confounded lands? (November 24, 1906)

Just as we anticipated and duly foretold in these columns over and over again. The persistent "FEATURING" of the C.P.R. irrigation ditch has accomplished its blighting work and done it well. In the new geography just issued for use in the Canadian public schools the statement is made that this—OUR—section of Alberta is "ABOUT TO BE RECLAIMED BY IRRIGATION," thus conveying the pleasing impression that Calgary is in the arid belt.

This is entirely the fault of the dunderheads who took it upon themselves to handle visitors in Calgary last summer and the summer before. Every man-jack from the east who looked to be of any consequence was shoved into a rig and

Some men never work harder than when they are doing useless things without pay.[7]

R. B.: "She loves me, she loves me not, she loves me——."

district without irrigation is 35 bushels to the acre; oats, 43; and barley, 32.

The natural possibilities and actualities in the grain-growing line in South Alberta are not advertised. Whereas—

The C.P.R. Irrigation project is heralded to the uttermost ends of the earth.

And there you are. (December 8, 1906)

Bennett hasn't yet caught Calgary in the mood of not being able to forgive herself because she never elected him to the Legislature. (February 23, 1907)

We were wrong in stating last issue that R. B. Bennett is a silent partner in the Alberta Hotel Company. He is not a partner, but has such confounded close business relations with the outfit that an outsider would naturally gain that impression. (February 23, 1907)

On the awful tidings of the impending death-blow reaching Calgary, the lumbermen were seized with a panic and held a hastily-summoned meeting in the Caledonia Block (Liberal Club Rooms?), with Mr. Grogan in the chair.

hurried out to see the ditch. Few escaped. Even as we write, there is an Alberta exhibit of grain being shown off in Chicago to advertise the C.P.R. Irrigation Scheme, although not one single solitary ear or grain has yet been grown on their irrigated lands.

Everything has been Ditch, Ditch, Ditch. Passengers on through-going trains look up and read "C.P.R. Irrigation Lands" in enormous letters on top of a C.P.R. building. By night the sign is illuminated! The Calgary district has become indelibly associated in people's minds with Irrigation, with the consequent broadcast impression that we cannot grow anything here without expensive artificial irrigation. Now it appears that they even have it so recorded in the Canadian School Books!

The reputation of this part of Alberta as a splendid grain-growing country has been sacrificed to help sell C.P.R. property. The average yield of wheat in this

There is little or no fun in loafing if you can't bother somebody who is busy.[8]

They decided to fight the prosecution tooth and nail, and R. B. Bennett was selected to do the fighting for them, his teeth and nails being in perfect order. (August 24, 1907)

Our good old friend, the irrigation ditch, which has provided us with so much excellent copy in the past, is now quite worth going out to visit. The company's demonstration farms, which are in actual operation this summer for the first time can now give strangers visual proof of the abundance and variety of crops that can be raised in the vicinity of Calgary. We sing the beet sugar in gloriam Beiseker and Davidsonem in excelsis. (August 24, 1907)

The average man tries to console himself with the belief that he isn't half as big a fool as he used to be. Look at R. B. Bennett, for instance. (September 5, 1908)

The C.P.R., like most corporations, is a cold-blooded outfit. When there is a bad wreck the conductor, engineer and the whole bunch, barring the newsy, are hauled onto the caret and put through the fourth degree. One gets fired, another suspended, and there is hell a-popping.

But let an engineer, by cool-headedness and presence of mind, stick to his post regardless of imminent danger to himself, and do the right thing at the right moment and thereby save the company hundreds of thousands of dollars, to say nothing of saving human lives, the company never lets loose a word of appreciation. It would be undignified. And besides, engineers and firemen are well paid to jeopardize their lives for the company. Oh, certainly.

What prompted us to write the above was the quick work of Engineer Pratt the other night while rushing passenger train no. 3 into Calgary at a thirty-mile clip to make up time. Through the negligence of a switchman, who has since ducked his nut, a switch was left open in the east Calgary yards at the curve just east of the bridge. Into this dived Mr. Passenger train, the light of a switch engine less than a hundred yards away! The fireman and a helper jumped, the former being killed trying to make his friend, who was a green hand just learning the work, jump first. The engineer must have done some lightning thinking, for when the two engines came together the speed of his train was less than six miles an hour and the headlight of his engine was not even smashed. This is what baseball fans would call "pretty work." The fact that Engineer Pratt stayed with the job, with death a four to five favorite in the betting, cuts no ice with the company. (July 29, 1911)

In days gone by, the *Eye Opener* has ever and anon experienced hard feelings towards R. B., but time has healed all that. In any event, our respect never wavered, which all by itself is pleasant for both to look back upon. Were we to be

It's a waste of time telling a man he is a liar. If he is, he knows it. [9]

asked what is Bennett's chief qualification to represent a western constituency in the Dominion parliament, we should say that it was his clear discernment of popular rights and his gift of fighting eloquence. This is a powerful combination. (August 12, 1911)

Vote for R. B. Bennett, who may one day be prime minister of Canada. (September 16, 1911)

R. B.'s majority over Vannie ran within an ace or two of 3,000. Mr. Bennett's position as a public man is thus one of undoubted security. A great career lies ahead of this man. If he develops as consistently as he has done in the past ten years and keeps his health, there is no telling to what heights he may attain in the councils of the nation. While McCarthy had to fight along the difficult lines of obstacle and impediment, Bennett steps on to a path that has been levelled off. Calgary has elected a man whose sense of duty will never fail and whose sincerity of purpose is above question. (October 28, 1911)

Publicity is certainly more interesting when the impetuous R. B. splashes about in it. (March 23, 1912)

The solitary figure toiling up the heights is R. B. Bennett. (August 3, 1912)

R. B. Bennett will stir up the criminals at Sherman Rink Tuesday night. Now, don't get on the prod. The animals are the other fellows. (November 2, 1912)

"R. B." is slowly convalescing after his long illness and will hie himself to Atlantic City as soon as his physician permits him to make the journey. The sea breezes and jass bands should pull him round. "R. B. " is certainly badly needed back in public life and the sooner he recovers his health the better it will be for us all. There are too many duds around. Too many wise guys with no wisdom. The western situation calls for a Bennett. (May 31, 1919)

RICHARD the LION-HEARTED

Daniel McGillicuddy

The October 6, 1908 edition of the *Calgary Daily News* left Bob Edwards in a swivet. Over the course of a 1,500-word poison-pen letter, someone dubbed "Nemesis" accused Edwards of being a libeler and a character thief and a coward and a liar and a drunkard and a dope-fiend and ... ah, read it for yourself. (It's a real piece of work.) Edwards took immediate legal action. *Daily News* editor Daniel McGillicuddy was arrested on October 7, 1908 and charged with defamatory libel.

For someone purportedly proselytizing from on high, McGillicuddy sure loved every second of the spotlight. His paper devoted the front-page to the ensuing trial, and he hilariously, and liberally, reprinted[1] portions of the Nemesis letter whenever possible. (A prolonged variation on the old "Are you upset because I called you a jerk, or because I said your breath reeks?" routine.) Much of the trial was spent trying to prove what everyone knew: McGillicuddy and Nemesis were one and the same.

A jury found McGillicuddy guilty of libel (fine: $100), but it was a bittersweet victory for Edwards. His professional reputation was scrutinized during the trial to the degree that the jury accompanied its verdict with "a scathing criticism of the journalistic methods of the *Eye Opener*, and suggested that its editor should be notified that unless he amend in that respect the paper would be suppressed."[2] McGillicuddy, naturally, spun his loss into a moral victory, further admonishing Edwards in a second letter.[3]

Clearly wounded by the affair, Edwards temporarily relocated the *Eye Opener*[4] to Ontario, but he was far from silent—as the following jabs (including filial potshots directed at Owen McGillicuddy) show. Unlike the Bennett feud, Edwards pursued this one to his grave—even though he outlived McGillicuddy by a decade.

[1] Examples are too numerous to mention. Basically any issue of the *Calgary Daily News* from mid-October to mid-November, 1908 carried detailed mention of the goings-on, and heavily quoted the Nemesis missive.
[2] *Calgary Daily Herald*, November 12, 1908.
[3] *Calgary Daily News*, November 23, 1908. This letter, however, bears McGillicuddy's own name, and his confession to having penned the Nemesis article.
[4] "The humiliation was too much and Bob left Calgary," recalled Robert Pearson ("Bob Edwards and I").

The science of living consists in not being a dead one.[11]

Real Reputation Of The Man Who Is
Very Busy Blackening Characters

The Calgary *Daily News*
Tuesday, October 6, 1908

To the Editor of the *Daily News*.

Sir—For years the city of Calgary and the province of Alberta have been cursed with a make-believe journalist in the person of one Robert C. Edwards, who has brought disgrace upon both city and province by bringing out, semi-occasionally, a disreputable sheet the mission of which has been blackmail and the contents of which were slander and "smut."

During a number of these years I have waited to see some action taken by the authorities to suppress this journalistic hermaphrodite and his infamous sheet, but I have waited in vain. The authorities are afraid to move because some of their own skirts are not clean and they fear the vengeance of the journalistic bully: the Citizens' league is a "false alarm" when real work for moral renovation is required; and the Ministerial association has been too busy dealing with the "Organic Union of the Churches" and such like complex questions to give time to the squelching of a moral leper and the eradication of a vile publication that has done more harm to the moral uplift of the community and brought more disgrace upon the fair fame of the city of Calgary than all the other vile agencies in the city combined.

It is only a week or ten days ago since a couple of ordinary blackguards were fined severely by the police magistrate for peddling obscene literature in Calgary. Why are not the police and the magistrate equally strict with the output of the putrid brain of Bob Edwards and the printshop of J. J. Young—for my information is that the *Eye-Opener* is printed at and mailed from the *Herald* job room?

I know that during the past few days copies of the filthy sheet have been hawked about not only by boys on the street, but by men who have been looked upon as reputable citizens and even members of the executive of one of the political parties of the city. Yet no effort has been put forward to put the dirty sheet under the ban and to fine the blackguards who are responsible for its production, as was done to the fellows who peddled the obscene literature in Calgary a week or ten days ago. It seems to me that this question is up to the morality department, the Citizens' League, the Ministerial Association and Magistrate Crispin Smith.

From long experience, however, I know that nothing will be done by any of these agencies, and I have determined to take hold of the matter myself by going after the figurehead whose name adorns the publication column of the *Eye-Opener*. I know that skinning a skunk is not a very pleasing occupation, but I know also that it is a very necessary one at times and that profit to the public results from the operation.

Now, I should like to know by what law, divine or man-made, does this ruffian, Edwards, constitute himself the keeper of the morals of not only Calgary, but Alberta and Canada at large? Who is he that the people should take his ipse dixit on matters of moral and political rectitude? What are his antecedents and other qualifications to give him the right to sit in judgment upon others? These are questions that will occur to every right-thinking man who looks into this subject and after they have done so I am willing to ask each and every one of them whether or not they approve the publication of a filthy sheet such as the *Eye-Opener* undoubtedly is by a creature whose literary fulminations cannot but create the impression that he was born in a brothel and bred on a dunghill.

Who is the terrible giant who would give the impression that he possesses the power to frighten the people by bellowing B-E-W-A-R-E! BEWARE? His alias is R. C. Edwards and his reputation was on the black list in the United States long before he saw the province of Alberta.

With his upbringing from the slums or his antecedents before fleeing from Spokane I will not at present speak. I will deal with him since he came to Alberta and trace his career at Strathcona, Wetaskiwin, High River and down to the present time when—miserable wreck of a depraved existence that he is—he seeks to make a living by scribbling rubbish that would turn the stomach of a professional refuse handler. As this will be merely the opening article of a series dealing with the record of this dealer in literary carrion I will only touch upon a few of the topics that I intend going into at length later on.

First I want it to be known that Robert C. Edwards is a "four flusher," a "tin-horn" and a "Welcher," where poker debts are concerned. I will give the dope in full later on.

Second—He is an ingrate and when I give the readers of the *Daily News* the story of his treatment of Jerry Boyse, they will see that the dunghill breed sticks out of him on every side.

I intend to show that he is a libeller, a character thief, a coward, a liar, a drunkard, a dope-fiend and a degenerate, and I hold the cards to play the game.

That he is a degenerate no one who has the slightest opportunity of seeing him can doubt, and the way in which he divides his time between the Jap-houses and the hospital admits of no doubt. In Paris it is well known that there are two kinds of degenerates. The "Apaches" are the thugs who rifle, rob and plunder the community in the criminal portions of the city. They resemble the "Hooligans" who infest Whitechapel in London. Edwards if he were in London or Paris would not be able to enroll in either the "Hooligans" or the "Apaches." He is a physical coward and could not qualify for a position where nerve was required. Why someone has not "batted his block off" before now is one of the things I don't understand, for while he goes up and down with what he considers to be the swagger of a Bowery tough he is a physical coward of the meanest type and a ten-year-old boy, possessed of the courage of a jack-rabbit, could spit in his eye with impunity and Edwards would sprint in the opposite direction.

But in Paris and in London there is a class of degenerates for whose ranks this unmitigated blackguard, character thief and slime-dealer could easily fill the bill. This class is known as the "Epicureans." They are the bestials in mind and body, and they carry the mark of their sin with them. They are so constituted after years of attachment to their infirmity that they cannot tell the truth and their moral sense is absolutely obsessed. Oscar Wilde was proved to be one in the English courts. "Monk" Widdows, another sweet-scented specimen of the genus—well known in Ontario twenty-odd years ago—was another. Many of your readers will remember the crusade of Oscar Wilde in America in the interests of sweetness and light and "Monk" Widdows' efforts in improving the moral condition of the country are well known. Widdows was convicted of an unnamable offence in Ontario and was incarcerated in the Central Prison for two years, after which he went to Britain and by a strange coincidence was a fellow-prisoner with Oscar Wilde for degeneracy in Portland prison.

I have given these instances to show that when a man, particularly one with a pretence at literary effort, becomes degenerate, he usually plumbs the lowest depths and no one who has any knowledge of this scamp Edwards will fail to believe that he has very nearly reached the bottom. He has all the earmarks of the degenerate. He takes no pleasure in the society of men of his own age except when he is drunk; he is morbid and taciturn when not under the influence of dope; his voice even has lost the manly ring and he purrs now with the velvety persistence of a house-cat before a porridge plate—he has even captured Oscar Wilde's lisp. Usually the fate of such unfortunates is poison, the pistol, the razor or the rope.

And when he goes hence by any of the routes mentioned none will regret his departure. He has alienated any feeling of pity that might have been evoked by the malignity with which he has pursued a number of the most prominent and most highly respected citizens of this city, as well as many outsiders. He has assailed in turn such men as John S. Dennis, R. B. Bennett, Hon. W. R. Cushing, Premier Rutherford, Wm. Georgeson, R. J. Stuart and scores of others in libellous articles and disgraceful cartoons; and surely all of those who have been thus attacked by this professional rib-stabber have not been offscorns and deserving of the vile abuse that he has heaped upon them.

Before concluding this letter, allow me to say that when I alluded to Edwards as a "figure-head" of the *Eye-Opener* I know whereof I speak. Any bright matter that may appear in that sheet is not the product of his hand or brain. He it is who is supposed to furnish the filthy end of the sheet, but even in that line he is forced to borrow vile stories and to levy weekly tribute on a London "pink 'un"—*The Winning Post*.

More anon.

NEMESIS

Here is a beautiful little poem that was sent to us at the time directoire gowns were all the fashion. We mislaid it, but unexpectedly found it again. It is not by Owen E. McGillicuddy, anyhow.

Mary had a little lamb,
Its fleece was white as snow,
It used to butt in every place
That Mary used to go.

Mary fleeced her lamb one day,
And shopping went to town.
She bought herself a new sheath skirt—
A split directoire gown.

But still sheep's eyes are made at her,
And rude men jeer and gloat;
Though Mary has her lamb no more,
She's everybody's goat.

For the sheath skirt is the latest cut—
It's cut almost in half.
Who gives a d— for Mary's lamb,
When we see Mary's calf. (January 1, 1910)

The inevitable has happened. The sheet known as the *Calgary News*, of which that old liar McGillicuddy was put in charge for the purpose of sandbagging western people who had the courage to expose Clifford Sifton and other members of the rotten Ottawa gang, has gone up the flue. It is now in the hands of a receiver and L. F. Clary, solicitor, has been appointed Liquidator. The old hypocrite, of course, was not fitted to conduct a newspaper, but was admirably equipped to run an obscene and libelling sheet for shameful purposes. Incidentally we may say, in writing the obituary of this blood-sucking fraud, that he has for years lived on pap handed out by politicians. We write "30" to this old dog's career with a great deal of satisfaction and had it not been for the favoritism of the judge before whom he was convicted of libelling us, he would have been wearing stripes in the penitentiary two years ago. Wonder how his imbecile son, Owen, the Train Dog, is taking the family misfortune? (October 15, 1910)

Tell us, is there anything at all that old Dan McGillicuddy has a hand in that isn't putrid? Having done his best to ruin the editor of this paper, in return for money paid him for that purpose, he now passes on to bigger game in Frank Oliver. He has evidently fallen down on this also. A man with more practice in blushing, when he finds himself unsuccessful in a stunt of this nature, would seek the deepest seclusion known and then would go still further into the woods. It is commonly predicted that this malicious old beast will commit suicide before the year is out.

And yet, innocent though Frank Oliver may be of the slightest wrongdoing, this ugly charge of McGillicuddy's cannot fail to stick in spots. There are always people of cheap, semi-ready natures who are ever willing and ever eager to believe evil reports of a man, especially if it be sufficiently spicy and ruinous to make conversations and

Life's sideshows cost us more than the real circus.[12]

secure free drinks. We have been through the mill and know but too well the distress of mind endured by the victim. When a man is guilty of misconduct he usually doesn't give a damn, for the man who commits dishonorable and unworthy acts is probably not very sensitive anyhow. But the man conscious of complete innocence feels utterly helpless and undone, scarcely knowing what to do under the circumstances or which way to run. He fancies that every man he meets on the street thinks him guilty and feels instinctively that he is being pointed out with the significant whisper, "That's him." You bet, we know all about it and can sympathise with Mr. Oliver with a comprehending heart. (May 6,1911)

Poor old McGillicuddy has broken out in sores again. Heigho! At the age of three score and ten many a man reminds us of an experiment that failed. (August 2, 1911)

Poor McGillicuddy! Poor, poor man. His "charges" were going to ruin Frank Oliver and lose him his Edmonton seat and lo! a bland electorate returned Frank by the largest Liberal majority in Canada. McG. is now indeed "out of it" for all time. The public can take our word for it that he will get nothing from the Conservative party. (October 28, 1911)

So those green-eyed sumphs up at Edmonton killed the Calgary University

bill by a vote of 17 to 15. Well, this makes things so much the easier for us Conservatives down here at the next political election. We know where we are at now.

It will have to be "Calgary College" now instead of "Calgary University," but once affiliated with the famous McGill (not McGillicuddy) University, students will be able to pass McGill (not McGillicuddy) examinations and receive McGill (not McGillicuddy) degrees. This should place Calgary College on a higher level in the popular imagination than the Strathcona institution, where the papers for degrees will probably consist of "Why is a hen?", "Who killed Cock Robin?" and kindred posers. Strathcona degrees will soon become a joke. It is too near Ponoka.

Here is a sample of a Strathcona University examination paper for the B.S. degree:

English Composition.
Write 300-word eulogy on Principal Torrey and explain why he is.
Is what?
Parse sentence. "Good grammar teached here."
Is the word "punk" a predicate, superlative, or past participle?

History.
Give brief life history of Principal Torrey.
When did Principal Torrey draw up the Magna Charter?
Give date of Johnson-Jeffries fight.
How long did the Seven Years War last?
Write what you know about Adam and

and the valley of the Bow. The right men are behind it and will be more zealous than ever in furthering the interests of Calgary's seat of learning. They are now on their mettle. After all, it is only the matter of a couple of years when there will be a change of government and then Calgary will come into her own so far as the University is concerned. So cheer up! (February 10, 1912)

Dan McGillicuddy is reaping the reward that goes with that kind of a career. (April 20, 1912)

Eve, and their antecedents.

Give date of battle between Edmonton and South Edmonton for possession of Land Titles Office.

Who stormed the heights of Torre's Vedras?

Geography.

Where was Principal Torrey born?

Name principal rivers in Principal Torrey's bailiwick.

Who were the Torres Straits named after?

How far is Athabasca Landing from its furthest subdivision?

What distance is the North Pole from the South Coulee?

Is Calgary on the map?

Name the capital of Alberta.

Of course, the above are only a few samples, but they will give you a line on the outfit up north. Calgary College will now go ahead and erect a splendid institution on the heights overlooking the city

The *Eye Opener* has enjoyed a rather stormy career and has been set upon by the enemy from time to time with great ferocity, but it has ploughed its way successfully and undismayed through the rough waters, to the manifest disgust of those who sought to put it on the bum.

The McGillicuddy attack was the worst, but as this individual was merely the tool of others higher up he is more to be pitied than blamed. A man rendered desperate by financial reverses is liable to do any old thing. Seeing that he is now down and out it would be ungenerous to say what we think of him.

We have been defendant in three libel suits during this ten-year period, winning two and losing one. This makes our batting average .666. The one we lost occurred a few weeks ago and was all over a josh story about an imaginary boozological yachting trip into which we

As for the blind leading the blind, wouldn't it be hilarious to see those famous blinds, Blind Justice, Blind Cupid, and Blind Pig, trying to lead one another?[14]

rashly ran plaintiff's name, and not meant to be taken seriously. Indeed it was so obviously a josh that the plaintiff seems to have been the only one that did take it seriously. At all events, everyone around Calgary saw it in its jocular light, knowing it to be only one of those imaginary yarns of which we write ever so many during the year to amuse our readers. We were only too willing to make amends for the offence given by signing an apology, for which, it is needless to say, neither the words nor the music were by us. Gilbert wrote the words, and John L. Sullivan the music.

The Killing of Dan McGillicuddy

In signing that apology, which our friends the enemy love to call "abject" we acted on the advice of our legal adviser, who is no fool. He explained that if the other fellow didn't know a josh when he saw one, that was our misfortune, not the other fellow's.

A number of Grit newspapers at the coast promptly jumped on this apology as an excuse to roast the stuffing out of the *Eye Opener* and its editor. The roasters, however, happened to be small fry, so no harm was done. It has always been our misfortune to be attacked by the minnows of the profession.

A successful journal, like a successful man, has to be prepared for attack from the incompetent ones who have failed. That goes with the business. The man who runs a newspaper, especially a weekly which has missed fire and fallen flat with the public and is losing money every time he prints, cannot help but regard with a bilious eye the man who has made a success and who has captured the ear of the public all over the Dominion. There is a certain pathos about their chagrin. There is, for a fact.

In years gone by there possibly was some excuse for roasts of the *Eye Opener*, but not of recent years. We cut out the rough stuff long ago and now the paper is welcome in hundreds and hundreds of happy homes all over the land. One of our more recent subscribers, in fact, is Lieut. Col. Lowther, of Rideau Cottage, Ottawa, who managed the western tour of his royal highness.

Only last Sunday an article which appeared in the *Eye Opener* formed the basis of a sermon preached from a local pulpit. The subject was a serious one and treated of the passing of parental control incident to the disintegration of the home and of home life. It was the clergyman himself who informed us of this, warmly commending the spirit of our article. So you see, we are not as tough as some

There are times when we should be thankful for what we fail to get.[15]

sissies would try to make out.

The paper was duly restored to the privilege of the government mails and its circulation has risen (since the Reformation) from 18,000 to 35,000. Our Calgary publishers will vouch for this circulation.

Well, then, having got these few remarks off our chest, we beg to return thanks to the readers of the *Eye Opener* for their generous support through fair weather and foul. It is sometimes hard to fill the paper with stuff that will be of equal interest to readers in Toronto, Ottawa, Winnipeg, Calgary, Edmonton and Vancouver, but we shall continue to do the best we can. The best can do no more. Thanking you, one and all, we will now conclude with the last act of "Lucy Marsh, the Prune Hater's Daughter." (November 2, 1912)

Hell got a new settler last week. (December 21, 1912)

In another column we publish a photo of the new building erected and now occupied by The *News-Telegram* Company. It gives us special delight to make public record in these columns of the success achieved in Calgary and throughout Western Canada by this brilliant daily. It is now recognized as the spokesman for the Conservative party in the West and commands a tremendous local circulation on account of its up-to-date methods of procuring and disseminating the news of the day. This paper is today a very different proposition to what it was under the regime of that defunct old blackguard McGillicuddy. (June 27, 1914)

With McGillicuddy in hell and ourself in the legislature, why worry. (*Summer Annual*, 1922)

All the fun of staying out late at night is lost when there is nobody at home to make a fuss about it.[16]

THE EYE OPENER AND ITS EDITOR

The *Calgary Daily News*
November 23, 1908

The *Eye Opener* has had a severe shaking up and its "figure-head" takes some two pages of the sheet to let its readers know that he is severely injured and to exhibit his wounds, bruises and putrefying sores.

He runs amuck and attacks not only the author of the original letter, which showed him to the public as a liar, a coward, a character-thief, a bulldozer, a blackmailer and a good many other things of a discreditable nature, but he endeavors to cast a dragnet to draw in anyone whom he desired to cast slime at. The writer's sons, his lawyers, the reporters of his newspaper, the witnesses, the judge, the jury—all are made marks for the falsehood and invective of this character-thief and coward. This certainly does not gain anything to Edwards in the shape of public sympathy and only goes to prove that when the *Eye Opener* was attacked as an immoral and lascivious sheet and its editor pilloried as a mental degenerate and moral leper, the designations did not even being to give an idea of the low depths to which he had descended.

Why doth the heathen rage and this person imagine vain things?—to paraphrase a familiar quotation. I will give the reason.

Some seven weeks ago, after giving some thought to the subject, I came to the conclusions that the *Eye Opener* was a disgrace to Canadian journalism and an injury to Alberta province, and that its editor, morally and intellectually, was a standing menace to all that was decent and of good report. For years he had terrorized the Territories by his bulldozing and blackguardedly methods and had polluted the minds of old and young by republishing ribald stories and obscene paragraphs from a salacious sheet called the *Winning Post*, published in London, England. These stories and paragraphs he changed to suit the locality and passed them off as his own—dirty and all. And this is the man who raises his hands in holy—or unholy—horror against the crime of plagiarism. Why, half of his sheet is plagiarized and a large part of the remainder of it is written by an outsider in Winnipeg—the man who wrote the defence of Edwards in the *Saturday Post*. Edwards is a cheap skate with no newspaper experience and who, when the *Eye Opener* goes out of business—as go out of

KINDLY READ THIS FIRST

The facts re. the editor of the Eye Opener and one McGillicuddy are as follows:

McGillicuddy wrote an article in his paper, the Calgary Daily News, containing a series of infamous charges against the personal character of Edwards, which he circulated broadcast throughout the country.

Edwards promptly brought action against McGillicuddy, for libel, but before the case could be brought before a Supreme Court judge the horrifying charges had a full month in which to soak into the minds of the people.

During this interim, McGillicuddy spread reports that he had dozens and dozens of witnesses and stacks of affidavits to prove every charge made. "We have the goods,' was the way the old liar put it.

When the trial commenced, McGillicuddy, through his lawyer, E. P. Davis, of Vancouver, coolly admitted that the charges were baseless. He confessed that he was a malignant old libeller and took everything back, pleading that he did not intend that the same meaning should be attached to the charges that the prosecutor (and the public) attached to them!

At the close of the trial Judge Beck made the following statment: "I think it is only fair to Mr. Edwards that it should be publicly known that during the course of this trial the counsel for the accused asserted that it had not been the intention of the letter in question to charge Mr. Edwards with the abominable crimes that were suggested in it."

The jury found McGillicuddy guilty of libel without justification, and the old codger was thereupon fined $100 or in default two months' imprisonment with hard labor

Edwards character is thus cleared and McGillicuddy has crawled back into his hole. Here endeth one excitement. Bring on the next.

business it will—could not obtain a position on a solitary paper along the entire route between Victoria and Sydney. His only experience in newspaper work was in Strathcona, Leduc, Wetaskiwin and High River, and where his end wasn't peace nor his haven glorious in any of them, notwithstanding the benevolence of Jerry Boyce and the other kind friends upon whom he sponged, and whom he still leaves unpaid. At this stage of the game he divided his labors between the pastepot and scissors, the hotel stable and the bar.

Before the jury it will be remembered that the lawyer for the defence drew attention to the "creed" of Edwards, which had been conspicuously printed at the head of his paper, to show that he feared not God and cared not for man, woman or child. This unmitigated blackguard hand endeavored to give the impression that the blasphemy was all of his own—that he was a real bad man for whom earth or hell had no terrors and heaven no recompense. And what happened when his own lawyer was addressing the jury and when he adverted to Edwards's "creed"? Mr. Nolan simply admitted that it was not Edwards's creed at all—that it was simply stolen—that Edwards had not the brains to evolve the "creed"—that once more the shears and the pastepot were editing the *Eye Opener*.

And this is the journalistic viper who spews up heroics against plagiarism. As I have already said, the blackguard is a journalistic misfit—a newspaper sharp who, lacking brains and education, has to live by the wits of others, and in choosing the pabulum to suit his public has to rely upon a prurient mind and a disordered mentality to help him in his purloining of filth and obscenity.

But Edwards claims to be a man of culture and of breeding. His name as given by his counsel is Robert Chambers Edwards, and they say that, in his cups, he claims to be a grandson of Robert Chambers of the great publishing house of Chambers Brothers, of Edinburgh, Scotland. Shade of Ananias! can this be so?—that the prurient-minded, rotten-hearted, paranoically-inclined, so-named Robert Chambers Edwards is of kin to the clean, healthy, sober, honest, upright publisher who made the publishing house of Chambers Brothers one of the brightest and best in the annals of the literary world? I doubt it, and have every reason to believe it to be an impossible thing. R. C. Edwards, in his pollution, related to Robert Chambers, the uplifter of his fellows? It cannot be. It is enough to make the body of the grand old man to turn in its grave.

As to the original letter regarding Edwards, it stands. An effort was made by the prosecution to attribute a false meaning to the "Epicurean" paragraph, but even that attempt to sidetrack the real meaning was taken from the plaintiff by the statement that what was imputed by the counsel for the prosecution was not after all what was set forth in the original statement.

The original letter sent Edwards to the hospital. The Terror of the Plains, who, according to his "creed," feared not man and honored not God, was knocked out in the first round. For about seven weeks the *Eye Opener* was out of commission as a purveyor of filth, and for a goodly part of that period the bum editor of the sheet was laid up for repairs.

One letter was sufficient to show the yellow streak that permeated this four-flusher through and through—one letter proved that Edwards was an ass in a lion's skin, or, to change the metaphor, a dunghill bird masquerading in peacock's plumage. This notorious individual, who had never spared man, women, or child in his displays of vituperations, ran to cover when he was attacked after his own style, yelled for the protection of that law which for years he had mocked to score, and finally broke down physically and had to be sent to the hospital for special treatment. Truly, a dead game sport of the cuckoo variety.

Well, he invoked the law and what did he get for his pains?

The plea of the defence that he was a degenerate and dissolute person was allowed by the judge.

Witnesses swore that Edwards had libeled them and had endeavored to blackmail the C.P.R. by threatening not to support their solicitor (R. B. Bennett, K.C.), unless sales of the *Eye Opener* on trains were allowed.

The jury brought in a verdict censuring Edwards for publishing a blackguardedly sheet, using the following language: "As citizens of Calgary, we desire to place on record our disapproval of obscene and suggestive articles and illustrations which appear in the *Eye Opener*, and we respectfully request your lordship to caution the prosecutor against publishing any more such articles; and, if persisted in, it should be suppressed."

The Judge agreed with the recommendation of the jury and

afterwards stated that Edwards "was a man entitled to very little consideration (if any)."

Edwards has to pay his own costs, which is certainly one way to bring supreme happiness to him, for which he is no doubt devoutly thankful.

The *Eye Opener* has been debarred from the use of His Majesty's mails.

The C.P.R. have under consideration the question of disallowing the sales of the *Eye Opener* on their trains.

Edwards has been forced to admit in the *Eye Opener* that it was rotten in the past and promises amendment as follows: "This paper will be run henceforth on strictly legitimate lines, with risqué and objectionable matter entirely eliminated. This we do in deference to the criticism handed out by the judge and the jury in the recent trial."

In these circumstances I am at a loss to see wherein anything in the shape of a victory has been gained by the *Eye Opener* or its "figure-head"—for I cannot dignify this nonentity by calling him a journalist. Edwards's claim of being exonerated reminds me of the fight in which the celebrated "John Phoenix" stated that he came out victorious. He said: "We caused our despised assailant to injure his knuckles by hitting us several times in the face and then when we clinched we fell to the floor dragging him down on top of us. Then we inserted our nose in his mouth and held him down in that position until the police came upon the scene and rescued him from our clutches."

Edwards is a coward and a blackguard still and he shows it when he attacks the members of the family of the writer and others who had no connection with the writing of the letter. The writer of this is the author of the original letter and the same was stated in court. He has made up his mind to send Edwards to the hospital again and again until that ruffian is put out of business and the *Eye Opener* is suppressed, and having put his hand to the plow, he is not going to look back. He takes all responsibility and will fight it out on this line until the work is done. What is more, he is going to do it single-handed and alone. No human being except the writer knew on the morning of October the 6th, that the letter was written, no one knew until it went to the printers that the letter was to be published, no one outside of the writer is in any way responsible; and the question of the costs in connection with driving the blackguard sheet into decency is one that is to be settled by the writer alone and without any outside assistance, notwithstanding all foolish statements to the contrary. Edwards has no more right to drag in outsiders in the fight than it would to drag in his brother Jack, who passed from this vale of tears by the wood-alcohol route. I will keep Robert Chambers busy until he follows suit, leaves the country or becomes decent.

The days of this scamp are numbered in western journalism. There is no more need for "wild and wooly" newspapers in the west than there is for the old-time desperado who belonged to the plunderbund. And on this line I beg to quote from the *Winnipeg Saturday Post,* Edwards's apologist, the following: "I do not know of a Canadian newspaper from coast to coast that had the moral courage to come to his (Edwards') defence."

All honor to the Canadian press which refused to recognize in this brazen bummer and bulldozer a fellow craftsman and brother in the profession of journalism, and which by its action practically admitted that the heretofore Terror of the Plains was getting what had been coming to him for a long term of years.

There is another feature that I may as well deal with in passing. This fellow Edwards poses as an authority on politics and on sport and yet knows no more about either than he does about the life and habits of "grandfather Robert Chambers." He has made a living by being willing to support either political party in the past, irrespective of principle, and I have been told that he was on the payroll of one of the parties during the campaign recently closed at $100 per month—drunk or sober—and that the money came from outside. If this be true then the party that put up the paycheque was certainly a victim of false pretences. Edwards doesn't know a Tory principle from a liberal plank in a platform. He is as ignorant of the political situation in Canada or anywhere else as is a pig on the way to an abattoir. The only thing he does know is to do any kind of dirty work he is employed to do, on the principle that the ox knoweth his owner and the ass his master's crib. This was clearly demonstrated when inside of ten days before the last provincial election he made a volte face because he could not bulldoze the C.P.R. This showed that the blackmailer had no political principles, no integrity of character but was in the market for sale to the highest bidder, and then this hireling prates of integrity, of honesty and of square dealing!

It is not necessary for me to take up any more space on this occasion in making further reference to this journalistic malediction. I do not as a rule waste so much powder and shot on such a miserable coyote, but I feel that duty rests upon me to put this animal in the class where he belongs, and I intend to do it every time he lifts his morally leprous head.

As to the publication of the *Eye Opener*, as was stated in the previous letter, that sheet has no habitation or home, no plant—nothing that should give it status as a newspaper. It was printed last issue on the Herald Co.'s press, of which William Southam, Hamilton, is president. Mr. Southam and his sons are known to be newspaper men above reproach, but unfortunately they may make mistakes in selecting managers for their outside papers. This appears to have been done in the Calgary venture. If the Southams are satisfied, nothing will suit me better than that they continue the course which their local manager is following. It certainly will not injure the *Daily News* when the public learns that the *Eye Opener* in an output of the *Herald* press.

It was my intention to round up the whole herd on this occasion, but this epistle has already taken up more space than I intended to give to the party of the first part, and books would not hold what can be written about him. As to his local associates, "there's a reason," as the cereal advertiser would say, why at this juncture they will receive only "absent treatment." 'Tis sufficient to say that they know why and their friends know why. As to the night-writer—or is it night-riter?—at Winnipeg, I will allow him to stew in his own juice until a more convenient season; but I know the gun story and other incidents and may feel disposed to let the public know of them later on.

D. McGillicuddy.

E. P. Davis

Although over before it began, a third *Eye Opener* lawsuit warrants mention. During the "Nemesis" trial, Daniel McGillicuddy enlisted Vancouver lawyer E. P. Davis, among others, to testify as to Edwards's journalistic debauchery. True to form, Edwards never forgot Davis's criticisms. Over the following four years, he took occasional digs, culminating in a fanciful story about the lawyer being marooned on an island. An obvious fiction, it nevertheless pushed Davis to the edge. He brought criminal libel charges against his foil, but Edwards avoided a trial by issuing an apology—it's an extraordinary document not just as a rare Edwards *mea culpa*, but for so explicitly laying bare of the *casus belli* behind the smear campaign.

A very amusing incident occurred during our stay at the Elysium. It appeared that a party, which included T. F. Brockett, the broker; James Kellarty, the real estate man; a third man whose name we didn't learn; and E. P. Davis, the lawyer, sallied forth in a launch for a day's outing. We did not see them leave but those who did say that the barge they were towing was pretty deep in the water. A quarrel occurred on the home journey, said to have been due to the sarcastic line of conversation put up by Mr. Davis. He had his three companions right on the prod to such a degree that they deliberately marooned the great lawyer on Deadman's Island, leaving with him a case of Scotch whisky and a corkscrew, but no grub. They landed him on the little island after dark, with a parting injunction to go to h—l.

Being pretty well soused themselves, Messrs. Brockett, Kellarty, and the other fellow, did not remember the next morning what they had done the night before. So poor old Davis was literally left stranded with his case of Scotch.

Along about Wednesday, the disappearance of Davis began to cause comment in the city and preparations were made for a searching party. Then it suddenly came back to Mr. Brockett that Davis was marooned on Deadman's Island. He had his friends immediately set forth to the rescue and it was well indeed that they lost no time. When they arrived on the scene the sight that met their gaze was of such a nature that they didn't know whether to laugh or cry.

There was E. P. Davis running about the island stark naked, with only his spectacles on, armed with a club and striking right and left at imaginary snakes. The twelve bottles were empty. It was with the greatest difficulty that the unfortunate man could be induced to enter the

In this world of strife a man must be either an anvil or a hammer.[17]

launch, but a few stiff hookers, of which he was sadly in need, calmed him, and he returned peaceably to the city.

The authorities at the hospital had him pretty well straightened out before we left Vancouver so that by this time he is, no doubt, busy handing out bunk in the law courts as if nothing had happened. There is nothing like being used to the D.T.'s is there? (August 3, 1912)

EYE OPENER PUBLISHER APOLOGISES FOR ATTACK ON A VANCOUVER MAN

Calgary Herald
October 12, 1912

The action for criminal libel entered by E. P. Davis, K.C. of Vancouver, against R. C. Edwards, publisher of the *Eye Opener* in this city has been withdrawn. The basis of the withdrawal was the receipt by Mr. Davis of the following apology:

The Apology
E. P. Davis, Esq., K.C., Calgary,

Sir:—I beg to offer you my sincerest apology for a vile attack on you which appeared in the *Calgary Eye Opener* (of which I am the publisher) under date of August 2, 1912, for the publication of which I was yesterday committed for trial on a charge of criminal libel.

There was not a particle of foundation in fact for that attack and I never believed there was, neither has there been any foundation in fact for the various other attacks on you which have appeared in the same paper during the last four years.

I have never known you personally and have never had any dealings with you, and my sole motive for these attacks was that I thought you had criticized my paper too severely in an address you made to a Calgary jury some four years ago.

I promise not to mention your name again or to refer to you in any way directly or indirectly in any future number of the *Calgary Eye Opener*, or any other paper that may be published by me.

I authorize you to publish this apology in any way you may think fit.
Yours truly
(Sgd.) R. C. Edwards.

Witnesses:
(Sgd.) P. J. Nolan, Barrister
James Short, Barrister.

It's a fellow who wades in shallow water who stirs up the most mud.[18]

CHAPTER SIX

A Lovely Little Tablet of Corrosive Sublimate

In which the editor of the E.O. himself (applause) furthers the legend of ... the editor of the E.O. himself (wild applause)

"Some men spoil a good story by sticking to the facts."
—*Eye Opener*, January 25, 1919

Are you constantly being passed over for promotions? Do you strive to cuddle a little closer with your baby, only to be rebuffed by derisive glares & mocking laughter? Sounds like you need self-mythology, old sport!

Although painfully shy[1] in person, Bob Edwards used self-mythology to turn himself into a Larger Than Life Western Character. Close study of the chapter at hand will reveal how to—

☞ Relay memoirs of cheeky doings!

☞ Refer to reasonable subscription rates whenever possible!

☞ Revel in negative criticism!

☞ Refer to reasonable subscription rates whenever possible!

☞ Sing your own praises as if oblivious to the heavy crush of self-doubt!

☞ Spin personal health crises into slapstick farce!

☞ Refer to reasonable, etc. etc.!

Results guaranteed within weeks, unless you blow it like you do everything else.

---

[1] References to Edwards's reclusive nature are legion. A typical example is found in Grant MacEwan's ... *And Mighty Women Too* (Saskatoon: Western Producer Prairie Books, 1976); currently in print as *Mighty Women* (Vancouver: Greystone Books, 1995). Margaret "Ma" Murray recalls meeting Edwards while dining with her husband in a Vancouver hotel. Despite being her husband's good friend, he bashfully refused an invitation to join them. He instead sent two bottles of champagne to their table, while he dined in solitude nearby.

Next week will be the anniversary of the birth of the *Wetaskiwin Free Lance*. Congratulatory baskets of flowers can be left at our boarding house. All votive offerings in the shape of bottles had better be taken round to the office, where instructions have been left with "Grassy" as to their disposal. They will be given to the poor. (*Wetaskiwin Free Lance*, December 8, 1898)

--- ---

The Rise and Fall of the *Wetaskiwin Free Lance*

For the benefit and behoof of people who imagine there is glory in running a paper out west we beg to append a few remarks with a view to correcting that impression.

For a couple of long, weary years, (they were the usual length, but ah! so long after all) we conducted a rag called the *Wetaskiwin Free Lance*. It made us more famous than rich.

The town, which no one in his proper sense had ever taken into serious consideration before, emerged from the obscurity in which it should have remained, into the broad light of notoriety. People clamored to know where Wetaskiwin was; also how to spell it. Children cried for it. The subscription list jumped from 210 to 248. Immigration agents throughout the country aver that their lives were rendered intolerable by the incessant inquiries about Wetaskiwin, and as for Whyte, Kerr and Forslund, they aged rapidly during our efflorescence. However, the thing is busted now, and farmers are returning to their homes.

Here is how the "thing" was run: In the case of births there was a pseudo-facetious formula which it was death to dodge. "John Podgers is wearing a broad smile these days. It is a girl." This was supposed to be very funny, and we had it set up in plate. It was usually good for two subscriptions. One for his folks in Dakoty and one for her folks in Minnesoty.

Going beyond the formula, however, was very disastrous. Reporting a school exhibition one issue we chanced to allude to a Miss Mabel Johnson's rendition of "Curfew shall not ring to-night" as an astonishing performance. It most certainly was.

Her brother came around next day and swung his right for the jaw, landing heavily. In the mix-up we got decidedly the worst of it, though for a few moments we flatter ourselves we kept him hustling to keep on his feet.

Those particular features got to be very common before we got through with it. The most uncomfortable situation connected with the position was the receiving of visits from clergymen when suffering from a jag. We could live a Godly, righteous and sober life for four days at a stretch and our only visitors would be the local sports who, to do them justice, would not dally after ascertaining that the editorial department was dry; but the moment we acquired a good healthy jag in company with some congenial spirit and felt like yelling, in would

Acting on the advice of our lawyer we have cut out half of our stuff this week. Perhaps it is just as well.[1]

walk a parson to consult about the Ladies' Aid.

Those who think a western editor's bed is composed of Gloire de Dijon roses are certainly laboring under a misapprehension.

Theatrical troupes who came along were the only redeeming feature in connection with the miserable business. We could always shake them down for lots of passes. In one instance the whole town was deadheaded into the school house on our passes. He was a hypnotist and earned his living by making passes, but he could not have waxed fat on those sort of passes. He had an awful time the next morning settling for the hall, but we gave him a good write-up, mentioning to the people that his only equal in the hypnotic line was Charcot of Paris. He was very grateful, and gave us his autograph to an I.O.U. for two dollars as a memento.

The man who objected to our description of his singing in the choir of the Methodist church is happily dead. He gave us a lot of trouble while alive; also a pain. (*Winnipeg Free Press*, May 27, 1899)

The starting of the *Breeze* has been attended by a few complications owing to the editor, while on a business trip to his Calgary publishers, catching the grip and having to go to the hospital. The first issue was duly produced and sent up to Wetaskiwin but as I pen these lines in my room at the General I cannot say for certain whether my friends have been thoughtful enough to take out the parcel from the express office and do the distributing act. If they haven't this will give the other feller, my hated rival of Paper No. 3, a chance to get in some very fine work. The first issue will be distributed anyhow even though it be a little late.

Though I took no luggage down to Calgary during my late visit I lost no time in getting the grip. At the Hospital they were a trifle leery about admitting a patient from the north owing to their unbounded faith in the smallpox report promulgated by a Calgary doctor, but inquiry through the phone made it all right. It appears that inquiries were made from three different parties, and, curiously enough, elicited the same reply in each cases. I am ashamed to say what these replies were, but they did me a grave injustice. It really was the grip. The insinuation was that it was a case of seagramalaria. Wouldn't that jar you!

It is almost a pleasure lying sick in the Calgary General Hospital, where everything is so clean and comfortable, and one departs full of gratitude for the many little acts of kindness and graceful attentions shown by those in charge. They do numberless things for their patients that they really don't have to. Miss M. J. Carswell and her genial lady assistants perform their duties—some of which must be exceedingly repellant to the gentler sex—with unfailing cheerfulness and good humor. A chinaman, who will shortly be on the missing list, was among those brought in while I was there. He

The editor of this rag is beginning to be loved for the enemies he has fooled.[2]

received as careful attention as any of us Caucasians. Professional nursing may be a noble calling, but were I a young lady I believe I should prefer typewriting, even in the office of a Calgary lawyer. (*Wetaskiwin Breeze*, March 23, 1901)

A rancher of Dried Meat Lake writes to say that the *Breeze* is about the crawliest mass of literary putrescence he has yet struck. There is nothing so terrible as ignorance with spurs on. Our correspondent, whom we know well by reputation, should give that breed back the horse he stole from him last fall. Obliterating brands is a serious offence. (*Wetaskiwin Breeze*, March 25, 1901)

Wetaskiwin is the one and only town in Alberta which has three newspapers. I was furtively hoping that the *Times* might prove a little on the pork, but, so far from being that, it bids fair to keep me humping to hold my own. In order to do this I have engaged a creamy-complexioned lady to do a society column for me every week. She applied for the job herself. Her first stuff will appear next week. It is liable to be awful the same. She says she writes copy in a tea gown and slippers. Call and see her. Our room is Number Nine, Driard hotel. (*Wetaskiwin Breeze*, March 25, 1901)

That gruesome ghoul out at Duhamel who refused to take the *Breeze* out of the post office could not have paid for it anyhow. The only time he was worth anything was when a $25 reward was out on his rapidly decaying carcass 10 years ago down round the Knee Hill country when horses were easy. (*Wetaskiwin Breeze*, April 18, 1901)

From the light and dry way in which our publisher cut out the racy paragraphs from the *Eye Opener* last week we may presume that it will henceforth be safe for ladies to subscribe. We know they read it. (April 4, 1902)

A certain curiosity having been expressed as to how the editor of the *Eye Opener* spends his time in High River, we beg to state that he rises every morning contemporaneously with the opening of the bar. After partaking of a jolt, he communes a while with the bartender and then has another jolt. This makes him a new man and he has to stand the new man a jolt for luck. After a few more desultory jolts he goes into the dining room and throws in a little breakfast, not infrequently throwing it up afterwards. Thereafter he secures a cigar and takes a walk across the bridge to the Squaw Patch to lecture the Indians on the curse of intemperance. A few more jolts and luncheon comes on. After this function he takes a siesta and as many jolts as happen his way. At four o'clock the school children gather below his window and sing the national anthem. A carnival of frightful jolts follows, and if he has a few minutes to spare

After reading the Eye Opener *and thoroughly digesting its contents, go and see Zinn's Dancing Girls at the Lyric. They're great.*[3]

he writes stuff for his great moral journal. After a hearty supper he engages in a few games of seven-up, a mild form of excitement which involves considerable drinking. Seven or eight nightcaps brings the day's labor to a close and the editor retires for the night. It is a strenuous life. (April 11, 1902)

We are delighted to learn that some awful stories were circulated in High River about the editor of this truly Christian organ before he arrived on the scene of his present labors. It proves the old axiom that the more virtues a man has, the more glaring are his shortcomings. One might well reason that the possession of as many virtues as we have, while no doubt exciting envy, should excuse us in certain faults. But it is not so. Of those who have, much is apparently required. Yawp! (May 30, 1902)

Yes, yes. This paper will appear henceforth with unfailing regularity. Horace says: "Mingle a little folly with your wisdom." We have been following this advice with considerable ardour, but find that it don't pay, so we propose trying the converse of the proposition as an experiment. If you get your paper regularly you will know that it is working all right. (January 2, 1903)

The *Okotoks Times* draws attention to the fact that the *Eye Opener* in its Union Bank advertisement has omitted mention of Okotoks in the list of branches, and complains that the omission is due to a narrow-minded jealousy on our part. And this after all the nice things we said about them last week. Et tu, Okotoks! Why does not the *Okotoks Times* work its rabbits' foot on Mr. Durnsford, the manager of the Okotoks branch, and get an ad all to itself? Hanged if we can afford to advertise Okotoks institutions free of charge. (August 8, 1903)

Perhaps it may interest our readers to learn what it feels like to be poisoned, from the experience of one who has just been there. We are the party. Moi qui vous parle. Through mistaking a box of tablets in a little drawer in our bedroom we swallowed a lovely little tablet of corrosive sublimate. This was in the dark watches of the night last week.

The proprietor of our hotel had formerly occupied the room in which we repose and write guff, and had some corrosive sublimate knocking around which he had used during the scarlet fever epidemic, for disinfecting purposes. We also had a box of tablets (for sleepless nights) knocking about somewhere, and in rummaging around in the dark through the bureau we ran on to what turned out to be the wrong box (which, by the way, we never knew the existence of) and took a tablet, washing it down with a mouthful of water.

To illustrate the grave import of this mistake we have only to mention that an

Originality is merely a new way of expressing an old thought.[4]

internal dose of this stuff, which is one of the most dangerous of poisons, should be one-sixteenth part of a grain, liberally diluted with water. One grain is considered a fatal dose for an adult. WE TOOK SEVEN.

To be more exact, the tablet contained 7.1, or a little over seven grains. There was no diluting about our dose. We took ours straight.

No, we didn't need a brick house to fall on us. A case of this kind calls for no guessing contest. When the merry little tablet, which had dissolved in the mouth, struck our peritoneum and gastro-jiminywhiskers we knew just too well that Death had opened the bedroom door and stepped in.

The problem now was to overpower the grim intruder. As luck would have it, Dr. Ernest Wills, lately from England, our new doctor in High River, was in the hotel and we knew the number of his room. He tumbled out with the good natured promptness which is characteristic of all doctors when aroused from their slumbers and came toddling along. In the meantime we were doubling up and giving a really superior contortionist performance, retching and wobbling about in great shape. We pointed to the little box. He took up a tablet and glanced at it. Thereupon he left the room in a hurry.

While he was gone we picked up one of the tablets and eyed it curiously, wondering what deadly stuff could be concealed in such an innocent-looking little thing. In a few minutes Doc was back with a whitish mixture which he got us to down. Bow wow wow! Then another tumblerful of white mixture, then another, and yet another.

"What was it I took, Doc?"

"Hot stuff."

"Anything dangerous?"

"Oh no, only corrosive sublimate. Splendid stuff to take. They kill rats with it."

"Then I suppose I'll be pushing clouds in about ten minutes."

"Oh dear no!"

"How much of it kills a man?"

"One grain, according to medical experience."

"And how much did I take?"

"Seven."

Well, we hung there in the balance for a couple of hours. It is a curious fact, but the actual fight with Death, when he is liable to give you the half-Nelson and throw you any minute, does not produce fear. When there is but the twinkle of a star between you and the boneyard, your mind becomes very cold and collected. It is not half so fearsome as it is cracked up to be, especially to a young Christian who has led so virtuous, noble and exemplary life as we have.

The fight was hammer-and-tongs while it lasted, but having a good second in Doc, we won out. Had we lost, it would have been a case of the *Eye Opener* suiciding, sure. We know how dearly we are beloved by some people here. As it was, some disappointed yaps—mostly female—added sweetness to their weak-

It is hard for a man to support sealskin on a muskrat salary.[5]

tea talk by saying: "Did you hear about the editor of the *Eye Opener* trying to poison himself?" Besides yaps, this town and neighborhood has its full share of yahoos and buzzardheads. (September 5, 1903)

There is absolutely no truth in the malicious report that a file of the *Eye Opener* was publicly burned by the common hangman in front of the parliament buildings at Ottawa last month. Parties circulating this report, which is calculated and probably intended to prejudice the moral status of this paper, will be prosecuted. It is inconceivable to what lengths some people will go. (October 17, 1903)

A somewhat inconsequent petition has been gotten up and signed by several parties in High River requesting the postmaster general to have the post office removed from its present quarters. There is no complaint embodied in it against the postmaster and his assistants. The secrecy with which this merry little "knocking" document has managed to live for the last six weeks (being born on October 6th) is evidenced from the fact that we never heard anything about it 'till the other day. Hanged if we know why it has been kept so dark. There is surely nothing to be ashamed of in a movement purporting to be pro bono publico.

Though started on the 6th of October, this document has only eight or nine signatures. It speaks of the post office as being in "a dark and remote corner of the High River Trading company's store, causing distress to the public." We admit that there is room for improvement in the matter of accommodations, and the postmaster himself is quite alive to the fact also, but the facts are these that the substantial addition to the north end of the store which was in contemplation for post office premises this summer had to be delayed until the inspector arrived and was able to examine the plans. The inspector came too late for anything to be done this fall. However, he was perfectly satisfied with everything connected with the running of the High River post office.

It is a citizen's privilege to sign any old petition of which he approves, but it does seem a pity in a little place like High River where we should all pull together that movements of this nature cannot be conducted openly and above board. Suggestions for the public weal should not have to be made with shame-faced secrecy nor carried out through the dubious system of what in slang lingo is known as "knocking."

Certain of the signatures betray the fact that the object of this petition is to have the present postmaster removed. During the last six months there has been a curious animus against anything and everybody connected even in the most remote and indirect manner with the *Eye Opener*. The High River Trading Co. has absolutely nothing to do with the *Eye Opener*. Kickers should not visit the sins of this Moral Weekly upon innocent par-

Few men are able to appreciate getting the short end of a joke.[6]

ties. (November 21, 1903)

Monte Carlo has made a profit of $7,000,000 during the past year. But that will not keep other people from thinking they can go there and beat the game. A good many years ago, while living at Nice in the south of France, we used to go by train to Monte Carlo every morning and do a little piking with five-franc pieces, the lowest they will allow you to stake at roulette. We did all right for a while, but on the last—the very last—visit to the casino we had to hoof it all the way back to our diggings in Nice, busted higher than a kite. No, we never returned to try and win it back. (January 9, 1904)

At least we have never violated the ethics of the west by being too good. This paper, however, will come out henceforth with unfailing regularity, even though we have to reform and die young. (February 20, 1904)

The *Eye Opener* had a slight ginning up from the postal authorities last week on account of the irregularity of its publication. It appears, according to legislation, that a paper which poses as a weekly and receives postal privileges as a weekly, must come out weekly and not semi-occasionally. Our infuriated subscribers thus have cause to rejoice, for we shall have to come out once a week now whether we like it or not and whether there is anything to write about or not. It

is a confounded nuisance but it can't be helped. (August 25, 1906)

In order to keep pace with the exigencies of modern journalism which demand a special mammoth edition every time the fire bell rings, the *Eye Opener*, not to be behind at—ah—this jungchah, steps into the breach, so to speak, and unfurls its banners to the teaming billows of a healthy and multitudinous public opinion. (Hear, hear.)

We are going to leave it at that. (September 22, 1906)

Our readers will pardon us this week for having such a devil of a lot of ads, but we want to make a little dough out of the paper just for once to see what it feels like. That fat ad on the fourth page simply had to go in. Moreover, our artist, George Fraser, is off on the coast, so that the *Eye Opener* is not so profusely illustrated as usual. Another saving. We are going to make a killing this turn out of the box and, altogether, stand a darned good show of getting that overcoat. (October 6, 1906)

A Merry Christmas and a Happy New Year to all those who have become our friends through this little paper. May God bless you and may He incidentally damn our enemies. (December 22, 1906)

The bona-fide circulation of the *Eye*

Some men and women are like silver plated knives. They look bright, but they are usually dull.[7]

Opener is now well over the 10,000 mark. It reaches and is read by about 40,000 people. For corroboration of this 10,000 feature, we refer doubters to the *Calgary Herald*, which prints and publishes the *Eye Opener*. The subscription price should be $10 per annum, but owing to slight irregularities in its appearance and an occasional punk issue, we only charge one plunk. (December 22, 1906)

That Edmonton weekly publication which recently printed some personal rot about the editor of this paper, publishes an apology for same its issue of today, Saturday. The editor frankly admitted his error and was willing to make amends. (February 23, 1907)

That insufferable bounder, Bill Georgeson, of whom we had to speak somewhat sharply in last week's issue, got wind of what was in the *Eye Opener*, before it reached the 'Peg, and bought up all the papers consigned to Morris & Taylor, our Winnipeg agents. Probably he was tipped off by wire from Calgary.

Why Morris & Taylor should calmly hand over these 1,500 *Eye Openers* to Georgeson, when they are under contract to supply so many copies to half of Winnipeg, we do not know. Perhaps Georgeson scared them into selling the lot to him. That remains to be seen. Georgeson got away with the papers anyhow, paying for them all right enough, and not one *Eye Opener* of last issue was circulated in Winnipeg at all. Our Leland Hotel news agent, Mr. MacDonald, who handles 400 of our papers, writes to say that, finding there were no *Eye Openers*, the public concluded that we were off on a drunk, and made no bones about saying so either. This grave imputation has caused us no end of pain. But we cannot allow Georgeson to put it over us twice. Not on your life.

Georgeson's remarks, made in a public speech in Winnipeg, about "the black-leg methods of the *Calgary Eye Opener*," were published in the Winnipeg newspapers, and read by perhaps a hundred thousand people throughout Canada. We would be simply crazy to submit to such defamatory language. (March 9, 1907)

Facts about the *Eye Opener*.

Its circulation, bona-fide, is 12,000.

The Herald Publishing Company, which publishes the *Eye Opener*, will corroborate this statement.

The price is $1 a year.

Payable in advance.

Payable in advance.

Payable in advance.

These are about all the facts necessary to spring just now. (March 23, 1907)

The editor of this paper has been laid up by a severe illness for the past five weeks and is far from himself yet. Readers of this paper are therefore asked to overlook the shortcomings of this exceedingly bum issue. (June 13, 1907)

If many people were to think before they speak they would forget what they were going to say.[8]

There is some rascal prowling around Saskatchewan taking subscriptions for the *Eye Opener*. We beg to warn people throughout the country that there is no one authorized to take subscriptions for the *Eye Opener*. Of course, this does not include personal friends who are good-natured enough to pick up an occasional subscription for us in their travels, but we have no regular authorized agent out on the road at all. Any one passing himself off as such is a fake and should be arrested. (August 24, 1907)

The price of this paper is one dollar a year. It ought to be five, but we knock off four for irregularity. What's that? Oh, yes, in advance, certainly. (August 24, 1907)

It has often occurred to us that the name of this paper is an unfortunate one. There is nothing dignified about the title "*Eye Opener*." Public speakers who occasionally would like to quote some of our wise remarks, hesitate to do so, because they know full well that the moment they start to say, "I have it on the authority of the *Eye Opener*," or "Only the other day I saw in the columns of the *Eye Opener*," the audience forthwith begins to grin and some d——d fool with a jag on sings out, "Wot's the matter with the *Eye Opener*?" There is, as we say, no dignity to the name. People are used to the old stand-bys, *Gazette, Herald, Review, Star, News*

and so forth. Village weeklies are usually called the *Clarion*, the *Bugle* or the *Voice of the People*, but they are neither here nor there. It is too late now to change the name of the *Calgary Eye Opener*. (May 17, 1908)

Did you ever run a little local paper in a small burg along a branch line of railway? We have—at Wetaskiwin, Leduc, Strathcona and High River. It is the greatest fun imaginable, especially when you are on good terms with the bartenders. In order to make a pecuniary success of your sheet, and get the ads, you must pursue a laudatory policy and sing the praises of everything and everybody in sight.

Here are a few samples of the kind of guff we used to get off at Wetaskiwin in order to propitiate the Furies and secure a few subscribers:

For Concerts—Patti, Nilsson, Tietjens, Van Zandt, Albani and Trebelli, all rolled into one, singing in the zenith of their powers, are not to be mentioned in the same breath with Miss O'Shaughnessy who sang last night in our hall. Miss O'Shaughnessy, who created quite a furore in South Edmonton last year by her marvellous recitation of Sullivan's "What is Home without a Doorknob," is without doubt the most wonderful cantatrice (of the kind) in this or any other country. The singers and accompanists showed themselves to be the greatest singers and accompanists of the age, and

Many a fellow has more money than brains, who isn't rich, either.[9]

a hearty vote of thanks was passed on behalf of everybody in sight. The sum of $.50 was taken in, which will be applied towards adding a wing to the Home for Fallen Dining Room Girls.

For Dances—The famous Bradley Martin ball, to say nothing of the Duchess of Devonshire's masquerade which created quite a sensation in London last season, were cast completely into the shade last evening by the dance given in the Shea-Miquelon hall. The costumes were ravishing, and as one walked through the brilliantly lighted rooms adorned with rare and costly exotic plants, listening to the intoxicating strains of Mr. Dan Oleson's violin, one could imagine himself in fairyland. A recherche supper was gobbled up with great gusto, and did great credit to the genial—and so on.

Election of a Dog Catcher—Mr. Skiff, our talented fellow-townsman, was yesterday elected to the onerous office of dog catcher. It is only fitting that all these years of unremitting toil in the political arena should culminate in Mr. Skiff's appointment to this high office, and we feel sure that we are voicing the sentiment of the whole community when we say that he is eminently fitted for the place. That Mr. Skiff may pass down through the vista of life with joy and happiness, and fulfil his solemn trust as dog-catcher with satisfaction, to himself and the dogs, is the earnest wish of the *Clarion*, the *Bugle*, the *Snifter*, or whatever your bum rag is called.

Receiving a pass from the C.P.R.—It affords us unbounded satisfaction to be able to hold up our right hand and state conscientiously that the service of the C.P.R. is undoubtedly the most perfect in the whole of the civilized world. Trains run like clockwork at a phenomenal rate of speed all over the system, within a fraction of schedule time. The lines of the C.P.R. form a perfect network all over Canada, and it is a pleasure to know that they are doing well. This is due to the excellent roadbed, the colored porters, and the really beautiful ties, each and every one of which are worth a dollar. The popularity of the C.P.R. is explained by their give and take (especially take) way of doing business, their kindness to shippers, their total sinking of self in their anxiety to please. May they live long and prosper. (July 18, 1908)

The Hon. W. R. Motherwell, minister of something or other in the former Saskatchewan government, on August 13 got the following off his chest:

"The *Regina Standard* quotes me as saying, 'I do not take much notice of the *Standard*.' That is true. I do not. But I would rather depend on the *Standard* than on the *Calgary Eye Opener*."

That's all right old cockie, but we helped put you where you belong anyway—on the scrap pile. (September 5, 1908)

A man seldom attempts to escape any temptation that looks good to him.[10]

Whenever we make a mild protest to our publishers about the cost of producing the *Eye Opener* they always tell us about the awful increase in the price of paper, owing to the denudations of our forests on which the pulp factories are dependent. Think of what it must have cost centuries ago to produce a paper when all writing was done on bricks! The *Babylon Eye Opener*—printed, or rather written on bricks or tablets of stone—preferably bricks, because they were cheaper—must surely have sold for more than five cents. Strange that no early documents have any mention of youths of the B.C. period, rushing about the highways and byways crying "*Babylon Eye Opener*! 45 shekels—all about Sir Frederick Herod and Clifford Beelzebub! *Eye Opener*!!" (December 18, 1909)

Again, once more, for the hundreth time, we warn our readers in Vancouver not to pay more than 5 cents for copies of the *Eye Opener*. We learn that the kids out there are at their old tricks of selling this paper for 10 cents. Kindly notify us if those little imps are continuing to pull off this holdup game. This sort of thing queers the paper and makes our readers sore. Our agent gets the papers at the same price as all other agents, who seem to make plenty of profit at the regular 5-cent price. (August 13, 1911)

Since the last Dominion Election the *Eye Opener* has been denied the privileges of the mails. This will be straightened out first crack out of the box. Perhaps the Postal Authorities were justified in what they did—we are ready to admit that they were—for we sometimes got pretty rough; but within the past few years the character of this sheet has changed and it is now well called the Great Moral Weekly of the West. It is quite as moral a publication as the *Christian Guardian* and a darned sight livelier, and has the *Fireside Companion* skinned forty ways.

During a stormy career of close on to ten years the humble individual who runs the *Eye Opener* has accumulated a bunch of enemies who, if stretched out lengthways on the ground, would reach from Calgary to Banff, and back again as far as Morley. We now wish all such enemies to be our friends. Let us call it a stand-off. If those whom we have lambasted hell out of will forget it, we shall freely forgive all those who strove so vainly to put us on the bum. In effect, the *Eye Opener* celebrates the great Conservative victory by granting a general amnesty to all its enemies and will be glad to receive the same generous treatment in return. There is only one man barred, and you can guess who it is. Every one else we wish to regard as a friend, and it is our heart that speaks. This goes. (October 28, 1911)

How strangely the wheel rolls round, stopping over and anon at the lucky star—for somebody. But a short while back there was talk of R. L. Borden being

Oh well, speaking of certain cabarets, it's hard for most of us to be good when we have a chance not to be.[11]

removed from the Conservative opposition leadership; now he is prime minister at the head of an abnormally strong government.

To come nearer home, but a short while back the editor of this paper was struggling through some terrible storms, his paper being denied the use of the mails and its very existence threatened; now the *Eye Opener* is firmly re-established at the old stand, is back on the mails, and is enjoying the biggest circulation it has ever had since its inception—27,000. Now bark, ye dogs! (December 30, 1911)

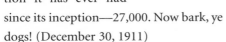
Well, they had no one to blame but themselves.

Speaking of reading, it may interest some of our more morbid readers to know that the last thing read by Pidhoney, the man who was hanged in Winnipeg three summers ago, was a copy of the *Eye Opener*. The night before his execution, Pidhoney could not sleep, and after tossing restlessly till well on towards morning, he got up and asked his death watch for something to read. The guard could not leave him to get a book, but he happened to have a copy of the *Eye Opener* in his pocket. This he handed to Pidhoney, who was soon engrossed in its contents. When the priest arrived about six o'clock the condemned man stuck the paper in his hip pocket,

and actually mounted the scaffold with a bit of the *Eye Opener* sticking out. We were present at the hanging and noticed that Pidhoney had a newspaper of some kind in his pocket, but did not know until afterwards what it was. The doctors found it while examining the body to see if life was extinct. It was noticed that Pidhoney was snickering to himself about something while standing on the trap, and the officials were not a little mystified at such a flippant exhibition. There was rather a good article about Sir Frederick Borden in that issue, if we remember rightly. (December 30, 1911)

Our old friend, Mr. Mecklenberg, the well-known eye specialist, who for many years has been making professional trips through the West, has recently been the victim of what might be called an "advance impersonator." An optical imposter has been visiting the towns on Mr. Mecklenberg's itinerary a few days ahead of that gentleman, tacitly allowing people to labor under the impression that he was the real Mecklenberg and in consequence getting lots of custom. This man was finally arrested at Trochu on a charge of obtaining money from residents by representing himself as the one

The way of the transgressor is very popular.[12]

and only Mecklenberg. This is not the first time this old-time optician has been the victim of persons trading on his reputation and he is getting rather tired of it.

The editor of the *E.O.* himself has been impersonated at various times and in various provinces. A few years ago some chap went through the province of Saskatchewan like a dose of salts, claiming to be Bob Edwards and collecting subscriptions for this paper. He even had the cheek to forge our name to receipts for the "one plunk." To make matters worse, he took pains to foster the illusion by getting very drunk in every town he visited. This was the unkindest cut. Fortunately he only visited the smaller burgs. We put the police on the fellow's trail but nothing ever came of it. For months afterwards we were receiving letters from indignant subscribers in Saskatchewan and parts of Manitoba, wanting to know why in hades they hadn't received the paper. One very wrathy correspondent even wanted to know if we had not sobered up yet. Deucedly familiar chap, that.

Another time, some six or seven years ago, we were impersonated for weeks and weeks in the city of Winnipeg by an uncommonly tough looking individual, who claimed to be the editor of the *E.O.* and who bummed probably over a million free drinks on the strength of it. One day a year or two later, while residing in Winnipeg, this party was pointed out to us in the Queen's hotel, sound asleep in a chair. Poor chap! We presume he had to have the booze or bust a gut.

There have been several other impersonators of our humble self besides those mentioned. The worst about it is that, from descriptions received, every one who ever pretended to be the editor of the *E.O.* was some dilapidated rummy of ruffianly appearance, usually drunk and given to borrowing quarters. Several well-known Winnipeggers with whom we later became socially acquainted, told of their experiences with at least one of these drunken, borrowing imposters posing as your uncle. Not very pleasant, this sort of thing. (June 27, 1914)

We have received an excellent article on the war situation from a gentleman who lives on a ranch near Wetaskiwin, but hesitate to publish it. Everybody who has an occasional effusion printed in this paper seems to get so swelled up over it that he goes capering all over the place shouting that he is writing all the dope in the *Eye Opener*, and then borrowing money and cadging drinks on the "glory" of it. We have been a victim of this sort of thing recently and don't care to take any more chances.

One chap whom we had befriended, to an extent which we could ill afford, was good enough to write a few articles for the *Eye Opener*, excellent articles too—as we thought, by way of repaying our kindness—and unbeknown to us he was at the same time scampering around telling our astonished friends that he was "getting out" the *Eye Opener* and was not

It is unwise to measure a man's intellect by the volubility of speech.[13]

being paid and would they mind letting him have a five-spot or a ten-spot as the case might be. He certainly was an unmitigated exaggerator.

Thereafter, through our agreeable personal relations with the powers that be, we got him a responsible position at the city hall, but alas! he stole the funds and was sentenced by Magistrate Sanders to one month hard labor and had a devil of a time of it generally. All of which goes to show that a four-flusher never prospers—for long. The price of ingratitude is always a stiff one. (November 21, 1914)

Last month the *Eye Opener* commenced its fifteenth year of publication. (Applause.)

Considering the way the little paper and its editor have been buffeted about, they are both doing very nicely, thank you. (Renewed applause.)

Not having kept the early copies of fyle we were uncertain as to the exact date of the initial number, but when Mayor Costello presented us the other day with a bound volume of the first two years of publication we found that operations began March 2, 1902. (Loud cheers.)

Complaint is sometimes made about the irregularity of publication. This can be explained very simply in a comparatively small western community where there is not much doing, there is sometimes absolutely nothing to write about. As in social life when you have nothing "worth while" to say, you may as well keep your dam mouth shut: so in journalism, when you have nothing of interest to write about, you may as well—better far—not write a line.

During these fourteen years strenuous attempts have been made from time to time to put the *Eye Opener* out of business. Most of those responsible for these pleasing efforts are now either dead or down-and-out. (Wild applause.) Few newspaper men in Canada have withstood the hammering and battering that the editor of this paper has been subjected to, but we can now afford to laugh pleasantly and say, "It was all in the game." So what is the use of referring to it at all? (A voice—"None whatever!")

The most painful thing to us, as an Edinburgh Scotchman, in connection with these varied and unique experiences, is our utter disillusionment with respect to the Canadian judiciary. One can only speak with precision of things as one finds them through personal touch, and we certainly found this phase of western civilization in sad need of improvement. Prejudice and political bias should have no place on the bench. (April 8, 1916)

Subscribers to the *Eye Opener*, whose subscriptions have run out, are earnestly requested to cough up for another whack at the Great Moral Weekly. (October 5, 1918)

Starting in High River, in March, 1902,

It is as easy to talk as it is difficult to say something.[14]

with a circulation of 230, this rag embarked on a wild career, full of adventure by and land and booze, plunging ahead regardless of the most appalling obstacles and finally reaching a circulation averaging, with the usual fluctuations, 20,000 copies. In sending your congratulations please don't forget to include a bottle, not necessarily for publication but as an act of good faith.

The *Eye Opener* is going strong these days. No home is really complete without it. In days gone by it was the fashion to speak of this paper as a tough publication, given over to objectionable stories and so forth, but it has happily outlived all that and is now not unfrequently quoted from the pulpit in order to point a moral or adorn a parable. A parable with *Eye Opener* trimmings is some parable. Our readers comprise saints and sinners alike, especially saints, and the advertising rates are reasonable. We strive to please. Say when. (March 15, 1919)

The following messages of congratulation on the occasion of the *Calgary Eye Opener*'s seventeenth birthday have been received at this office:

From David Lloyd George, Paris

Hearty Congratulations on Seventeenth anniversary. It marks red letter day in Canadian journalism. All Paris rejoicing. Gala performance at opera tonight when the Maple Leaf Forever will be sung by Signors Borden, Sifton and Madame Golightly.

Ah, there!

From King George, London

Her majesty the queen and myself join in wishing the *Calgary Eye Opener* many years of happiness and prosperity. After the War Cry it has been the greatest influence for good in the English speaking world and has formed a delightful link between Canada and the mother country.

From Pope Benedict, Rome

Vox populi ne plus ultra hic jact pro bono publico. Sine qua non post obit sic itur ad astra nem com. Pax vobiscum, O Oculus Openarius, duces tecum e pluribus uum penna, pennae, pennae, pennam. Nunc est Bibendum.

From Captain Ponsford, Edmonton Penitentiary

Your many friends here join me in wishing you and your paper many happy returns of the day. The *Eye Opener* still remains the favorite publication here and is especially popular with murderers. It reconciles them to death.

You can't judge a man's brain power by his tongue power.[15]

From Premier Stewart, Edmonton

Your seventeen years of journalistic activity marks an epoch in the world's history. Great events have happened during this period to disturb the world. A terrible war has torn the world asunder, thrones have disappeared, law and order threatened with bolshevism, society menaced, but thank God we still have the Public Utilities Commission. Hearty congratulations.

From His Excellency, Lieut-Governor Brett, Edmonton

Never thought you would live to see your seventeenth anniversary. Am strongly in favor of beer and light wines. My government is passing many beneficial measures this session and I have just signed an order-in-council directing Providence to grant us a bountiful harvest next fall. Hope this meets with your approval. Kindly reserve me two ringside seats for the Anderson-Noyes bout on twenty-seventh. Wish you continued success.

From General Sam Hughes, Ottawa

My God! Is that rag of yours still running? (March 15, 1919)

Some years ago we went out of our way to write a special criticism in the *Eye Opener* of Olga Nethersole, when she presented "The Redemption of Evelyn Vaudray" at the Grand. This must have been a damn fine piece of work on our part, because it was reproduced in *The Bookman* of New York, an ultra-high-brow publication of tremendous authority, as a "specimen of dramatic criticism that might well serve as a model for some of our more pretentious critics on the New York press."

We have this copy of *The Bookman* in our possession.

The writer went on to say that "Over the literary quality of this sample of dramatic criticism, there can be no quibbling, no dispute. And, in spite of the traces of colloquialism that may be observed, it may not be fairly urged that it is not without proportionate traces of clear judgement and common sense."

The only thing that annoyed us about these flattering remarks in *The Bookman* was the appalling sentence: "The criticism appeared in the journalistic organ of Calgary, a small mining town in the western section of Canada." (April 5, 1919)

Fame has come to our doorstep at last. It has been a long time coming, but so long as it has come at all everything is all right. Some men have cigars called after them. We go these gentry one better. In a letter from a rancher friend, W. Austin Brown (returned officer and a good head) may be found these words: "My two-year-old colt, 'Bob Edwards,' is turning out a beauty. He is a fine little fellow and will be a big horse next year." (November 1, 1919)

The editor of this extraordinary rag has some explaining to do, to account for the

Some men are pleasant enough to talk to, but rather disagreeable to listen to.[16]

long gap between last issue and this one. The fact is that our health partially broke down and the Doc suggested that a spell of sea-level might bring us back to par. He was right. Accompanied by the missus we made a bee line for the coast and now behold! here is the dam old paper out again. Just prior to this we had paid a visit to Toronto in connection with this summer's "Annual." Ontario would make anybody sick just now. (April 30, 1921)

The other day we ran across a copy of the old *Free Lance*, a weekly journal published by ourself in Wetaskiwin some twenty or more years ago. This particular number is dated May 6, 1898. Wetaskiwin at that time had a population of about 300 and everybody was busted higher than a kite. Our office was in a butcher shop which had just been vacated by the butcher who had gone broke. His sign remained over the door and we wrote our stuff on the counter where he had been wont to chop meat. Great place for inspiration. The following paragraph will explain itself.

"We take this opportunity of announcing that the beautiful painting of a bull's head over our new office does not signify that it is a meat market. It was once, but not now—not now. People wandering through our portals in search of pork chops will have to go empty away. Our patience, as it is, is well-nigh exhausted by little children coming in and rapping on the counter with a dime,

while we are dashing off an editorial on C.P.R. atrocities, and calling for ten cents' worth of liver."

We said we were all broke in Wetaskiwin in those days. This is quite true. The butcher had providentially left us a stove and a chair, but the difficulty lay in getting wood for the stove during the winter. It so happened that Constable Ketchen of the N.W.M.P. had his barracks next door and all his wood was provided by the government. This wood he got sawed to the proper stove lengths by stray prisoners or half-breeds. Our neighbor on the other side was an Englishman named Keble, who bought and sawed his own wood. Well, we didn't do a thing to those two woodpiles. Many a dark night when the town was asleep, also Ketchen and Keble, we sallied forth and laid in a supply of fuel. Neither of our genial neighbors caught on to our depredations until we mentioned it ourselves, when spring arrived, in the following paragraph:

"Now that the winter has come to a close we beg to thank the various owners of woodpiles in the vicinity of our office for all the wood we have stolen. Although not caught on any occasion, we consider it our duty to express our grateful appreciation of the wood. It was all right. The only improvement we can suggest for next winter is that Mr. Ketchen get his wood cut a little shorter and Mr. Keble, his a trifle longer."

Nowadays a man would be sent to jail for this sort of thing. Ketchen, the

The louder a man talks the easier it is to discredit anything he says.[17]

Mountie, not having had to saw his own wood, was easily placated. All we had to do in his case was to set 'em up a few times down at the hotel. Keble, on the other hand, who had had to saw his own wood and didn't drink, was rather inclined to grumble at first, but beyond remarking that he thought it d——d cheek on our part, he soon got over it.

These certainly were happy-go-lucky days. Whenever a new subscriber drifted into the office with a dollar, we instantly abandoned all business for the day and convoyed the subscriber down to the hotel, where the dollar was duly blown in. Did a man, through some happy streak of fortune, come into possession of, say, five dollars—which was damn seldom—it became known all over town immediately and the local sports could be seen converging towards the hotel from all directions at an exceedingly rapid gait. Many of those to whom we are here referring as "local sports" are today prominent businessmen in various parts of the province and well-blessed with this world's goods, to say nothing of overdrafts at the bank. As for ourself, we should worry! (*Summer Annual,* 1922)

That was a very kind obituary they published of yours truly in the *Vancouver Sun* of Monday, June 26th, lamenting our untimely death from pneumonia and attendant complications. True, we were pretty sick, but to die on the eve of a Race Meeting were unthinkable. The pari-mutuels will gather in our two-spots as usual. This is official. (July 1, 1922)

The editor of the *E.O.* has been a pretty sick man for some time past, but is rounding to nicely. Ellis, the hangman, has been wiring constantly from the east, making anxious inquiries. This is the last word in human rapacity. What's the hurry, anyhow? (July 1, 1922)

Grey matter is all right in its place—and so is the long green.[18]

Gloating over Pictures of
the Hootchee-Kootchee

In which your uncle rails against sexual predators,
police brutality, land-sharks, movie-house
chatterboxes, & other big issues of the day.

"Have been told that it looks more respectable to have a solemn paper
once in a while."

—*Eye Opener*, January 1, 1910

Life isn't always prunes & giggles. Bob Edwards knew this to be true, which is why
he took time to address serious social issues of the day. You, too, would do well to
familiarize yourself with matters such as—

☞ Lazy pedagogy makes children dumb as sticks!

☞ Physicians are quacks because they can't properly diagnose smallpox!

☞ Automobiles are a cottage industry of misery!

☞ Step lively lest hospitals become exclusive to the wealthy elite!

☞ Bastard offspring deserve child-support, too!

☞ Wireless telegraphy scams are bad!

Consider it your civic duty. The jokes will return in the next chapter.

In a private house in Calgary the other day we saw a child trying to interest herself in an advanced and dull history of Canada. To our mind one of the most fatal mistakes of the popular methods of education, is the teaching of names before things and without things. The natural child has absolutely no interest in abstract knowledge. His or her inexperience gives them no interest in the storing up on knowledge, of which he or she can make no immediate use. Compelling children to learn by rote, to learn as a parrot learns, is the great bane of our educational systems.

The children who sit listlessly on the benches of our public schools, are children who have been drugged with rote study, and who have been blighted by the repression of their natural inquiries after knowledge. The children are blamed, scolded and punished for stupidity for which they are no more responsible than the freckles on their faces. (*Wetaskiwin Free Lance*, December 8, 1898)

Doctor Macdonald's official visit up north to investigate a smallpox scare is not the first one of its kind. Some twenty-five years ago (I may not be exact as to time) there was a really serious outbreak of smallpox amongst the Indians east of Wetaskiwin. Many of those who died were buried on Pretty Hill, others being consigned to the blue waters of Bittern Lake. An official from Winnipeg was sent but to see about it. His report was much more remarkable than Doctor MacDonald's and, if I remember, ran something after this strain: On the hundred and twenty-first day out we camped on the top of an ice-bound rock in a drenching rain, no shelter, and surrounded by a hungry horde of grey wolves. Old Pierre Cafe-au-lait, most faithful and resourceful of guides, killed two of our horses, ripped them open, removed the intestines and into the hot reeking insides of these animals we crawled, sleeping in warmth and comfort till morning. Next day we made but slow progress owing to a blinding sleet, and Pierre and I sat up all night drinking pain-killer to keep warmth in our bodies—poor Pierre occasionally chanting "Alouette, gentille alouette"— listening to the shrill cry of the grizzly, the deep baying of the coyote and the wild roar of the chipmunk. Next morning we pushed on, arriving at our destination at twelve by the sun. Ascertaining that the disease was in truth smallpox (I got Pierre to go into a tepee and look), we started back at five minutes past twelve on our return journey. I arrived in Winnipeg after untold hardships, put up at old Cap. Douglas', and sent round my report to the Commissioner by the bell boy. The Commissioner subsequently congratulated me on the success of my trip, adding that the only reason he had sent me out was to get the laugh on a rival politician who claimed that the disease raging amongst the Crees was only the blind staggers brought on by Hudson's Bay rum, aggravated by Perry

Doctor Macdonald announces that Mount Vesuvius has the smallpox because it is in eruption.[1]

Davis' Pain Killer. He was heartily glad to hear it was the smallpox.

Twenty-five years later, in almost the same vicinity, another outbreak is reported. An official doctor goes out and reports that it is a mild form of smallpox, another doctor goes out and says it is a mild form of chicken pox, and yet another (who is suffering just now from severe cold in the head) insists that it is Gerbad Beasles. All well known physicians of acknowledged skill too. The people themselves say there is nothing the matter with them at all. What are we to think? (*Wetaskiwin Breeze*, March 13, 1901)

With the advent of the automobile Calgary advances another stride as the logical leader in all that is good, fashionable, immoral, gay and joyous in the Territories; and by way of further justification for the auto's introduction we have only to mention the two hospitals, the coterie of skilled surgeons, the coroner and the police magistrate and the patriotic, progressive, prosperous, perspicacious, popular, potent, powerful politicians of that beautiful and lovely city who will now have the honor of passing by-laws regulating the auto's speed and incidentally fixing the fines. (November 21, 1903)

Believe us, gentle reader, whatever we say and whatever we do, is said and done with a single eye to Calgary's welfare. The citizens of this town are all too good natured and easy-going. They are prone to think that if their own private businesses are running smoothly, everything is hunky dory. Every thing is far from being hunky dory when, through their own neglect, indifference, and habit of electing popcorn vendors and peanut-roasters to run the town (to say nothing of the inevitable contractors skirmishing around for business advantages thus obtainable), they allow the civic pot to boil dry and crack. (November 19, 1904)

Well, we have done our duty in the matter of calling attention to the excessive cost of the necessaries of life in Calgary, but nothing will come of it. The Board of Trade cannot take it up for the reason that most of the merchants who do the wolfing belong to that illustrious body; nor dare the two daily newspapers handle the subject for fear of losing an advertisement or two.

A lone weekly newspaper, at the risk of pecuniary loss to itself, shows the easy-going public where they are being soaked and the editor is told a hundred times a day on the street that his contention is just and proper and he is earnestly recommended to keep on giving 'em 'ell, but the whole matter drops into the abyss of public indifference through lack of support from the quarters most affected and from the local press.

The daily newspapers here are altogether too much under the domination of the respective business offices. No

Things are very quiet in the east just now. Molson's Bank has not been robbed or buncoed for two months.[2]

Citizen: " Say wow! Miss Calgary I'm being badly bitten!"

public abuse can be exposed if it affects in the slightest degree the interests of an advertiser. The city's last scandal was handled without gloves because none of the participants happened to be contributors to the revenue of either paper. Hornby has nothing to advertise, so there was no hesitation about holding that gentleman and his horse up to public ridicule. The city council gets fits from the daily press on the slightest provocation. Only one alderman advertises, and that on a small scale. Were they all good fat advertisers, their deeds in the council would be endorsed holus-bolus.

The way the papers do it is like this,— a man comes into the office with a real, genuine, bona fide grievance which affects the public generally. The editor in his own mind recognizes the justice of the complaint and the need of remedy. For business-office reasons, however, he dare not tackle it, but agrees to insert a letter on the subject if the complainant will sign his own name to it. As no one pays much attention to personal correspondence in a paper, attributing kicks to the enlarged state of the kicker's liver, no result is achieved. It is indeed a pity that the Calgary dailies cannot rise superior to the submissive and timid methods in vogue with our downtrodden friend, the village weekly. (February 4, 1905)

⸺

The *Calgary Herald* is certainly acquiring a very bad habit of giving opinions and making statements one day, and then switching around a few days later and saying something diametrically the opposite.

Last Friday they published an interview with C. H. Munroe, of the Munroe & Munroe outfit which is at present unloading Wireless Telegraphy stock at $3 a share on a guileless prairie public, an interview which was most damnatory so far as Munroe and his semitic coadjutor were concerned. At least, they protested very vigorously about it as soon as it appeared in the paper.

The interview began with Munroe stating, in answer to a question as to what eventually became of the money, that the

Anxious Inquirer: No. A floozy is not a person who has the floo.
Your informant has been stringing you.[3]

cash went to pay the underwriters, and the interview concluded with an admission by Munroe that the firm of Munroe & Munroe got all the money!

Of course they get all the money.

The editor who did the interviewing told Mr. Munroe that "some dissatisfaction had been expressed by the shareholders to whom his man Robinson sold stock in Calgary some time ago," to which Mr. Munroe replied that he was aware of it and that this was the very reason he had come out west, to see the shareholders and explain everything satisfactorily.

How the New Yorkers would laugh if they heard this.

On the Monday two days later, the *Herald* came out with an article whitewashing Munroe & Munroe and stating that the shareholders were perfectly satisfied. The article is so laudatory that these two men will most assuredly have it reprinted in the local papers of every western town they visit on this trip. It certainly does not harmonise even a little bit the tenor of the Friday interview.

What, might we venture to ask, was the cause of this sudden and mysterious change on the part of the *Herald*? We should have imagined that the protection of the Calgary public would have been the *Herald*'s first duty and consideration.

And why, oh why, have these New York high-financiers come thousands of miles out to the Rocky Mountain belt to peddle shares? Cannot they sell 'em nearer home? Surely Munroe & Munroe, late of the busted haberdashery concern in Montreal, have not been long enough in New York to be regarded with distrust? Perish the thought. In fact, tut, tut.

Another inconsistency of statement in this, Munroe in his advertisements claimed that he had come out west with a view to looking up suitable locations for the establishing of permanent wireless-telegraph stations. How does this chime in with his statement that the trip was specially made to give satisfactory explanations to disgruntled shareholders?—an apparently frank and honest attitude which proves that gentleman's subtle adaptability to and mental readiness for unlooked-for contingencies.

The explanation of Munroe's visit west will be found to be commonplace enough. His firm did so well last February taking $30,000 out of Calgary alone, that he, Oliver Twist-like, came back for more.

Mark you, we do not say that the shares they are selling are not all right legally and technically. They probably are. But are they worth $5? A short while back they were advertised in Winnipeg for $3. Suppose you wanted to raise money on your ten $3 shares tomorrow in the open market, could you get $50 or $40 or $30 or $20 or $10 or $2.50? That is what we would like to know. It would be most interesting to learn what infinitesimal sum of money Munroe & Munroe paid for that which they hauled out here to unload.

Last week we gave our readers the character of the firm of Munroe &

The movie actor has one great advantage. He can never hear the audience whisper "punk."[4]

Munroe as depicted by the financial editor of the *New York World*. Today we give a few observations on the same firm by Thomas W. Lawson, as may be found in the May number of *Everybody's Magazine*. (June 24, 1905)

Emma Goldman is to be here tomorrow (Sunday) to lecture on Alcoholism. Whoa, Emma! You better go back to Chicago and lecture there to the thugs and thieves of Halstead street and South Clark. Canada has no time for such as you, Emma.

It is a well-known fact that William McKinley's assassin admitted having been inspired to commit the cruel murder of the president from hearing a lecture given by this same harridan. She was likewise very conspicuous in connection with the Haymarket riots in Chicago, when a number of policemen were deliberately assassinated by means of nitro-glycerine bombs. For these murders four anarchists were hanged—Fielding, Spies, Parsons, and one other. Ling, the fifth assassin, committed suicide in his cell a few days prior to the day of exectution. (June 15, 1907)

We hate to be always showing people up, but some one has to do it.

There is a real estate man in this city—drop around and we'll give you his name, if you want it—who succeeded in putting his hired girl (English) on Queer street. This was bad enough, in all conscience;

but, what is worse, he was not man enough to look after her when the inevitable consequences loomed in sight. The poor girl, who is now near her confinement, hired a little cottage on Sixth avenue and, in spite of appeals to her betrayer, passed three days without anything to eat. Some one happened to learn of her condition and went to the real estate man about it. At first he denied all connection with the affair, but on being told of certain letters written by him, in the possession of the girl, he finally acknowledged the corn. The unfortunate young woman is now in Mr. Woods' Rescue Home.

It seems strange that the *Eye Opener* should be the only paper in Calgary to mention these things. Other papers report drunks most faithfully, and thefts and assaults, but they sidestep the gravest crime of all, the ruining of innocent girls. Ministers, also, are chary about tackling this sort of thing. We are not publishing the name of the guilty party in this instance—though we will promptly tell anyone who happens to ask us—but we give warning that the next case of this nature that comes to our notice won't be handled so gently. The only thing that keeps us in check now is the fact that the party is a married man and there is a no use bringing about further distress.

The *Eye Opener* does not wish to assume a Pecksniffian role, but we ask any right-minded man in Calgary if it is fair to get a girl on the bum and then refuse her support in the way of grub and funds

Contentment is sometimes the result of being too lazy to kick.[5]

during her period of trouble. As far as the general immorality of the thing, we don't care a snap of the finger about that. It is none of our business. (July 13, 1907)

In a previous issue we had occasion to draw attention to the case of a local real estate man and his rascality towards a young she-male. In withholding his name, for the sake of his family, we gave due warning that the next man we heard of implicated in any such deviltry would not be so lightly treated. So here goes.

There is a man—real estate, too, we fancy—named L. A. Babbitt, whose place of business is in the Pitman block. He duly got around a young girl employed at one of the city hotels in the good old way, making all sorts of promises and jollying her along in great style. As soon as she found herself in trouble, this man tried the black pill elimination act, but without success.

Then he made arrangements to place the girl in a certain questionable maternity home which within the past year or two has been moving about erratically all over the city—one of those maternity homes where the cases are all night cases and male troubles. Discovering the true character of this place, the girl (who, in spite of her subjugations by the smooth Babbitt, was good at heart) went to the hospital. The child fortunately died soon after birth, having apparently caught a glimpse of the isolation hospital out of the window. This contretemps freed her from the burden this scoundrel was going to have placed on her for life.

Prior to entering the hospital, the girl was in the Woods Rescue Home, that blessed haven for all such as are in distress, without money or without friends.

The girl is now working again and keeping straight as string. Personally, we don't remember ever having seen her, but we have the facts down very fine and are ready to substantiate them at a moment's notice.

Now, this sort of thing has got to stop.

What consistency is there in raiding the joints across the river in the name of morality, and at the same time allowing to go scot free the men who go around seducing the decent young women of Calgary? This is a matter that the ministers and the police should wake up. Why should all this particular kind of work be left to the *Eye Opener* to do? Every time we try to bring about a social reform by calling a spade a spade and giving the brutal facts, we run a hot chance of being put off the government mails. These smooth Johnnies we speak of are surely far more dangerous to a community than a hundred burglars or con men, and they should be arrested and punished accordingly. (August 24, 1907)

There is a bunch of Spokane land sharks in town that will bear watching. They are smooth as they make 'em and are preparing for a raid on the public's money in the spring. We here by serve notice on this bunch of advertising sharks that whenever they attempt to put on any of

Give us the flowers now and you need not bother bringing any to our funeral.[6]

their sky blue Additions this spring, we will investigate and expose every one of them. (January 13, 1912)

A certain real estate man in Calgary who is known to his associates far and wide as "Honest John," on account of his favorite text in the Bible, "Suffer the suckers to come to me," has been guilty of the most serious crime known to modern society, that of getting found out. "Honest John" originated a syndicate of himself and four leading citizens of Calgary to buy a certain corner and was entrusted by the syndicate to do the buying. This he did for $80,000, receiving from the vendors the usual five percent for making the sale. He then put it in to the syndicate, his own syndicate, for $100,000, thus skinning off for himself some $20,000 from his partners' pockets. This smooth piece of work soon leaked out in real estate circles. We are surprised at John, Honest John. We are, for a fact. He reminds us of the famous poem:

"John, John, the piper's son.

Stole a pig and away he run." (January 27, 1912)

If Mayor James Findlay, of Vancouver, has any political ambitions he may as well pigeonhole them. His career as a public man was nipped in its bud two Sundays ago by the blighting agency of his own pigheadedness. Acting presumably under his orders, the police undertook to prevent a demonstration of Vancouver's unemployed on one of the open spaces of the city. Not only did the police smash innocent onlookers over the head with their batons, knocking some of them senseless, but a bunch of mounted police charged into the terrified crowd acting like drunken Cossacks. One report says:

"The horses plunged into the heaving human mass. Men were knocked senseless by the indiscriminate use of the policemen's batons and whip-stocks by the onslaught."

Reactionary methods such as these are not to be tolerated for a moment in Canada.

Not satisfied with turning the police loose on the harmless demonstrators and innocent bystanders, the Seventy-Second Highlanders were under orders with twenty-five ball cartridges for each man! The question agitating the minds of Vancouverites is, who issued the mobilization orders for the troops? If it was Mayor Findlay, then it may be presumed that he was panic-stricken and lost his head. Which is not a very creditable performance for the chief of a great city like Vancouver.

For the general information we should explain that there is a large number of unemployed in Vancouver this winter and the meeting was called by the local labor delegates who had attended the recent labor congress at Victoria and incidentally interviewed Premier McBride with a view to seeing what measures the provincial government would take to provide for the commencement of public works in

Every man should master the art of concealing his bloody ignorance.[7]

order to ameliorate the condition of the unemployed. The premier had intimated that immediate steps would be taken with this end in view.

It was to deliver this message of hope to the hungry that R. P. Pettipiece and J. H. McVety called the meeting. Such a gathering should have called for kindliness and sympathy on the part of the authorities, not blows and curses. When Mr. Pettipiece got up to revive their hopes of obtaining employment by telling them of his satisfactory interview with the premier, he was promptly pinched. A bunch of prominent labor men were taken into custody at the same time.

This unparalleled treatment of the labor element will rankle for many years. It will not help the Conservative cause in the province either, to any alarming extent, for Mayor Findlay, who was at the bottom of it all, is head of the Vancouver Conservative Association. His political finish has been accomplished by a blunder which he will never be able to live down this side of the grave. He ought to be heartily ashamed of himself.

Even in London, the centre of Empire, parades through the streets and public demonstrations on the part of laborites, of unemployed, and of strikers, are freely permitted by the authorities. Trafalgar Square and Hyde Park are the favorite points of rendezvous. Of course, the metropolitan police are on hand to prevent obstreperous conduct, but their methods of handling large crowds are characterized by skill, good temper and a trained

intelligence which is lacking in the ignorant slobs who get on to the police force in Canada. (February 10, 1912)

The license department in Winnipeg is a funny outfit. They have a department to censor moving picture films. Every now and again in Winnipeg some picture gets in that needs clipping. It is clipped. The clipping goes on for a year, and all the clippings are kept.

Then what happens?

The city hall sanctions a private view of the pictures. Now, the fun lies in the fact that the people who have been railing against improper pictures are the very ones who attend these private exhibitions! When the private show was pulled off recently in Winnipeg at the Bijou Theatre, the place was jammed to overflowing with the moral lights of the city. Representatives of the best-known charitable organizations were also present, gloating over pictures of the hootchee-kootchee and all the rest of it. They are a bunch of libidinous hypocrites. That's what they are. (April 20, 1912)

We draw particular attention to the beautiful raft of oil ads in this issue. You must really excuse us for subordinating the reading matter to advertisements just this once. It is our only chance to make a little piece of change out of this oil delirium. Of one thing you may be sure—every oil ad you see in this paper is that of a good sound company. The men behind each

Never exaggerate your faults; your friends will attend to that.[8]

178

company advertised here are responsible Calgary business men, well known to everybody. No wildcatters are allowed to wander in these columns. (May 23, 1914)

One of the foulest exhibitions of man's inhumanity to man is on the eve of being pulled off in Calgary,

The gallant hero bombed the dug-out and slaughtered 37 Huns who refused to come out"

Barbarous! barbarous!

Will he be arrested, too?

Forrester

During Recess at Recent Trial
(Interpreter reads news of the day to Esquimaux murderers)

with the full knowledge and connivance of the council and commissioners, and the *Eye Opener* hastens to make the matter public before it is too late. The aggregation of so-called Christians—or bunch of rummies, whichever you prefer—whom you elected to run the city, are busy constructing a stronghold of police tyranny and cruelty compared with which the Bastille and the Black Hole of Calcutta were joy palaces.

If you don't believe this, go down today, as soon as you have read this, and look over the dank, dark, dismal cellar-basement of the new police station where they are installing the iron cages, and see what you think of it. It is a disgrace and will grow into a foul scandal if not knocked on the head. There have been a number of scandals in Calgary in bygone days, but they all pale before this one.

This unspeakable hole in the ground is being packed jam-full of small iron cages, with narrow alleyways between the rows.

In winter, when the windows are shut, this dungeon will be in total darkness unless artificial light is brought into play; and such air as they can pump in will neither relieve the physical distress of the unfortunate prisoners nor modify the horrible stench which must obviously permeate the place during the hot days and suffocating nights of summer.

It will be no time at all before this black cellar is swarming with vermin. No real fresh air can ever find an entrance here. Not in winter anyhow. Abandon air all ye who enter here. It seems incredible that preparations for the infliction of such monstrous cruelty upon human beings should be allowed to proceed. The people of Calgary did not vote money for the reproduction of the Black Hole of Calcutta. Prisoners are human and entitled in a Christian country to human treatment. If this dark, unhealthy, sickening basement is actually put into operation as a local prison, the *Eye Opener* and

The first two letters in the name of Okotoks are certainly very misleading.[9]

the *Eye Opener*'s friends will undertake next fall to sweep out of official existence every alderman whose term then expires and who has shared responsibility in this diabolical crime against humanity. (June 27, 1914)

There is a firm in Calgary which is paying its employees by cheque (for their own convenience) and making them pay the 2 cent war tax on same. This is pretty small business. If an employee's cheque is $25.00, he gets $24.98. The firm in question has, we understand, received important orders in connection with supplies for military purposes from the government. The employees of this concern should, on principle, decline to accept these emasculated cheques or else demand their full pay in coin of the realm. It may be a small matter, but the smallness is all on the side of the firm. (June 12, 1915)

The *Eye Opener* takes this opportunity of warning all and sundry to have nothing to do with a gold mining company promoted by one James Malcolm, now operating in Calgary. Never mind why we issue this warning, but whoever you are, fight shy of it. (April 20, 1918)

As the General Hospital has been run, it is little more than a hotel for sick people —rich sick people. There has been a place for paupers, but for the great mass of self-respecting people who will not accept charity and yet cannot afford to pay fees of $14 to $35 per week (which is about 60 per cent of the population], no accommodation is available.

It is run on the hotel plan, too. For instance for the private and semi-private ward patients paying fees of $18 to $35 per week, a dietician is especially engaged to prepare tasty food, but for the general ward patients, corned beef and cabbage, fish and such like are swizzled out in huge cans by a cook—sometimes a Chink.

It isn't a question of how sick you are, but how much money you have. (December 7, 1918)

We don't know what the function of the Bar Association of Calgary may be, but it strikes us that one of its functions might well be that of controlling the predatory instincts of some of its members who make a specialty of police court work. As it is, the unfortunate malefactors who for one offence or another land in the coop and have to appear before the magistrate, get soaked by their lawyers most unmercifully. There should be a scale of fees in this business established by the Bar Association.

It is the easiest thing in the world for the lawyer to scare a man or woman in trouble into thinking that their offence is a hundred times graver than it actually is and that the difficulty of getting them a light sentence or an acquittal is something tremendous and the fee, payable in advance, will be $50 where it should be

It is a waste of life to be sensible all the time.[10]

$10, and $100 where it should be $25. An excited person in the toils, all nervous and worked up, will cough up almost any amount for legal assistance.

Women of easy virtue are shining marks for some smart gentlemen of the legal fraternity. These ladies usually have a wad and it is apparently an easy and simple job for the forensic magicians of the police court to get it, leaving only enough for the fine. Whether the Bar Association considers these hold-ups ethical or otherwise, we cannot say, but it strikes us that a standard scale of fees might safeguard the interests of the scared-stiffers. (March 15, 1919)

The Calgary Gas Company is the most cheeky, impertinent, dislikeable public service corporation that ever cursed these parts. No one can get any satisfaction out of them. They simply gawk at you and say, "Well, what are you going to do about it?"

During a recent cold snap, when half their customers were freezing to death, Manager Coste's residence on Mount Royal was kept as warm as a pie. How we happen to know this is because there were a couple of parties at his house during the bitterly cold spell and everybody was as comfortable and cosy as a bug in a rug. (March 15, 1919)

At least half a dozen times each year we draw the attention of our movie theatre managers to the advisability of throwing

on the screen an admonition for silence on the part of the audience. In the regent theatre the other day, during the progress of the Caillaux Case, we had to move to another seat five times before striking a spot where our immediate neighbors were mannerly enough to refrain from chatter. At the Allen theatre this week we simply had to get up and leave the theatre altogether.

Movie managers should take better care of the fans. There is surely something more to "managing" than simply taking in the dough at the little wicket and grinding out the picture on a bit of cheesecloth. All that is needed is a sign stuck up somewhere so that everybody can see it, asking the people to maintain silence and not disturb their neighbors. It is not much to ask. A sign of this kind would cost about six-bits to have printed. The directors of the Allen and the Regent should call a meeting of their boards and authorise these disbursements. The combined outlay would not come to more than a dollar and a half. Half a dozen admissions would pay for this, each house going half, the Allen to pay seventy-five cents and the Regent the same. Of course this might involve a little trouble and some extra bookkeeping, but it would be worth it. The fans would greatly appreciate some attention to their comfort. (March 15, 1919)

By the way, who is the owner of the Victoria Block on 8th Avenue. Can he be

All that country has to do to improve the Government at Ottawa is to change it.[11]

aware, whoever he is, of the dive that has been running for a considerable time on his upstairs premises under the camouflage of a toothpulling parlor? This joint, and the fat greasy gink who runs it, has been giving the city police no end of trouble for some time past. Indeed, the toothpuller in question was treated to a rather painful interview with the chief of police in the latter's private office a few days ago, when he was given a sharp final warning. Is it not time that this unsavory person was ordered to leave the city? (April 5, 1919)

Who was the Calgary dentist who insulted a girl employee of a certain hotel in Edmonton, not far from the C.P.R. depot, some time ago? This man asked her to bring some ice-water to his room and when she did so grabbed her by the leg, with the remark, "You're some chicken!" It is gratifying to know that she instantly smashed him in the face. Can you guess who the man was? Yes, that's just who it was. (August 9, 1919)

Women will never make good on juries until they get to be as ignorant as men.[12]

CHAPTER EIGHT

The Builder of Bum Jokes

In which the village weekly editor gives away dogs,
cooks cats, & likens the Kaiser to a skunk.

"Weekly publications—or bi-monthlies like our own—should be commentators or prophets, never chroniclers of news. Nothing is news in these rapid times after the sun has gone down on it. Yesterday is already history."

—*Eye Opener*, July 8, 1916

Oh! what could be grander than the freedom to indulge whim & whimsy? Precisely. Bob Edwards knew well this simple pleasure, peppering his broadsides with rants & ravings & gags oft apropos of very little.

It is hoped the following miscellany will provide aficionados of words & punctuation with many minutes of jolly diversion. While reading, keep the following home study questions in mind—

☞ Is it good or bad to lose friends to Death's icy touch? Explain.

☞ Does anyone fare worse than a newspaper editor? Why not?

☞ Is worry conducive to good health? Are you certain?

☞ Is marriage preferable to the bachelor life?

☞ Nudity. Yes? Or no?

☞ I yawn frequently when commencing to sing. What will prevent this?

Did it ever strike you—you, gentle reader, who have lived in Calgary for say ten or twelve years—what a lot of our old friends with whom we used to joke and carouse are lying cold in death out in the cemetery? We made up a list of them the other day and have been in the blues ever since. What strikes us most forcibly is the quickness with which the dead are forgotten in this western country. "Old Jorkins has gone toes up." "Too bad—booze, I suppose?" A string of buggies, filled with men talking real estate, follow his remains to the graveyard, and pouf! He passes completely out of memory. Were we to die tomorrow the only remark passed would be—"When are they going to plant the———? I wonder where I can rustle a buggy."

Which of us will be picked off next? (*Wetaskiwin Free Lance*, March 24, 1897)

The other day a prominent citizen was talking to us on the subject of incorporation. The only thing we can think of as being in favor of incorporation at present is that, were we incorporated, we would be in a position to have an ordinance passed prohibiting the whistling or singing in the public streets of a horrible song entitled "Oh, I'm A Hot Thing," much in vogue at present, and on a par with that other miserable effusion, "A Hot Time in the Old Town Tonight." To be every man (or boy) is supposed to have an inalienable right to the acoustic properties of space, but under desperate conditions his right might be knocked from under by a properly worded ordinance. (*Wetaskiwin Free Lance*, December 30, 1897)

Holiday making in a small community is always of restricted order. There is nothing mixed about it. There are the two elements we all know so well, they don't intermingle, and each runs its little race for all it is worth on separate tracks. There is the church element, whose holiday festivities are of such a lively order as to horrify and astonish everybody, including the participants. In the nature of things there must be a certain amount of gaiety and pleasure. How poverty stricken must be the soul that does not recognize this necessity and throw itself heartily into the work of helping forward a good time. There is no set of conditions for holiday making, and if we cannot have the traditional customs of the season, let us make our own good time. The open fire, the Yule log (whatever that is) and the mistletoe, are not for us. All we have is the little old turkey and ourselves. Whatever we have, whatever we lack, the quality that makes the occasion is the spirit we bring to it. A few congenial spirits can celebrate the season away off in a log shed as heartily as can the Prince of Wales and his swift set at Sandringham. (*Wetaskiwin Free Lance*, December 30, 1897)

There is no doubt but what the lack of a marked individuality leads to a happy,

Bankruptcy is when you put your money in your hip pocket and let your creditors take your coat.[1]

peaceful and contented life. Those of a passive temperament who humbly follow a simple unobtrusive routine in their daily lives, who never get into snaps, jackpots or tight boxes, never commit themselves, who say nothing but saw wood, whose coming and going is not noticed, whose presence or absence is not marked, who never make much money, and yet, are never in debt, they are the happiest of us all. By never leaving the harbor they escape the rocks against which more active and aggressive members of society bump their heads. Men of weakly defined character, good-natured nonentities with no fiery impulses or nonsense of that kind, who cut little figure in their native towns, to whom the usual objects of existence offer no attractions, these are the lucky ones. To them belong the steady honest jobs, to them three squares a day and innocent slumber. Would we were like them. It would be money in our pocket. Instead of being in debt about fifty, we would probably only owe about five or ten. (*Wetaskiwin Free Lance*, June 15, 1898)

In the stampede after money the little old country editor soon gets trampled under foot. No one fares so ill in a crowd as this man who is wedged in the middle, and the sooner he races his way to the outskirts—even by retrograde movements such as slinging whisky and operating the pasteboards—the better it will be for his peace of mind. Why should a man, for the sake of the unremunerative glory of being a village editor, stultify himself, his principles and his character by allowing a cloud of debt to gather over his head; a cloud that will surely some day burst and drown him out like a rat. (*Wetaskiwin Free Lance*, September 29, 1898)

Often in our moralising fits in these columns we have made reference to the futility of worrying. What indeed is there worth worrying about in this blessed country! If one is really desirous for worrying, is not happy unless worrying, anxious to worry, there are women built that way, let him go to a country where there is something worth worrying over. We have been in this country going on five years now and have yet to find the man, the condition, or the circumstance, no matter how untoward, that has succeeded in causing us a moment's worry. And yet we have been "up against it" all the time. The only man who could come anywhere near it is the Chief of Police. (*Wetaskiwin Free Lance*, December 1, 1898)

Speaking of grub, is it not awful how tasteless all the meats are out in this country? Beef, mutton and pork are all the same if you shut your eyes. This is no doubt attributable to the lack of grain feeding. But strain your imagination into fancying yourself back east (far back) sitting down in a cozy little restaurant with a pleasantly jagged friend, to perfectly grilled, tender, luscious steak, cut thick,

One trouble with the bar-room as a "poor man's club" is that the annual dues are considerably higher than those of the rich man's club.[2]

and the deferential waiter by your side opening a bottle of Hass. You will excuse an old man's tears. The steak question out here is a fit subject to wrestle with, a tough subject, but as I am boarding at an hotel from which I am liable to get chucked at any moment, I deem it wise to defer any remarks till some later date. Suffice it to say that the best part of a hotel steak is the fair lady who serves it. (This should make me solid at court for a while.)

Although this is a vegetable country all right enough, one never by any chance sees a good potato. Wet seasons. The onions are coarse and woody. But it will never do to write in this querulous strain with new settlers coming in every day. The cue of a local paper should be to idealize the potatoes and rhapsodise over the onions. Pass the butter please. (*Wetaskiwin Breeze*, March 25, 1901)

There is a great dearth of books in this town. Nils Schmidt has a fair assortment of paper-bound works, but there do not appear to be such things as private home libraries from which one can occasionally borrow a Shakespeare or a Dumas. I do not possess a single volume of anything myself, not even a Bible, but were I to marry and establish a home of my own, you bet a library would be the first thing I should collect. All the wedding presents would be at once raffled off, and standard authors substituted. The usual set of plated knives and of forks would be good for

Robinson Crusoe; the pair of pillow shams could be exchanged for Carlyle's *French Revolution*, and so on. But the ponderous tomes of the giants of literature are perhaps not absolutely necessary in a town which boasts of so many high class newspapers as Wetaskiwin. Yawp! (*Wetaskiwin Breeze*, March 25, 1901)

When some poor devil goes and makes a bad break which lands him in trouble, his lapse from grace is heralded far and wide in inexorable detail. Not so in the case of the smooth well-to-do guy, who has friends at court. His peccadilloes are casually referred to in a whisper over a glass of beer, chuckled over, and the gentlemanly bartender, with a knowing smile remarks, "That feller's all right." (*Wetaskiwin Breeze*, March 13, 1901)

Undoubtedly the pleasantest feature in connection with the daily humdrum is meeting a man whom one knows slightly and who insists on showing you his team. With a sigh he says, "If I only had a mate to that black! The black's all right. I got hornswoggled on the pinto, but you bet I got even with the —— ——————. There was a feller from Dakoty last fall who—" and so on. As those sort of men never by any chance set 'em up, admiration for their shocking scrubs is neither general nor enthusiastic. (*Wetaskiwin Breeze*, April 18, 1901)

Bluff is often a good substitute for brains.[3]

Some old crook from Dakota, hearing that Edward Nunneley (that innocent young man) had a bunch of horses here, desired to procure some of them without paying. The Dakota man indulged in the present fashionable craze in the States of kidnapping. The amount demanded was $100. Mr. Nunneley accompanied the gentleman like a lamb, because he had a bot. As soon as the bot was done, however, Nunneley kicked Dakota out of the rig and drove back to town. This is a poor country for kidnapping. (*Wetaskiwin Breeze*, April 18, 1901)

Mr. W. H. Todd has invested in a ferocious bloodhound. It is one of the most dangerous propositions to bump into after dark that has ever afflicted High River. When you are hungry, and want a nice cold bite, go and seek Mr. Todd's dog, and he will attend to you. (March 4, 1902)

From observation we have arrived at the conclusion that the reason married men make so few "breaks" as compared with single men is because their wives interpose and prevent them from making fools of themselves. A sound argument in favor of matrimony. Therefore bring on your spinsters and let spinsters be brought, and in the bringing nothing bring but spinsters, spinsters, spinsters. Oh for a spinster, ye Gods! (July 25, 1903)

"Yes, gentleman," said the stranger looking for a business location to a committee of the Okotoks Board of Trade, "I have looked over your town and have practically decided to locate here. Having studied the life of Okotoks pretty thoroughly within the past week I am confident I can do well here and shall at once send for my family."

"What business do you follow, sir?" asked a member innocently.

"The embalming business." (August 8, 1903)

A debate was held this week at a meeting of the High River Young People's Society on the question of which was preferable—Married life or Single. Had we been privileged to participate in this debate we should unhesitatingly have taken the side of married life. We should have taken this side on the ground that marriage is a good business investment. Like appearing regularly in church, it pays.

Listen awhile till we unburden our alleged mind. Marriage has its sentimental, practical and expedient sides, but none of them can outweigh its business advantages. A single man may make good money, but what in nine cases out of ten does he do with it? Blows it, to be sure. The expenses when around with the "Lessavnutheround" boys are also notable for their magnitude. In an event, dear Lord, the money does not linger long.

Mark well that we are speaking not of the immaculate and innocuous member of the Young Men's Beef Tea Society, but of the average human bachelor who feels

Occasionally a man is clever enough to know how important he isn't.[4]

his life in every limb and declines to be a terrestrial angel.

Seldom if ever does he save, unless just before a race meeting when he has the fatuous expectation of putting the bookies out of business. In a town of any size most of one's bachelor acquaintances who hold good positions are constantly borrowing from each other and flying kites, and although they have only themselves to look after seem to be always in the hole. The single man is too apt to fancy that if he is not a bit of a sport he will not be "in it." Being a bit of a sport, however, usually costs a trifle over what a fat salary comes to.

In theory, the untrammeled young man with no mouths to feed and only his own clothes to buy, with no expenses but his own support—in theory, we say, this single man should be able to lay by quite a wad. But does he? The very first time he draws the third ace, pouf! Away it all goes.

He who is married has something tangible for which to save big money. Moreover, he has a home, and in this one respect alone has a decided edge over the poor devils of bachelors whose leisure hours after work are perforce spent in crowded hotel offices or in the unlovable precincts of a bum boarding house. The only advantage enjoyed by the bachelors is that there are no tidies on the backs of their chairs and no perambulators to fall over when arriving home from a St. Andrew's banquet.

Many a man has been drawn into the boozestrom and other dissipations for which he had no natural bent simply because he was lonely. By marrying a sensible young woman whose tastes do not run too much to pink teas, the inconsequent bachelor reforms unconsciously, becomes at last of real use in the community and even stands a very fair show of some day being asked to give a reading at a church social—the ultima thule of bucolic ambition.

By all means, therefore marry and God bless you. If one is to believe all one reads, it is more easy for the girl to find a husband. All she has to do seemingly is to write her name and address on an egg and await developments. (November 21, 1903)

As the West is a great place for people cracking jokes and telling funny stories it may be as well to give a few hints as to how to receive the jokes and stories, without losing dignity. When a rich man springs a chestnut don't interrupt to tell him you heard it as a child at your mother's knee, but follow him with an air of extreme attention and when he reaches the climax burst forth with—"Ha ha ha! Ho ho ho! Haw haw haw! That's the best I've heard yet—Oh ho! That's worth a drink— what's yours? haw haw, that's pretty good—a little soda water in mine?"

A mediumly well-off man's joke calls for "Ha ha, not bad. I guess we can stand a drink on that."

In the case of a salaried man's story you need not go further than "Ha! Pretty

One good thing about a dog fight is that the dogs engaged in it do not go around and talk for publication after it is all over.[5]

good yarn that—looks like as if he would have married the girl, eh?"

When you have reason to fear that the story teller is merely talking you into good humor to make a touch, take out your watch and back away, saying "Well, I'll hear that another time, old chap. I'm five minutes late now—so long!"

The humorous tale of the busted individual, which is liable to be really worth listening to, must be met with a slight cough. If he looks dry, you may stand him a drink. But take a cigar yourself and discourage further conversation. One's dignity must be upheld at all hazards even in the West. (June 25, 1904)

Only the other day, not barely two weeks ago this Eau Claire outfit raised the price of their alleged lights 2 per cent. And such light! Some people actually turn the light out to read. (November 19, 1904)

Whenever a man scratches his back on a post, he says to himself "God bless the Duke of Argyll!" In like manner, whenever you stumble over an obstruction on our dark streets you may likewise exclaim "Gol darn Cushing!" (November 19, 1904)

The Scottish game of curling is not much of a game for spectators. In order to enjoy the game you must be right in the thick of it yourself, scuttling over the ice in a state of tremendous excitement, sweeping frantically with a broom in front of a moving curling stone amid wild cheers of "Soop 'em up! Soop 'em up! Hoot mon! Soop 'em up!"

At night, over a bowl or two of whusky, you bring up the old dog and rabbit question by claiming that if so-and-so had played as advised by the skip, the result would have been vastly different. Then after twenty or thirty more whuskys you retire to bed extremely well satisfied with the yourself.

Next morning, after the affable hotel clerk has screwed your hat on to your head with a monkeywrench, off you hie to the rink again, broom in hand, for another soop 'em-up fantasia on the ice.

Curling is no doubt a very exciting game to those who are easily excited, but it cannot hold a candle to hockey. Indeed, it bears about the same relation to hockey that catch-the-ten, old maid or patience bear to stud poker. (January 28, 1905)

One of the great advantages in the rapid increase of population in Calgary is the relative lessening of local gossip. One's acquaintances cannot keep tab on one's actions so accurately or get next to one's bad breaks in a big crowd. A woman may be indiscreet and her indiscretion gets lost in the shuffle. A man may get off on an elaborate bender and only a few are aware of the painful fact. Give us a big crowd every time. Hoopla! (January 28, 1905)

Sooner or later a wise fish runs across a bait that fools him.[6]

Of course Wellman may reach the North Pole ahead of Peary, but it really does not matter much which of them wins out. On arrival they will find dozens of empty bottles of Kilmarnock lying around the base of the Pole, bearing silent testimony to the fact that the unspeakable Scot was there first. (August 24, 1907)

Whoever says that Calgary is not a metropolitan city does not know what he is talking about. The badger game was worked here some weeks ago, the victim—chump that he was—coughing up $800. (June 27, 1908)

The greatest fake of modern times (outside of the C.P.R. irrigation ditch) is the manner in which western municipalities are being held up for the entertainment of trainloads of alleged influential visitors. Take the excursions of so-called newspaper men from Newbrasky, Ioway and the two Dakoties. Anybody who can find amongst them the editor of any really prominent journal deserves a prize of $5,000 and an assisted passage to the Ditch. The only papers represented are such leaders of thought as the *Pumpkin Centre Bugle*, the *Hartley Clarion*, the *Grafton Prevaricator* or the *Cheeseville Sleeping Powder*.

The people who come out on those excursions belong to the impoverished country editor class and only take these trips because they cost nothing and give themselves and their wives a splendid jaunt which they could never otherwise undertake. Such stuff as they do write on their return merely describes the good old rollicking time they had and gives no information regarding the country which would induce any American farmer to make his home here. (September 5, 1908)

The nude, after all, is a relative term, and really implies and emphasizes the existence of clothes. Without clothes, there would be no nudity. For example, no one would speak of a nude cow, a nude elephant or a nude hippopotamus, and yet these creatures go around stark naked. Nudity implies that one has a wardrobe somewhere. (October 9, 1909)

There has been an awful lot of stuff written about Yuletide lately, and the Yule log. Over forty Christmases have passed over our frosty head and we have not yet the faintest idea of what Yule is. Nobody else seems to know either. A friend of ours who wrote a quantity of Christmas dope for one of the Winnipeg dailies, ringing the changes on good old Yule in great style, replied to our query in regard to its meaning with, "D—d if I know!" It surely can't be something to drink, because we are familiar with all the drinks and there is certainly none that goes by the name of Yule. Possible it may be intended as an expression of tender memory, the Forgetmenot and Yule Remember Me stunt. Anyhow, we give it up. If any one of our readers knows the meaning of this

A conceited man is one who wants to talk about himself when you want to talk about yourself.[7]

mysterious word, which bobs up so serenely every Christmas, and sends it in to this office, we will present him with a bottle of square gin and publish his photo on the front page. He must have absolute proof, however, and if his records have been left behind at Etah, the gin is off. (January 1, 1910)

We see that the *Winnipeg Tribune* is getting up a Contest ("most popular girl" or something of that kind), the prizes being trips to Europe, the Mediterranean, Egypt, Holy Land and other points of interest. Several other important newspapers in Canada are getting up similar contests.

The *Eye Opener*, in perhaps humbler fashion, must keep up with the times. It cannot afford to give pretty nurses, handsome salesladies and cute stenographers trips to Europe, but it can do the next best thing. The *Eye Opener* proposes to give prizes of valuable cats, dogs and birds to the six most popular bartenders in Winnipeg. Fill out coupon and enclose a dollar. The prizes are as follows:

Cats.

1st Prize, Black Cat—Until a year ago this cat was the ordinary backyard species, but one day got smelling too close to a sausage machine in a butcher shop. Small eater, as it hasn't so much to support as a cat with tail. Was formerly white, but overbalanced itself on the edge of a barrel of tar about a week ago. Is a strict teatotaller, as he was once struck on the head by a whiskey bottle. Beautiful singer of sad songs. Hell on duets.

2nd Prize, White Cat—Was formerly black, but recently fell into a pail of whitewash. At present rate of progress will lick itself clean in about ten years. Capital mouser, if mice are first caught in a trap. Fine singer. Would like to be won by bartender with a quiet home, as it makes quite enough row itself.

Dogs.

3rd Prize, Pure-bred Mongrel—Can trace its descent to the dogs that sympathized with Lazarus. Fine cat chaser and a rightful barker. Small appetite. Has been living lately on promises, hope and the smell of cooking. A recipe for mange-cure goes with the prize.

4th Prize, Irish Spaniel—Splendid coat, if it hadn't lost half of its fur through a kettle of boiling water falling over it. Has one eye in a sling, and a leg off. Otherwise perfectly sound. The winner of this valuable prize is respectfully requested to give it a bath.

Birds.

5th Prize, Rooster—A descendant of the bird that Peter heard. Starts crowing every morning at three punctually, so that winner never need be late opening up the bar in the morning. Extremely handsome bird, and would look fine with sausages and gravy round him.

6th Prize, Hen—Was a spring chicken fifteen years ago. Unrivalled layer; average for last five years, half an egg per annum. The winner of this prize is

Blessed are they who expect little, for they usually get it.[8]

respectfully requested not to drop dead when he sees what he was won. Sudden joy often kills. (June 18, 1910)

What impresses us most in current literature—such as we get in magazine articles and newspaper editorials—is the unnecessary amount of useless words used in expressing a simple proposition, or in telling a story. It is a vile custom publishers of periodicals have of paying by the word. It is as bad as the old penny-a-line stunt that was in vogue in the old country when we were a youth. In writing at a penny a line as reporter on a paper, you had to refer to a big fire as a "tremendous conflagration" and a fatal fire as a "terrible holocaust," if you wanted to eat all you wanted the next day, the result being that what should have taken about one stick ran four or five.

The rule of good writing is this: Write in the fewest possible words, and when you have written it stop and don't try to say it again. Write your stuff down and end at the end. The editorials in eastern Canadian newspapers are far too long, making irksome reading out of otherwise readable stuff. Our western editors have the right idea as to length, though it is no virtue on their part. Their habit of terseness and of coming quickly to the point is due to an unwillingness to allow too great a period of time to elapse between drinks.

In perusing a western editorial, the reader wonders at the strange abruptness with which it sometimes ends. Those in the business know exactly what has happened. A man has dropped in and suggested to the scribe the advisability of stepping over to the Bucket of Blood for a moment. The scribe, knowing what a moment means in such a case, says, "I'll go with you; hold on till I chop this thing off." He then adds a sentence or two and sends it down the chute, rises from his chair, puts on his coat, reaches for his hat and ho! for the Bucket of Blood. (August 12, 1911)

Come to Calgary, the Aquarium City, Full of Sharks! Boozorium Park!

Seize your opportunity! Do not delay!! Come early and avoid the rush!!! Yellow ball in the corner pocket!!!! Boozorium Park is the future residential district of Calgary, beautifully situated in the midst of the unparalleled scenic beauties of the baldheaded prairie, on a site famed for its badger and gopher holes and renowned in song and story for its entire absence of water. A pleasant place for a murder. Rural mail delivery service promised before close of century. Boozorium Park, owing to prevailing tranquillity, is specially adapted as a place of residence for those learning to play the violin and for those who may be desirous of studying the habits of range cattle. It is within the thirteen-mile circle. Ample room for a Carnegie library and bowling alley. Two lots have been donated by the owners for church purposes. Next ecumenical conference will be held at

Some men are known by the company they are unable to get into.[9]

Boozorium Park. A school is also in contemplation. For higher education come to Boozorium Park. Choice site for a home for inebriates. An automobile will convey you to Boozorium Park any day, provided you have the price to pay for it. Make your reservations tomorrow. An hour's delay may lose you a choice corner lot. BRING A FLASK!

Prices range from $175 to $350. TERMS EASY. One-fourth down, balance three, six and nine months.

BUNK, SOAKEM & CONTOK, Real Estate Agents, Calgary (October 28, 1911)

Advice for 1912: Do your share of work each day, pay your debts, save a little money, cut out the booze, talk only when you have something to say, don't get caught in a raid, look pleasant, and you will assist the world in growing better. (Loud and prolonged applause.) (December 30, 1911)

Ripe for the gallows:

All the restaurant chefs of Calgary, without exception.

The real estate man who tells you that you can double your money in six weeks by buying in his subdivision.

The Englishman who smokes cigarettes at your table in the restaurant between courses.

The man who stops you on the street to relate an alleged funny story when you are in a hurry.

The man who gives you the wrong steer by telling you that "the show at the Empire is all right this week."

People who come in late at the theatre.

The man who wants the editor to get after somebody, "but, of course, I don't want my name mentioned." (December 30, 1911)

A petrified ham has been discovered imbedded six feet in the south bank of the Red Deer River and there is much speculation as to which Calgary restaurant it escaped from. Served with cold storage eggs that have been lying in a cool place since the construction of the C.P.R. the delicacy should awaken tender memories in the breasts of some who have lived the bachelor life in Calgary. (January 13, 1912)

One of the saddest cases of suicide within our recollection occurred last Sunday evening when James L. Cameron, an old friend of ours and for years a respected citizen of Calgary, hanged himself from a tree near the south end of the C. & E. railway bridge. Mr. Cameron was around his usual haunts Saturday and appeared well and hearty. He was naturally of a jocular turn and had many friends. His untimely death will be widely mourned.

His body swaying in the early morning breeze was discovered on the Monday by the crew and passengers of the Calgary and Edmonton northbound. The train was brought to a standstill and

There are lots of great men until you get close to them.[10]

the conductor, followed by a number of passengers, hastened to the scene and had the body borne on a handcar to the station, whence it was removed to Shaver's Undertaking Parlors for the inquest. The news quickly spread over the city and the members of the lodge to which deceased belonged took charge of the remains and undertook arrangements for a suitable funeral.

Coroner Costello summoned a jury, of which Alderman T. A. P. Frost was foreman, and a rigid inquiry was instituted as to the causes leading up to the act of self-destruction. Several witnesses were called who testified that deceased was a bachelor in good circumstances, living in an apartment block with little or no worldly cares or worries. He was a man of cheerful disposition and was known to be kind to his mother, who resided in Brockville, Ont. A letter found on his person, addressed to the coroner, was finally opened in the presence of the jury and partly explained the rash act. It read as follows:

Dear Sir—This letter will be found on my person and should reach you in due course. I am taking my own life, not in a moment of passing insanity, but in a fit of terrible depression. My naturally cheerful temperament precludes any idea of degenerate mentality, my mind as a general rule being absolutely normal. So pray direct the jury not to return a verdict of suicide while temporarily insane. No man is saner than I.

Today is Sunday. When I arose this morning the Salvation Army band was passing my windows playing a frightful tune. This was a bad start. The Hudson's Bay restaurant, where I usually feed, was closed, and I partook of an exceedingly bum breakfast at a joint on Ninth Avenue and was overcharged by the waitress. On returning to my rooms I found I had nothing to read, so went out again to buy some papers and magazines. The hotel book stores were shut down tighter than Billy be damned. I then decided to get a box of cigars and pass the day in calm reflection and quiet contemplation. The cigar stands were also closed.

Returning to my rooms I took a seat by the window and watched the dreary groups of men who gathered on the street corners and huddled in doorways with nothing to do and nowhere to go. Pretty soon the church bells began to ring and I beheld a man who had flim-flammed me out of $500 the previous day walking down the street with an immense Bible under his arm. A feeling of intense irritation came over me, and I felt in all my pockets for a cigar to sooth my feelings. Nothing doing. I then put on my hat and sallied forth to see if the drug stores were open. Perhaps here, I thought, might be found some relief in the cigar line and peradventure the obliging clerk might even be worked for a glass of spiritus fermenti. Vain hope! The obliging clerk explained that while he was distressed beyond measure that he could not accommodate me with either of these commodities, he would be

It is part of human nature to think wise things and do ridiculous ones.[11]

delighted to let me have as much calomel and Seidlitz powders as I wanted. He said he had a fine lot of those delicacies. I then decided to take a brisk walk. No sooner had I made a fair start than I ran into a flock of people, all dressed in black and looking very lugubrious, on their way to church. I crossed the street and ran into another bunch. Turning down an alley I regained my rooms by a circuitous route and decided to go to bed. When half undressed I changed my mind and reclothed myself. It then occurred to me that a bachelor friend who had rooms on the same flat might possibly have a bottle of beer to spare, or perhaps a shot of booze. This man usually keeps a small assortment for emergencies. But when I entered his room he was fast asleep in bed and when I woke him up the first words he uttered were, "Say you haven't got such a thing as a drop of whiskey, have you, or a bottle of beer? I had a thick night last night." So that settled that.

The Salvation Army again passed my windows, the drum making a most diabolical noise and the trombone going oompa-oompa in great style. Once more I put on my hat and sallied forth. Groups of homeless men were collected in the entrances of moving picture palaces, looking at the gaudy pictures of the films to be put on the following day. What struck me more than anything else was the absence on the street of any one I knew. None of my social or business acquaintances were to be seen. They were no doubt comfortably ensconced in their cosy homes in the bosom of their families, or what is more likely, were playing billiards and quaffing goblets of Scotch and Polly at the club. Not being a club man, I felt lost indeed.

Lunch time came around and I entered another Ninth Avenue joint and downed a cup of unspeakable coffee and a chunk of apple pie with leather underpinning. On my way back I ran into the black-robed crowd returning from church, some of whom I knew and had to bow to. One man in particular I tried to stop, because I knew that he seldom, if ever, was without a flask in his hip pocket, but his wife was with him and he passed on. Ships that pass in the night.

A furtive visit to the various hotels produced nothing but disappointment. The proprietors, most of whom I knew, were all out driving in their automobiles, the outward and visible result of 15 cent beer, and I did not happen to know any of the clerks. At any rate, they all said the same thing, that "they didn't have the key."

The gloom deepened. A man for whom I have an intense dislike, and whom I knew but slightly, stopped me on the street and began explaining to me why Billy Manarey should be elected commissioner. That settled it. This was the last straw. I decided to go to some remote spot and in the cool shades of the evening end it all. Hell were a paradise to such a Calgary Sunday. True, Monday is tomorrow, but Sunday will come around again and I dread to face it. I am not a coward.

Remorse is memory that has begun to ferment.[12]

What man dare, I dare:

Approach thou like the rugged Russian bear,
The arm'd rhinoceros, or the Hyrcan tiger;
Take any shape but an Ontario Sunday,
And my firm nerves shall never tremble.

Unreal mockery, hence!

In my rooms I found a suitable length of rope, such as had enwrapped my trunks on many a well-remembered holiday, and wound it round the belt inside my coat. Then I sat down to pen this letter, my last farewell to the world. It will be found in my pocket. My affairs are in good shape and I am addressing a letter to my banker to act as my executor and devote the whole of my current account to the poor. This should buy at least three turkeys. Goodbye. Tell the Rev. Marshall and his co-stiffs that my blood is on their heads.

Sadly yours,

James L. Cameron

After a brief consultation the jury returned a verdict of "Death due to neurotic effect of a Calgary Sunday," with a rider to the effect that Calgary Sundays should be modified in their severity. The coroner agreed with the verdict and invited the jury out to have a drink. The funeral was largely attended and many wreaths were placed on the coffin as a tribute of affection and esteem. A message of condolence was forwarded to the sorrowing mother in Ontario, who, it is said, is prepared to bring an action for heavy damages against the Rev. Marshall and his co-stiffs. (December 6, 1913)

Mona Lisa, Leonard Da Vinci's famous portrait of the homely wife of a Neapolitan gentleman, which was stolen from the Louvre in 1911, has been discovered in Florence where it had been smuggled by an Italian who stole the picture for, as he says, patriotic reasons. The recovery of this ancient masterpiece will re-open the floodgates for a renewed discussion of Mona Lisa's enigmatic smile.

The late Walter Pater tried to explain this smile in a volume of about three hundred pages, but at the end of his labor Mr. Pater found the smile more perplexing than when he commenced his arduous task. Walter Pater was a bachelor. A married man would have known all about the smile the first time he saw it.

Literary critics who have attempted an account for the lady's levity of expression have suggested that while her portrait was being painted, the painter engaged a band to play ragtime music to prevent his model from going to sleep in the middle of a sitting. This explanation is plausible, but we have a shrewd suspicion that she is smiling at some funny story that has just been read aloud to her from the *Florence Eye Opener*. From the portrait it is safe to assume that Mona used to hit the can pretty freely. (December 20, 1913)

Character is what you are. Reputation is what you try to make people think you are.[13]

Open Letter to the Kaiser

Dear Kaiser:

After the creator had finished with the rattlesnake, the toad, the skunk and the rat, he took a day off and made the venomous species to which you belong and of which you are the finished product.

While I might perhaps be willing to admit that you are in some minor respects superior to the toad and the rat, you fail entirely to live up to the standard of the rattlesnake and the skunk. The rattlesnake is honest enough to give warning before it strikes, while the skunk—you know what the skunk does, don't you, old chap? It means well, anyhow.

Where others have hearts you have but a rotten tumor, and when the news of your inevitable assassination reaches hell the devil will close the gates and keep you out. This you may very properly regard as an insult, because Judas Iscariot was admitted without the slightest hesitation.

No ghastly criminal like yourself has a right to live so long as there is a rope strong enough to hang your carcass, and when your beer-logged soul leaves your body it will, believe me, have a whale of a time finding a resting place, unless, peradventure, it should seek repose in the dungeon cells of the new Calgary police station. Which were purgatory indeed.

Sincerely,

The *Eye Opener* (November 21, 1914)

Of course, in punishing the Kaiser after the war, one must not overlook boiling oil.

The buds on the trees are hesitating. Trees usually wait until they receive certain assurances of spring before permitting their sap to rise. Of course, the human saphead is on the job all the year round. (April 3, 1915)

What a lot of wondrous things have happened in our lifetime! Automobiles, electric light, electric street cars, wireless telegraphy, and more recently wireless telephony, X-ray apparatus, great medical discoveries, high explosives, submarines and air craft! These are but a few. All of which suggests the question—Have we made similar progress in the working out of human relations? We certainly have not. True, we are not guilty of a lot of the cruel and unjust things that disgraced former ages, such as religious persecution, burning witches and all that sort of thing, but there remain a lot of amazingly stupid holdovers.

The worst of these is war. In spite of a much vaunted civilization, nations seem

Gladness is appreciated only by those who know what sadness is.[14]

still committed to the plan of arranging international affairs by the awful process of murdering vast numbers of their best citizens. Cannot the ingenius minds that are capable of weighing and measuring the stars find out some other way of enabling British and German and Russ to live upon this pleasant earth than by astounding bestiality of war? (November 20, 1915)

Oh, you want to know what a highbrow is, eh? Well, a highbrow is a person who has a habitual attitude of contempt toward that which is popular and also a person whose education is generally beyond his intelligence. (April 8, 1916)

ANSWERS TO CORRESPONDENTS:
Sport, Edmonton: Record for high jumping is 1,000 feet, made from top of Eiffel tower, Paris, by a genial suicide.

Anxious Mother, Cayley: Name of lady in your village who gave birth to triplets eight years ago when Mrs. J. Prewen. It was her husband who got the sparkling jest about being full of prewens. He had a pretty wit.

Constant Reader: You lose. Shakespeare was not a Scotchman, although his talents would justify the supposition. He was an Englishman.

Phil Weinard, High River: You lose. Rainbow and Niobe were not won by the late Wilfred Laurier in a raffle. They were

The Rainbow, one of England's most venerable battleships, showing the Niobe how she put 'em over the French at Trafalgar.

purchased from England many years ago.

Petronius, Moose Jaw: The solar plexus blow was invented by Fitzsimmons. Some one has been stringing you. A left hook is not a demi-mondaine who has missed her train. (May 12, 1917)

The editor of the *Hootch Clarion*, who has been running country newspapers for years, offers the following summary of his experience:

Been broke 300 times.
Had money 65 times.
Praised by the public 6 times.
Asked to drink 8 times.
Refused to drink 0 times.
Been roasted 524 times.
Missed meals 0 times.
Taken for a preacher 11 times.
Taken for a capitalist 0 times.
Found money 0 times.
Taken bath 6 times.
Delinquents paid 27 times.
Got whipped 10 times.
Whipped the other fellow 0 times.
Cash on hand six bits. (June 28, 1919)

People no doubt often wonder how

How much does it cost you each year to be sarcastic?[15]

alleged jokes are built up. It goes something like this—are you listening?

The sad-looking man (professional funny man, of course) stopped before the bootblack's stand to have his shoes shined.

"And is your father a bootblack, too?" he asked by way of making conversation.

"No, sir," replied the lad. "My father is a farmer."

"Ah! A farmer?" cried the sad-looking man, as a spasm almost akin to joy spread over his features. Reaching into his pocket for notebook and pencil, he started mumbling to himself a sort of gibberish:

"Farmer, hey? Farmer—hay. Son, bootblack. Son shines. Ah! I have it. Your father believes in making hay while the son shines."

That's all there is to it. The builder of bum jokes goes on his way and if there is a drink anywhere in the offing, he moves in that direction. (July 17, 1920)

Sir Samuel Sims saw sweet Sara Sampson swimming. Suddenly she seemed sinking. Sir Samuel stood stunned. Striding seaward, spurning shingle, Sir Samuel swiftly swam Sara-wards. Sir Samuel skillfully supported swooning Sara; swimming shorewards. Sir Samuel successfully succored Sara. Seeming somewhat shaky Sir Samuel sampled some spirits—special Scotch. Sara saw Sir Samuel's self-sacrificing spirit: Sir Samuel saw Sara's sweetness. Sir Samuel soon sought Sara. Striding slowly, Sara sighed softly. Sir Samuel seemed speechless.

"Say something, Sir Samuel," said Sara.

"Say Sam, Sara," said Sir Samuel.

Sara, smilingly shyly, softly said "Sam."

"Sara—Sally!" stammered Sir Samuel. "Sweet Sara—sweetheart!"

Sara solemnly surrendered.

(Pleace ctop thic. We are chort of ccccc.—Printer.) (September 11, 1920)

SEASONABLE RECIPES

Pea Soup: Take a lot of split peas and dump them into a pot of water. Let it boil a week. If the peas show no signs of softening, boil for another week. Time is no object with pea soup. Add an old boot to give it body. Also a pinch or two of salt. If not to your taste, chuck it out the window.

Croutons: This goes with the pea soup. Take a loaf that is several days old and cut it into little cubes about the size of dice. Mark correct spots on cubes with India ink and put in oven till hard enough to crack the teeth. Guests can then extract them from the pea soup and agreeably while away the time shooting craps until the next course is served.

Hash à la Reine: See that the dog is a fairly fat one. Hit him over the head with an axe and allow him to boil three hours. Chop into mince meat and mix in a lot of potatoes, onions and sage. Serve hot. Cats take only twenty minutes.

Breaded Veal Cutlets: Select chops with nothing on them but bone and strips of

Sneers are the weapons of helpless fools.[16]

gristly fat. Camouflage alleged chops by smearing them over with thick layer of bread crumbs, then stick in the oven until somebody orders "Breaded Veal Cutlets." Serve and then stand aside and watch the poor boob picking away at it. It is quite a study and is good for sixty cents. Or you can lay an old leaf of lettuce on the plate and charge six bits. (*Summer Annual*, 1920)

An editor who started about twenty years ago with only 55 cents is now worth $100,000. His accumulation of wealth is owing to his frugality, good habits, strict attention to business and the fact that an uncle died and left him the sum of $99,999. (*Summer Annual*, 1920)

THE FAMILY DOCTOR

This department of the *Eye Opener* has been opened to meet the wants of those who cannot afford to pay the fees of a regular practitioner. They cannot arrest us for this, can they? Many queries have already been sent in and we shall do our best to answer them satisfactorily:

J. B. S., Red Deer, Alta.: Is strychnine efficacious in stopping ailments of the heart?

Ans.—If taken in sufficient quantities, strychnine will stop almost anything.

A. F., Edmonton: A man in this town is suffering from phlegm. He owes me five dollars, and seems unable to cough it up. What would you suggest?

Ans.—Give him a stiff does of salts

and he'll soon loosen up.

F. O. B., Okotoks: Am afflicted with prairie itch. What is a good thing for it?

Ans.—Try scratching.

Miss F. M. G., Lethbridge: I yawn frequently when commencing to sing. What will prevent this?

Ans.—Don't sing.

Mrs. J. F. M., Vancouver: A wealthy uncle of mine, aged 92, is run down; has poor appetite and takes very little exercise. Sleeps a great deal. Has hallucinations that his end is not far off.

Ans.—Make him hop into a cold bath every morning and run five miles before breakfast. If his will is made out in your favor, throw three or four whiskies into him and he will forget about the breakfast. Prepare a nice dinner for him and see that he gets enough whiskey so that he won't want to eat it. Between dinner and supper throw half a dozen more under his belt and after supper, which by this time he will have forgotten all about, give him a ten-spot and start him off down town. Phone a bootlegger to meet him at the corner of Hastings and Granville and when he comes home roaring and shouting at 3 a.m., put him to bed. Keep this treatment up for three days and then make your arrangements to winter in California.

R. Kellock, B.C.—Have a friend just commencing to have the willies. What ever shall I do? Have managed to cut him down to two bottles of Scotch per diem.

Ans.—Put some knockout drops into his Scotch so that he may obtain a little sleep. Shovel about half a bushel of calomel tablets down his throat, followed a few hours later by ten or a dozen Seidlitz powders. Let him have a stiff horn when he needs it, but not always when he wants it. Should he drop into a sleep, leave a jolt by his bedside for him to take when he wakes. Chances are he will drop off to sleep again after downing it. Avoid irritating your patient by telling him, during a vomiting

• • •
Ash Wednesday.

Self-denial Week in Calgary.
• • •

spell, that he should "cut out the booze or it will get him." He knows that as well as you do. Cheer him up by relating funny incidents connected with the last time you yourself had 'em. If he asks for something to read, do not give him a copy of *The Wide World Magazine* with the usual frontispiece of a hunter upset out of a canoe in the Congo river and a hungry crocodile making for him with wide-open jaws. Rather hand him a copy of the *Eye Opener*. It may send him to sleep. If there is any Scotch left over after his cure, you can send it to me. (*Summer Annual* 1920)

There are too many Canadian labor organizations controlled from the United States. Canada has recently had a humiliating experience along this line. An English orchestral conductor, engaged to come over with a revue produced by Trans-Canada Theatricals Ltd., was notified that he would not be allowed to fill the job because the rules of the American Musicians' Federation does not permit the members of that organization to play with a non-member.

In other words, a labor organization controlled from the United States has been able to prohibit a British conductor from conducting a British orchestra in a British country. What, then, becomes of the Union Jack? (October 8, 1921)

An old Wetaskiwin acquaintance, Charles Dunlop, has died and was buried last week. During our residence at Wetaskiwin Mr. Dunlop was one of our bitterest enemies, and there was no love lost between us. In the shadow of the tomb all is forgotten. Deceased had his faults. Besides being an inveterate rustler of young cattle, he made more than one mysterious shipment of horses. But the good traits of deceased greatly outnumbered his faults. We have long since overlooked his theft of a posy of flowers from a grave to give to the dining room girl of the Driard, and trust that no vandal will play the same

It is the things we shouldn't do that seem to make life worth living.[18]

mean trick on his own resting place. There is little likelihood, however, of there being many flowers placed over the tomb of such an ornery cuss as Dunlop. With cold wintry spring like this he is probably happier in hell than in Wetaskiwin. Rest in peace. (*Summer Annual*, 1922)

COOKING RECIPES

Bread Pudding: Gather up all the chunks of bread that have been left over on the plates for the past week and dump them into a bucket of water. Let them soak overnight and in the morning pound into a pulp with the butt end of an empty beer bottle. Take a handful of plums and chuck into the mess. Stir with a big spoon and add a little sugar. Dump into a pan and stick it into the oven. As soon as it begins to look a trifle less disgusting, take it out and serve it as plum pudding.

Stewed Chicken: Take the varicose veins of an aged chicken and wind them around the bones. Lay the flesh of the bird aside for private consumption the next day. Stick veins and bones in shallow pan and allow to simmer for a while, then serve in white sticky sauce. The latter can be procured in desired quantity from the Calgary Bill Posting Company Limited.

Pudding à la Reine: Take down flask from shelf and pour stiff horn down your throat. Whip five or six eggs into a fine lather and pour in a quart of milk. Add cupful of sugar. Have another drink. Add a little minced onion and the contents of a can of strawberries with pepper and salt to season. Flavor with vanilla and set away to cool. If the guests are not satisfied with this, tell them to go to hell and throw the pudding out of the window. Finish the flask.

Rabbit Stew: Take a good fat cat and give it a bat over the head in the cellar. Remove skin and dismember with sharp knife. Put in pan with a little water and allow to simmer slowly for a couple of hours. Season to taste.

Roast Turkey: Save up for months until you have price of good big bird. Then take money and send to Maple Creek for half a dozen bottles of Scotch. You won't want any turkey. (*Summer Annual*, 1923)

A drug store is a collection of bottles filled with poisons, presided over by a man who has a certificate to deal them out to whoever presents a little bit of paper made out by a man whose sole object is to conceal his purpose by writing in a dead language. More murders are committed in a drug stores than in any other place on the face of the earth. Even the soda water fountain is built of polished gravestones to typify its mission. Besides which, you must have observed druggists and undertakers all look alike. (*Summer Annual*, 1923)

Some favorite fiction:

"Yes, I Can Take a Drink or I Can Let it Alone."

If a man is always making new friends it is a sign that his old friends are onto him.[19]

"My Friends are Urging Me to Become a Candidate for the Council."

"No, I Wouldn't Go Across the Street to See a Prize Fight."

"I'm Always Pleased to Have a Friend Tell Me of My Faults."

"When I'm Thirsty Give Me a Glass of Cold Water Every Time." (*Summer Annual*, 1923)

So what, after all, does it matter how you act or what you do in this world, so long as you keep out of jail? You may have lived a most virtuous life, denying yourself many kinds of worldly amusements and enjoyments, because you were told by the preachers that true virtue lay in self-abnegation; but after you're dead, the community at large won't think any the more for it. Not they! They will shrug their shoulders and say, "that mutt didn't get much out of life anyhow."

The man who economizes his emotions, his money and his pleasures during youth and middle age gets as much satisfaction out of life as a man who is dieting does out of his dinner. Some clever man has said that the cost of living is just a little more than you can earn. It is begin-ning to dawn on people that the success-ful—worldly—man commands just as much respect as the successful business-man who is trustee of a church and therefore, very solemn. Even the young folks nowadays cannot fail to observe the silent admiration of the world for the successful scoundrel, the debonair master of craft who is morally, financially and perhaps politically opaque, but who floats on the crest of the wave to the gold-en shore, living on the fat of the land, whirling about in motor cars, and order-ing pints the live-long day. When the first mentioned and second mentioned are laid away in their graves, they are both at a par, their bones will rot and crumble into dust "just the same" and they are known no more. (*Summer Annual* 1923)

A man in trouble always appreciates a friend—until he gets out of it.[20]

CHAPTER NINE
Letters from a Badly Made Son

Being the collected correspondence of Albert "Bertie"
Buzzard-Cholomondeley, remittance man & gopher rancher.

The fashionable reader will find much kinship in the epistolary adventures of Albert "Bertie" Buzzard-Cholomondeley, the first great fictional character to spring forth from Bob Edwards's pen. Assuming, that is, the fashionable reader is—

☞ Unemployed, with no prospects!

☞ Not really interested in working in the first place!

☞ Unrepentant about fleecing the family fortune!

☞ A widowed father of two who faked insanity to beat a murder rap & then went on to impersonate a physician, only to next etc. etc.!

☞ Or simply a humourous social parasite slowly draining humanity's goodwill!

Essentially an extended promissory note, the ten-part series placed Edwards on the crest of the short-lived craze for RemitLit.[1] (He later rehashed the conceit for one-off "sequels" starring Percy de Witt Champneys and two mono-monikered chaps named Algie and, yes, Bertie.[2]) Seven of the missives are extant, and are herein reprinted in toto.

---

[1] Notable entries in the genre include W. A. Fraser's *Brave Hearts* (New York: Scribner's, 1904) and W. H. P. Jarvis's *The Letters of a Remittance Man to his Mother* (Toronto: Musson, 1908).

[2] Percy appeared in the January 28, 1905 *Eye Opener*. Algie and this other "Bertie" shared space in the October 19, 1918 issue.

First Letter

Peace River, N.W.T.

The Fall, 1902

Dear Father,

As you have not heard from me for some ten years I thought perhaps a line from me might be of some interest to the family, showing at least that I am alive and well. I often think of dear old Skookingham Hall and the splendid shooting. Is old John, the head gamekeeper, still with you? I ran across a copy of *Truth* a couple of years ago and noticed that Violet, who always was my favorite sister, was married to the Earl of Pocklington. I well remember Pocklington. He was my fag at Eton, and not a half-bad chap. There should be some fine shooting on his estate. How I should enjoy one of our good old grouse drives again! The only shooting I have done out here of late years has been at craps, a different species of game from grouse or partridge. I suppose my old steeple-chasers and hunters are all either dead or superannuated by this time.

I see by M.A.P., a copy of which I have just been loaned, that my dear mother is visiting the Dowager Duchess of Applecore at Cannes. Give her my fond love when you write and tell her wild young Bertie has not forgotten the time when she used to teach him to say his prayers, "Now I lay me," and tuck him away in bed. But about things in this country. The few thousand pounds you gave me to start farming with in Manitoba are duly invested in a farm. In farm labors I had several assistants, Hi Walker, Joe Seagram, Johnnie Dewar and Bennie Dikteen, men of strength and fiery temper. In place of regarding me as their master, they soon became My masters. So it was not long before I had no farm. I then quit farming and went tending bar for a hotel-keeper in the neighboring village whose prosperity seems to have dated from the hour of my arrival in the country.

The love of liquor which is inherent in my blood, and which I must have inherited either from yourself or from my grandfather, made me a failure as a bartender and I soon got the bounce. So I packed my things in a large envelope and hit the blind baggage for the West where I went cowpunching. Worked during the summer till the beef gather and lost and all my wages in one disastrous night at poker. After a long hard winter working as cookee in a lumber camp I struck for Peace river country where I now am, knocking life out to keep life in. You can get five-gallons of whiskey at a crack if you have a government permit—but that is by the way.

I am married to a half breed and have three ornery looking, copper-colored brats. We are all coming over to visit you at Christmas when you will be having the usual big house party at Skookingham Hall. I shall so like to see the dear old place again and my wife is most anxious to become acquainted with her darling husband's people and obtain a glimpse of

One can always tell when one is getting old and serious by the way that holidays seem to interfere with one's work.[1]

PUPIL-FARMING AT HIGH RIVER.

"Of course, this is awfully jolly, you know, but—er, by jove, I think I'd much wather be **tooling** a four-in-hand **down** to the Ascot races. I wondah how much of this beastly stuff—ah—constitutes a load!"

English society. The Hall will be quite a change for her from the log shacks and tepees she has been used to all her life.

If I only had about a thousand pounds just now with which to start afresh I would invest it all in cattle right away, settle down to business and forego the pleasure of a trip home and remain right here. But I do not know where to lay my hands on that amount. The climate here is lovely. With love and kisses to mother and the girls, believe me, dear old Dad.

Your affectionate son,

ALBERT BUZZARD-CHOLOMONDELEY

(October 24, 1903)

Third Letter

Edmonton, December 2, 1902

Sir John Buzzard-Cholomondeley,
Skookingham Hall,
Skookingham
Leicestershire

Dear Father:

Your second cheque for five hundred pounds received, making one Thou in all. Many thanks. Do not be alarmed. We are not coming over. I am exceedingly grieved to learn that my dear mother is suffering from nervous prostration and that my sisters contemplate entering a convent.

Most of the entries in the human race are also-rans.[2]

Cheer the family up by assuring them that my poor half-breed wife is suffering from acute alcoholism and is not expected to live. Even as I write, an Indian medicine man is beating a tom-tom by her bedside in an adjoining tent to drive away the evil spirits, though I fear her system is too thoroughly impregnated with spirits to yield to such treatment. I have let the children out on shares.

Both of your cheques I have had cashed in Edmonton on the outskirts of which thriving village we are at present encamped. So far I have only bl—spent about $600 of your generous remittance, having given away most of it in the fullness of my condition to the local hotel keepers. It is a traditional custom of this country to whack up one's wealth with the hotel keepers and deposit for safe keeping in their cash registers all funds not immediately required for grub.

I have materially altered my plans as regards investing my money in stock. Being anxious to die rich, I have decided, after a prolonged pow-wow with my wife, to start in the newspaper business at Leduc, an alleged town twenty miles south of Edmonton. I am assured by Mr. J. C. Crome of the Toronto Type Foundry, who deals in printing plants, that fortune far beyond the wildest dreams of avarice can be rolled up running a country newspaper in Alberta, especially with a plant procured from his firm on easy terms.

In this business one has to move around a good deal. After busting in one town, all you have to do is to start up in another. An experienced western newspaper man tells me that an editor may safely bank on receiving the same frank, hearty, whole-souled welcome in one of these hamlets as is accorded a new preacher. The new editor is "all right all right"—until he starts in collecting the dough. The moment he evinces a longing to be paid for his ads his finish is in sight coming down the pike. It is time to start moving the plant.

My newspaper friend informs me the first issue, on account of its novelty, is always a distinct success. Your rag is pronounced by sagacious gentlemen seated on barrels of salt cod to be "a real spicy little paper." Spicy is the word invariably used in this connection. A large portion of your time is occupied laying for the rubes as they come in from the country and bracing them for subscriptions. Mr. Jawkin Hakadahl, whose advent into town the previous Tuesday with a bunch of hogs was duly chronicled, subscribes delightedly of his own accord, as does also Hank Buckley whose appearance before the J.P. on a drunk-and-disorderly charge you charitably left out, while Mr. Chug Guszaack, whose daughter's cracked voice you have lauded to the skies as being one of the most pleasing features of the Methodist choir, buys a copy to send to his brother's folks in the Bad Lands of Bruce, Ont.

The second issue is not considered quite so good as the first. The third is conned with cold, critical, fishy, carping eyes, and by the time the fourth has come

Just about the time a man gets comfortably fixed in this world it is time for him to move on to the next.[3]

out and you go hustling around to collect for the ads, you are regarded as a detriment to the town, and your paper condemned as rotten by the gentlemen on the codfish barrels.

"Collecting for the ads, eh? Well, I think I'll have to discontinue mine for the present, but perhaps I may advertise with you later on in the spring. It don't do me a d——d bit of good nohow. How much was it—two and a half? Call around same time next week. Um—yes, it does look a little like snow, blamed if it don't."

When my month is up, I contemplate opening up at Bowden (the heart Bowden) after which I expect that a month at Gleichen should about complete my journalistic aspirations and deplete my purse sufficiently to put me on the same financial plane with other country editors. By this time also I expect to have acquired the limpid radiant style of writing so necessary to meet the refined literary tastes of the St. Henkines and John Calloways, the limpids on the codfish barrels.

As soon as the plant arrives at Leduc I shall pile in and give them a hot time. I have secured the services of an excellent compositor who learned his trade in the penitentiary while doing a stretch for horse stealing, and in order to establish a firm footing with the church element I have taken the precaution to have my wife interdicted. There is still the off chance of her getting over her present attack.

Love to mother and the girls. Drink my health at Christmas. I shall drink yours right now if the medicine man has not finished the jug. That reminds me I have not heard his tom-tom for several minutes.

Your affectionate son,

Albert Buzzard-Cholomondeley.

P.S. Have just visited the adjoining tent and find that my adored wife is on the prod and has laid out the medicine man. I think she is a little better. (November 21, 1903)

- - - - - -

Fourth Letter

Fort Saskatchewan

November 3, 1903

Sir John Buzzard-Cholomondeley,

Skookingham Hall,

Skookingham, England

Dear Father:

When you open this letter at the breakfast table do not read it aloud to mother or the girls. Keep the contents to yourself as you are the leader of the family. I am at present in the direst distress and have had to postpone indefinitely my newspaper venture at Leduc.

You remember me writing to you that my half-breed wife was very ill and was being attended by an Indian medicine man who beat a tom-tom by her bedside to drive away the evil one? Well, she's dead. Her untimely death affected me deeply. So enraged did I become after brooding over the maladroit practices of the tawny Aesculapius that I determined

The things that come to the man who waits are seldom
the things he has been waiting for.[4]

to kill him. Before doing anything rash, however, I consulted a friend, one of the most distinguished bartenders in Edmonton, who promptly offered me his profound sympathy and a small flask. His advice seemed reasonable enough. He said: "Shoot him by all means, but do as the gamekeepers in the Old Country do with boys bird-nesting. Don't use shot. Put salt in your shells and you will thus both scare and hurt the brute without getting yourself into trouble."

Returning to camp I loaded up a couple of shells with salt as per advice. I also put the little old flask out of business before I mustard up courage enough to pepper the gentleman with the salt. Then I let him have it both barrels, at a range of about three feet. He dropped like a log and never came back. He was stone dead.

Then began my troubles. The coroner examined the body carefully and the jury returned a verdict of wilful murder. I explained that I had only used salt, not wishing to do other than nip him a little. "Yes," said the coroner, "that may be so, but unfortunately you used rock salt." As a matter of fact, I didn't have any table salt. I am now incarcerated in Fort Saskatchewan awaiting trial. Owing to recent events in the Police I am chained to a ring in the floor of my cell and all visitors have to talk with me through a megaphone placed for that purpose on the top of a bluff half a mile from the fort. They are taking no chances. My bartender friend sent me a box of cigars to wile away the time and the policemen

smoked them all up to make sure there were no files concealed in the wrappers. It is a strenuous life. Think of your little Bertie occupying a murderer's cell!

Dad, I must have $1,000 immediately to secure the services of a competent lawyer from Calgary. There is a famous criminal lawyer down there by the name of P. J. Nolan whom I should like to get. All the best murderers of the west employ him. The few whom he fails to get acquitted without a stain on their character are singularly successful in escaping the hangman. They get off somehow. There is no doubt but what Mr. Nolan would accept a fee of $1,000 if I can give him reasonable assurance that it is all I've got.

On one occasion, so my friend the bartender told me through the megaphone, Mr. Nolan defended a man who had killed another by filling him full of buckshot. His line of defence was that deceased came to his death through natural causes, because how could a man be expected to live with half a pound of lead in his vitals? The jury took the same view and the murderer is now leading a virtuous life and travelling with a stud horse.

Dear father, it is essential to my safety that I be immediately provided with funds to hire this lawyer. The peculiar circumstances of the case admit of none other. The balance of your last cheque has been handed over to the medicine man's family as a grief-assuager, and I have not enough money to buy seed for a canary. Should I hang, the papers will bristle with lurid descriptions of the exe-

A man who goes out to meet trouble will have a short walk.[5]

cution and shocking headlines, all of which will be copied into English papers. The name of Buzzard-Cholomondeley will become a bye-word.

"Buzzard-Cholomondeley, son of old man Cholomondeley, hanged today! Painful scenes on the scaffold!"

"The Gates of Hell ajar! Buzzard-Cholomondeley strung up for foul murder! Says he had no table salt!"

"Buzzard-Cholomondeley, the gruesome ghoul, now pushes clouds! Makes farewell speech on scaffold advising young men to keep from drink. Claims he is prepared to die."

"Buzzard-Cholomondeley expiates horrible crime on gallows. Game to the last!"

"Buzzard-Cholomondeley, the assassin, in dying speech attributes his fate to refusal of father to provide funds for lawyer! Sympathy felt for doomed man! Indignation expressed towards unnatural parent!"

"Apotheosis of Buzzard-Cholomondeley! Scion of old English family sent to Kingdom Come for Brutal Murder! Death instantaneous!"

Now, dear father, can the family afford to be everlastingly disgraced for $1,000? Cable over the money at once. Sending by mail means dangerous delay. If I can secure P. J. Nolan I am saved. If not, I am a gonner. They say he won't save a man's neck on jawbone.

Dad, I may after all have to mount the scaffold. You may harden your heart and refuse to save me, but a spirit of resigna-

tion animates my being. Alone in the world, deserted by my flesh and blood, I place my wearied head on the bosom of God and put my heart close by the heart of my heavenly Father. The evening of my life has come and I am alone. Alone I drink in the solitude of my cell. There is nothing else to drink. Oh father, understand and grasp the fact that it is only one thousand dollars that stand between me and a dishonored grave. Cable it over at once and save.

Your wretched son,
Albert Buzzard-Cholomondeley.

P.S. If you think that my general deterioration deserves death and you decide to leave me to my fate, heed my last request and send the hangman a ten-spot, asking him as a special favor to keep sober for the event. As for me, it will be the last drop I shall ever take. Goodbye and God bless you. (January 2, 1904)

Fifth Letter
Calgary, November 16, 1903

Sir John Buzzard-Cholomondeley,
Skookingham Hall,
Skookingham, England

Dear Father: Your cable to the bank at Edmonton of $1,000 has saved my bacon and the honor of the Buzzard-Cholomondeleys. I was duly acquitted of the charge of murdering the Indian doctor who attended my late lamented half-breed wife.

Money that a man has saved represents the good times he didn't have.[6]

The money arrived in the nick of time and I at once put myself in telegraphic communication with P. J. Nolan, of Calgary, asking him to hasten up right away and try my case, mentioning as a fee the sum of $500. In declining to rescue me from the jaws of death for this amount he employed some metaphorical language symbolical of the season, suggesting that I was a frost and a cheap skate, so perforce I had to cough up the "thou" straight. How he knew you had sent me a "thou" I cannot say. Be that as it may, it is to his diabolical ingenuity that I owe my life.

Local Merchant: "So you are highly educated and would like me to employ you, eh? But, my dear young man, what do you know and what can you do? Nothing? I thought so. Good day."

* * *

Mr. Nolan after looking me over carefully and talking with me on general subjects, entered a plea of insanity. The fact of my being a bloody Englishman made the task an easy one for my learned saviour. On the morning of the trial he came to my cell with a pair of very baggy pants for me to put on, also a pair of leggings and a remarkably high white collar which made my ears stick out at right angles like the topsails of a ship in distress. Then he handed me a package of abominable cigarettes, with instructions to rise at a critical moment during the trial and crave permission of the judge to smoke them in court. If asked any questions I was to start a rambling harangue about gymkhanas and describe to the jury how I once at the Calgary fair rode a hundred yards, dismounted and undressed in front of the grand stand, drank a brandy and soda, dressed again, remounted and rode back to the starting point all in a minute and a half. I followed counsel's instructions to the letter and the jury never left their seats. They decided I had a violent form of dementia and that the Asylum for the Insane at Brandon was my proper sphere.

The prospect of passing the remainder of my days in a lunatic asylum was not an alluring one, but any old thing was preferable to being hanged. Mr. Nolan expressed the fear, as he pocketed your "thou" and bade me goodbye, that I might feel a bit lonesome at first in the asylum as, from what he had learned, I would be the only Conservative lunatic who had ever been confined within its walls, and added that the name of Buzzard alone would have the effect of making me a rara avis.

The following day, in charge of a North West Mounted Policeman, I start-

Most people who are old enough to know better often wish they were young enough not to.[7]

ed for the Brandon asylum, with the machinery in my idea box turned on at full pressure. The trip to Calgary was uneventful. While waiting for the midnight flyer going east, the policeman and I strolled leisurely up and down the platform. The butt of his revolver protruded temptingly from his pocket. There was no one on the platform at that late hour, and everything was quiet. We were just turning round close by the fence of the C.P.R. gardens when, quick as thought, I whipped out his gun from his pocket, and told him there was the twinkle of a star between him and his finish. Me to the Bug House? "Na na, my bonny Jean!"

Swiftly I steered him into a labyrinth of boxcars and made him peel off his clothes and hand over uniform, boots, hat and overcoat. At the same time I took off my own togs and ordered him to put them on. Thus we exchanged raiment. I was the policeman, he the lunatic. Right

Bartender : "Oh, you're very dry and are expecting money from home and want a drink on jawbone eh ? Well, there's nothing doin'. Scoot !"

carefully did I keep him—hazed amongst the boxcars in the darkness until the express came along, and for fear of possible hitches, did not board the cars with my madman (he was mad all right) till she was moving out.

In the pockets of my new clothes I found railroad tickets, money, warrant for my, or rather his, incarceration in the Bug House, and a set of shackles. I lost no golden moments shackling my man to the seat. Of course he kicked up a tremendous row and appealed for help to the conductor and passengers—knowing I couldn't decently shoot him in the car—but ha ha! My dear old dad, I was a North West Mounted Policeman and he was an insane prisoner. The brakeman even suggested knocking him over the koko with a coupling pin to keep him quiet. Happily for me we passed through Regina in the night. It wouldn't have mattered very much anyhow, as the police at that point are located away off on the horizon, miles from town and invisible to the naked eye.

I turned over my unfortunate victim to the asylum authorities at Brandon, explaining to them his pitiful hallucination about being a policeman, and got a receipt in full for the delivery of "Albert Buzzard-Cholomondeley."

Having the policeman's return ticket and his little wad of money I thought I might as well return to Calgary where no one knows me. It did not take me long to

What has become of the old fashioned citizen who used to sleep with his pipe in his mouth and set the bed on fire?[8]

rustle a suit of civilian clothes on my arrival there. The Fort Saskatchewan authorities will no doubt attribute the constable's delay in getting back to the usual drunk and may not get uneasy for a week or two. The Brandon people certainly won't catch on, because they will lay the ravings of the hapless policeman to the hallucination I told them about. You ought to be proud to have such a brainy son in your repertoire.

Now, look here, dad. Although I may not be dead, I am dead broke. The trick I have played is sure to come out sooner or later and I must get out of here. I cannot get out without money. Cable over another hundred ponds to take me home. I shall come alone, my two children being still out on shares at Lesser Slave Lake. Cable on receipt of this letter and I shall start right away.

I was deeply distressed to learn from mother's last letter that you were suffering from an ingrowing toe nail, but hope you will soon recover and live long to be an honor to your King and country. Don't forget the hundred pounds. Love to mother and the girls.

Your affectionate son,

BERTIE

P.S. I had to pawn that fine old watch you gave me years ago, an heir loom in the family. When the hundred pounds arrives I shall redeem it. What did I get on it? As full as a goat. (January 9, 1904)

--- ---

Sixth Letter

Calgary, March 17, 1903

Sir John Buzzard-Cholomondeley,
Skookingham Hall,
Skookingham, England

Dear Father: That hundred pound you cabled over for my return home was duly received, and many thanks.

I am sorry to again disappoint you and mother and the girls, but the fact is I have at last struck a bonanza which should enable me to return to dear old Skookingham next year a comparatively rich man. This I shall explain further on.

For the first few weeks after getting back here from Brandon where I left the policeman a prisoner in the Daffy House I had to lay very low to allow my whiskers to grow. As soon as I was sufficiently bewhiskered I discreetly keyed myself up into a pleasurable Dutch-courage frame of mind and sallied up town. In the various hotels I was rather taken aback to see Reward placards out for my arrest. The fellows at the bank smiled with ill-concealed amusement when I appeared at their counter for the dough, and the manager was so tickled that he put on a loose jacket and laughed in his sleeve. They evidently regarded my recent escapade as a huge joke. Nor did they give me away, God bless 'em.

By way of further disguise I went to a tailoring establishment and got myself togged out in a harmonious arrangement of baggy pants and yellow leggings. A

When a man gets into trouble the majority of those who call to sympathise with him are only after particulars. [9]

pair of pince-nez glasses perched on the bridge of my nose assisted the tout ensemble, while a blue tie with little dots completed the color scheme. I was then a Montmorency Curzon, fresh out from Cheltenham, England. "Crossed over on the Campania—they do you very well on that boat, you know."

After carefully wetting the new clothes with some ten or twelve whiskeys and sodas, I settled my bill at the tough old joint where I had been staying and moved to the Alberta. Here I was in the thick of baggy-pantses, independent all and sublimely indifferent as to whether school kept or not. One glance at my toggery and I was put up at the Raunchers' Club.

From their conversation at the club that evening I gathered that a great scheme was on the stocks. A new institution promoted by private funds was on the tapis. By keeping my ears ajar I gathered that they were contemplating hiring a large building on the outskirts of the town and turning it into a Dipsomaniac Asylum. One sigh enough for me. My chance had come and I rose to go.

Next day I casually ran into one of these gentlemen at the Alberta and explained my abrupt departure the night before on the ground that I was afraid they were talking private business.

"Oh dear no!" he laughed pleasantly. "It wasn't so awfully private. By the way what, might I ask, is the nature of your business? Don't think me rude."

"Not at all, sir. Before coming out here I was for a number of years super-intendent of an Inebriates' Home near Cheltenham."

"What?" he cried excitedly. "Inebriate Manager of a Home? The very man we're looking for. Come along with me—hold on, we better have a drink first. By gum, this is lucky! No no, this is on me."

The other gentlemen interested were delighted beyond measure that such an experienced handler of drunks had turned up so opportunely, and not a moment was lost in leasing a building for a term of years, furnishing it in hospital fashion with private wards and installing me as manager with full powers. Arrangements were made with a doctor for two daily visits, and a couple of husky male nurses capable of holding down the most obstreperous patients were engaged.

The location of the building is unrivalled, being up on the hill beyond the Mission Bridge, contiguous to two cemeteries and not too far from Irish's celebrated sporting resort. The institution was appropriately opened by the directors with an uproarious carousal which lasted two days.

A day or two after this carousal I inadvertently went off on a rather big lone spree at Irish's charming bungalow and by a singular coincidence was conveyed as the first patient into the institution of which I was acting-manager. It did look rather bad, certainly, but the directors simply roared with laughter and thought it a capital joke. I kept the attendants dodging bricks for a few days, but by the end of the week I was well again.

The man who would give his last dollar seldom possesses a nickel. [10]

Some of the directors having balked at the suggestive title of "Dipsomaniac Asylum," we cast around for a suitable and attractive name for the place. Some were for Rosenook Manor, others Least Dell, Pleasant View, Sunnyside, Château Boozenac and so forth, but our choice prevailed. The name decided upon was Tanglefoot Hall.

Tanglefoot Hall soon became the best patronized institution in the country. I adopted the Keeley plan of giving the patients all they wanted to drink as soon as they arrived, a scheme which added greatly to our popularity and attracted slobsters from far and near. Another of my plans was to humor the patients. If any of them expressed a desire to walk over to Irish's and whoop things up I accompanied them and joined heartily in their frolic.

The doctor is a most genial fellow, though he got rather crusty the other day when he drove out and found Tanglefoot Hall empty, all the patients, as well as myself, being down to Irish's holding an impromptu smoking concert. The attendants were on duty all right, but sound asleep and snoring away in the best beds. The doctor warned me that half the patients were liable to die on his hands if I did not follow his instructions, but I retorted that they would outwit him yet and keep on living. Cappie Smart, the undertaker, came out one Sunday, looked around and left with a broad grin. What he was grinning about, the Lord only knows.

Our woman cook remained one day and we now have a man cook. If he keeps on as he has been doing we shall soon have him as a patient.

The institution received something of a scare the other day when a man from the country mistook Tanglefoot Hall for the Holy Cross Hospital. He had the smallpox and was to be pitted. This gave everyone connected with the establishment an excellent excuse to kill any possible germs with alcohol, with the result that the evening wound up in a blast of revelry. The only real mishaps we have had up to date is one man who leapt out of a top storey window and broke his neck, another who cut his throat with a razor while the attendant was absent for a few minutes shooting craps with the cook, and some half dozen gentlemen who died of the jim-jams straight. So you see we are not doing so badly after all.

In addition to my salary I receive liberal subsidies from the wholesale liquor dealers down town, from the druggists, from Irish and from the undertaker. In a year I expect to be able to return home and settle down. I must close for the present as I hear a patient running about the corridor yelling like a Comanche Indian. He is probably seeing things.

Give my love to mother and the girls and remember me kindly to the dear old Rector. It is not unlikely that I may take holy orders when I return to England as I am naturally of a religious bent of mind and torn with anxiety for the moral welfare of mankind.

If you would like to buy a few shares in Tanglefoot Hall Co. Limited, send me a

It's awfully hard for the average man to look in a mirror and believe he was once a cute baby.[11]

couple of hundred pounds and I will get you in on the ground floor.

Your affectionate son,

BERTIE

P.S. I open this letter to mention that the president of this institution has just been brought in with a horrible attack of the Willies. He is in bad shape and the buzzards are wheeling in the sky. Don't forget to address my letters to "J. Montmorency Curzon, Tanglefoot Hall." (February 13, 1904)

- - - - -

Seventh Letter

Calgary, May 2nd, 1903

Sir John Buzzard-Cholomondeley,
Skookingham Hall,
Skookingham, England

Dear Father: I regret to state that the Tanglefoot Hall company, Limited, is busted. The patients, male nurses and other hired help, including the cook, have been removed to the hospital for treatment, all suffering more or less from a peculiarly violent form of the jumps.

The directors have tried to fix the blame for failure on me, on your Bertie, though they are ready to admit that I gave them a hot run for their money. From the auditor's report on the first month—indeed, we only ran a month—it appears that there was a ridiculous disparity between the bills for solids and the bills for liquids. Our charge for patients was $1.50 per diem, medicine, tapering-

off dope and little extras being thrown in gratis. The accounts showed that each patient must have put at least half a gallon of bug-juice out of business every day he was under treatment at the Hall. This seems to me to be a gross exaggeration, especially as regards the last week or ten days when the mortality was frightful, there being hardly any of our original patients left alive at all. There could not possibly have been over twelve gallons licked up during the last week by the survivors, unless the cook was trying to establish for himself a new record.

I told the directors frankly that my de-alcoholicing process may have been faulty, but that the dubious quality of the dope and the high altitude may have had something to do with it. An error gracefully acknowledged is a victory won.

The press and the public, however, have been giving vent to rather coarse expression of indignation, but I humbly bend my head to the storm and put my trust in the Lord. Censure is the tax a man pays for being eminent.

The couple of hundred pounds you sent out to invest in shares in the Tanglefoot Hall company, Limited, will come in handy for another scheme I have on foot. There is nothing bogus about this scheme. It is perfectly practicable. I propose going in for pupil-farming on a ranche adjacent to Calgary which I think I can rent at a nominal figure for a few years. My pupils will be young Englishmen of the greenest color obtainable. If I can get half a dozen sufficiently

Fewer flowers for the dead and more flour to the needy living might help some.[12]

green and possessed of sufficient long green I should be independently rich inside of a couple of years.

The wholesale liquor dealers of Calgary have promised to give me all the time I want until I get the pupils fairly started. "Excelsior" is my motto. Instead of remaining at the bottom of the ladder some men crawl farther down. But not so your Bertie. Upward and onward is the slogan for Albert.

The remuneration I shall receive from my pupils will be what is left over after Fred Adams and the other Calgary mixocographers, to say nothing of the wholesale houses and Diamond Dolly, have got through with them. The pay, no matter what it is, will be absurdly inadequate when one considers the fool questions I shall have to answer.

Several young English bloods are expected out here any time within the next few weeks with the intention of learning raunching, and it is with a view to nailing some of them to the cross that I have formulated this brilliant scheme. I think they will like my style, as I take mine straight. By way of evidence of my own

"Aw, me cheque's arrived Give me a brandy and soda and be demmed quick about it."

* * *

prosperity as attained in the west I can point with pride to my fashionable knickerbockers and paid-up meal ticket and assure them with pardonable pride that I started in life a bare-footed boy. The dolts will probably not reflect that it was extremely unlikely that I should be born with shoes and stockings on.

Cappie Smart, our genial undertaker, who made quite a stake out at the Tanglefoot Hall venture and has since made me a present of a box of cigars (El Peukos), is sanguine as to my success with the pupil-farmers. At least he said I ought to make quite a killing.

I trust, dear father, that you admire my nerve. Tomorrow I am to see the man who has the ranche to let. I understand that there is a commodious shack on the place and a little old barn capable of holding three or four cayuses of not over 15 hands. Also a small stack of hay in the corral. He has agreed to sell me a cute little buckboard guaranteed to hold two occupants, two demijohns, a fair sized keg and two cases of bottled beer, together with a couple of

We admire a good talker who knows when to shut up.[13]

nice gentle ponies which go well in harness and have been trained to stop dead whenever a man falls out of the rig.

I am gathering together a number of sporting pictures with which to adorn the walls of the shack and make the pupils feel at home over their toddy of an evening—pictures of Fred Archer the jockey, Harry Beasley the gentleman steeplechase rider, Persimmon the Derby winner, Mrs. Langtry, Charles Peace the murderer, Lord Charles Bereaford, Father O'Flynn winning the Grand National, the battle between Tom Sayers and Heenan, Nellie Farren of burlesque fame, Florence St. John, the late Marquis of Salisbury, Gladstone, Arthur Balfour, Bob Fitzsimmons, Joseph Chamberlain, Whittaker Wright, Lord Roberts, Dan Leno, the late Charles Spurgeon, Ernest Cashel and a facsimile of his Last Message and any other suitable pictures I can lay my hands on.

None of the land is broke yet, but it is not the land I am going to break on this farm. Give me time and a pupil with rich parents and I will make the pomp of cattle barons ridiculous. When the relief expeditions begin to arrive two years hence to take my pupils home I ought to be on Easy Street.

Society has not taken me up here yet. The ladies are very exclusive and strangers must be "just so" or take a back seat. As usual I had to put my foot in it first clatter out of the box by unintentionally offending one of the worthiest dames in town. She had been telling me about her daughter's unfortunate tendency to weep at a moment's notice over the most trifling mishap and had asked my advice as to how to keep back the tears. All I said was "Dam her eyes." It was an unfortunate mode of expressing myself and I was led back to the paddock.

Well, dad, this is all at present. Next letter I hope to be able to tell you all about my pupil-farming venture. I shall use your two hundred pounds to the best advantage, you may depend. The p.f. is the greatest get-rich-quick scheme I've struck yet. Love to mother and the girls. Your affectionate son,

BERTIE

P.S. The unfortunate policeman I left in the Brandon Lunatic Asylum is now doing a stretch of thirty days in the guard room up at Fort Saskatchewan. He puts in most of his mornings moving around the barracks yard with a wheelbarrow and shovel, cleaning up. The afternoons he puts in sawing cord wood. I feel sorry for the poor fellow. (February 20, 1904)

Tenth Letter

Calgary, Alberta
March 17, 1904

Sir John Buzzard-Cholomondeley,
Skookingham Hall,
Skookingham, England

My Dear Dad: When last I wrote you I was running the Black Cobra Distillery full blast in conjunction with my friend

---

A man's deafness has reached the limit when he can no longer hear a noise like a skirt.[14]

Courtenay. Since then I have sold out my interest and am at present worth all of $50,000. In consequence of this pleasant accession of wealth I am resolved to branch out and return on a visit to the ancestral home in England crowned with laurels and with honors thick upon me. With this laudable aim in view it is my intention to enter the Dominion Parliament, running on the Prohibition ticket. Money being plentiful, my chances are excellent.

As soon as the committees of the two great parties learned that I was willing to spend $20,000 on getting elected, they waited upon me and besought me with tears in their eyes to run on their respective sides. I told them they could not play me for a Cochrane.

The prohibition ticket I am running on is pretty sure to prove a winner, as the liquid I propose prohibiting in this case is water. The hotels will pull for me as one man and the local sports have promised to stand by. My committee is a singularly influential one, being composed of all the bartenders in town, with Fred Adams as chairman. Every man who steps into a hotel for a shot is presented with a quart of Black Cobra, with "Vote for Buzzard-Cholomondeley" blown in the bottle, together with a little circular containing my Electoral address. This latter effusion runs as follows:

Fellow Citizens: In soliciting your suffrages I beg to state that my attitude on all public matters will be one of unswerving adherence to my own individual interests. I believe in a public man getting out of it all there is in it. Let us be honest in our villainy. What is the use of me telling you that I will only stand for clean government when you know and I know that if the opportunity presents itself for making a stake at the expense of the people I will drop on it like a bee on a posy? As a good straightforward grafter I expect to make my mark in the House. I shall always be on the side of the government, so that if any horrible scandal should arise, a carefully selected commission of inquiry will whitewash me and make me clean. You will lose nothing and I shall be laying up treasure on earth that neither the moths nor the flies will corrupt.

I am a Prohibitionist. What I propose prohibiting is the reckless use of water. Its effect on the health, habits and moral character of the community is disastrous. Look at the interminable series of typhoid cases with which our hospitals are filled from month to month, people dying who never died before, young men and maidens who have not reached the middle arch of life passing away and going down to a watery grave. It is sad to contemplate the distressing results of the steady tippling of germ-laden water. Every sample of the horrid stuff shows the presence of colon bacilli and an excessive number of other bacteria, including pollywogs. If men would only confine themselves to a good stiff rasping old whiskey like Black Cobra, Calgary would be happier and better today. Any

The man who is always right is always a nuisance.[15]

germ that can live after a gulp of Black Cobra has struck it, must be a corker.

To further these principles I am in favor of keeping the bars open all night. By this innovation I expect to gain the gratitude of the drouthy voter and of the unfortunate man with the shake-shakes in need of a drink who roams the streets at 2 a.m. looking for relief. I propose erecting a beer fountain at my own expense in the C.P.R. gardens and having it playing there all the time instead of the band. Although my business connection with Black Cobra has been severed, I can still recommend it to the earnest Christian as a means of grace and as a hope of glory. It touches the spot.

I am in favor of abolishing the office of license inspector altogether and of appointing a water analyst with full authority to prosecute those responsible for distributing typhoid dope throughout the town. The young man alleged to have died last week from drinking Black Cobra confessed at the last moment that he always took water for a chaser. Rash youth! Perhaps, after all, he is better off in hell, where his opportunities will be but slight for indulging his unnatural craving for water. Had he lived, he might have grown up to be a burglar or a member of the City Council. You never can tell about these things.

I am in favor of rustling on the range, if you can get away with it. Every appeal made to me by horse-thieves to have their sentences quashed or mitigated will be promptly attended to. Alibis will be provided for train-robbers, thugs and murderers at the bureau of the prohibition association free of charge, and a bottle of Black Cobra presented to each and every constituent tangled up in a woman scrape. Doubtful voters get two bottles of Cobra instead of one. Ballot stuffers will get three.

On this platform I appeal for your support. If I prove recreant to my trust and false to my promises by becoming too darned immaculate, I shall be willing to resign. But there is no danger. I leave myself in your hands. Call at the committee rooms and get a bottle of Black Cobra.

Respectfully,

A. B.-C.

Perhaps, father, you think I am crazy to issue a brutally frank address such as this, but, believe me, the rank and file of the voting public in Canada have reached such a pitch of exasperation towards the smooth flannel-mouths who pose as saints on the hustings and turn out to be nothing more than common-place sinners when in office, that they are ready to welcome with open arms a man who is honest enough to announce beforehand that he is not seeking their suffrages for his health.

In addition to the allurements of my platform, the glamour of my wealth and the prospective tapping of my barrel will gain me hosts of friends. Money talks without stammering in this country. Money is the predominating factor in

The good don't die young at all. They simply outgrow it.[16]

western life and rules the situation. We have no aristocratic titles or patents of nobility—no stars and garters—and hence the money standard lends itself the more readily to the uses of the time as the simplest, if not the most natural, of all standards.

Although the church folk may rail at the devastation wrought by Black Cobra, yet the fact of my having made $50,000 out of it ensures me profound consideration at their hands and a warm welcome within the sacred circle. The power of money in the west is steadily augmenting. As the country gets populated the opportunities multiply. There are more people to do up.

Graft is the rule. Boodle is the stake. Were I to tell the people that I disapproved of that sort of thing and would not tolerate it in others, they would instinctively distrust me. So my Bismarckian tactics of artless frankness will win me the day. They remember their folly in returning Frank Oliver to parliament as an independent. That gentleman now is one of Sifton's staunchest henchmen, votes and speaks contrary to the mandates of his constituents, and, when protested with, grimly says "What are you going to do about it?" When I get in my fine work at Ottawa on the rake-off pile I shall not be ashamed to face my constituents later on, seeing that permission to steal and sell my vote at every opportunity was incorporated in my platform.

Your average reformer agrees that the devil must be fought with fire, but the rule in Canada is for the reformer, once in power, to set up for a devil on his account. I shall side in the House with whichever party is in power. The party in power is always the defender of rogues, because most of the clever rogues stand in with the party in power.

That beer fountain in the C.P.R. park I shall open just one week before election day and give the people to understand that I am presenting it to the city by way of perpetuating my memory, keeping it green and so forth. They will think the fountain is to go on for ever, like the brook, but the morning after the election no more beer will be forthcoming. Should remonstrances reach me I shall hand them out their own Canadian medicine as used with effect by all duly elected members—"Ha! Now you can go to blazes. You have elected me—there is no drawing back—I'll do just as I darned please for the next six years and you can go chase yourselves. No? Well, what are you going to do about it?"

So, father, you may expect a visit from me some time in the fall when you can introduce me to all your friends as the Member for Calgary. Love to mother and the girls. How did you like the case of Black Cobra I sent you? By the way, I saw by the *London Times* that a physician had been hurried from London to your bedside at Skookingham Hall. I hope it was nothing serious.

Your affectionate son,

BERTIE . (April 30, 1904)

Most men are ambitious to do those they have been done by.[17]

CHAPTER TEN

The Most Unfortunate of Men

In which your loyal correspondent regales the masses with the picaresque exploits of Peter J. McGonigle, hard-luck editor of the **Midnapore Gazette.**

> "Attempts to locate the Garden of Eden near Midnapore has some justification in the fact that Peter J. McGonigle, editor of the *Midnapore Gazette,* has the snakes."
>
> —*Eye Opener,* August 12, 1911

Once in a great while the reading public discovers a personality whose exploits burst forth as clear & fresh as sunrise on the prairies, whose life has the compelling grip & urgency of true genius. But chances are they prefer reading about a hapless schlub like Peter Jonah McGonigle, editor of the *Midnapore Gazette.* Wise to a good thing, Bob Edwards never wasted an opportunity to report his fictional peer's misadventures. Now: you, too, can—

☞ *Rejoice!* as McGonigle gives the keynote address to the Pan-Boozological Congress of Demented Bartenders!

☞ *Squirm!* as McGonigle extracts rats from his pants!

☞ *Stare at your shoe!* as McGonigle's easily distracted dog scandalizes a widow's reputation!

☞ *Emit noises of surprise!* when McGonigle is fatally felled[1] by an ivory-handled pistol!

☞ *React!* at McGonigle's exhumation & spectacular resurrection![2]

Alas, we shall never again see the likes of Peter J. McGonigle, a realist who never abandoned his ideals & an idealist who wasn't actually real.[3] Gone but not etc.

---

[1] For the intriguing backstory behind Edwards's decision to kill off his popular character, consult *Eye Opener Bob.*

[2] As this chapter makes clear, McGonigle's second coming was short-lived. Again, consult *Eye Opener Bob* for details.

[3] Not everyone got the joke. In the December 21, 1912 *Eye Opener,* Edwards recalled how "lots of readers thought that there really was such a person as Peter J. McGonigle, editor of the *Midnapore Gazette,* and often expressed themselves as appalled at our disrespectful manner of talking about him. Indeed the London (Eng.) *Morning Leader,* which somehow got hold of a copy of the *Eye Opener* and wrote a column criticism on it (date Dec. 21, 1907), commented on the brutal frankness with which a brother journalist (McGonigle) was treated and added that 'this sort of thing would not be tolerated in England for a moment!'"

The many friends of Peter J. McGonigle, editor of the *Midnapore Gazette*, will be glad to learn that he was able to leave the hospital this week. The delayed Christmas number of the *Midnapore Gazette* will appear next Saturday. Mr. McGonigle desires us to contradict the rumor that he attempted to cut his throat while in the horrors. He received a slight abrasion on the face from cut glass while springing through the window of his private ward while pursued by an imaginary herd of rogue elephants, but the story that he tried to sever his jugular with the penknife he cuts his tobacco with, is a canard. Mr. McGonigle is thinking of getting in a linotype machine as an addition to his already extensive plant down at Midnapore. His job department is already very up to date especially when the fonts are not pied. (January 12, 1906)

As banquets and luncheons seem to be the order of the day in Calgary, we offer no apology for presenting an absolutely correct report of a pleasant function which was pulled off last week.

The banquet tendered by the Calgary board of trade to Mr. Peter McGonigle on the occasion of his release from the Edmonton penitentiary, where he had spent some time trying to live down a conviction of horse stealing, proved a great success. Quite a number of prominent citizens were present, and, with Mayor Emerson in the chair, the songs, toasts and speeches passed off with all the éclat available at such short notice.

Letters of regret were read from Lord Strathcona, Earl Grey, Premier Rutherford, Charles Wagner, Joseph Seagram, Josh Calloway, W. Callahan, Col. G. C. Porter, W. F. Maclean, Joseph Fahy, Rev. John A. McDougall, Con. Leary and others.

Lord Strathcona's letter reads as follows:

John Emerson, Esq., Mayor, Calgary.

Dear Jack,—You don't mind me calling you Jack, do you, old cock? I regret exceedingly that I shall be unable to attend the McGonigle banquet at Calgary, but, believe me, my sympathies go out to your honored guest. The name of Peter McGonigle will ever stand high in the roll of eminent confiscators. Once, long ago, I myself came near achieving distinction in this direction when I performed some dexterous financing with the Bank of Montreal's funds. In consequence, however, of C.P.R. stocks going up instead of down, I wound up in the House of Lords instead of Stoney Mountain.
Believe me, dear Jack,
Yours very truly,
Strathcona

Joseph Seagram, M.P., wrote:

Dear Mr. Mayor,—Though unable to be with you in the flesh, my spirit is no doubt with you in sufficient quantities. Wishing Mr. McGonigle all luck in his

Every man thinks he is more important than his neighbor.[1]

next venture.

Yours truly,

Joseph Seagram

The sumptuous repast, of which we give the menu, was provided by Messrs. Wing and Kidney, the well-known caterers.

Soup

Bouillon Macaulaise

Skilly à la Matt

Fish

Suckers à la Hanson

Henglish Erring à la Hemerson

Entrees

Calf's head without brains, Commission style

Muttonhead Cutlets à la city council

Commission Croquettes out on the bias

Boiled

Owls, aldermanic variety

Roasts

Herald

Albertan

Eye Opener

Dessert

Assorted Fruit

Receptions glacees à la Grey

Kitheth à la Gillith

Cafe Chantant, with or without

Tea Deum

As the walnuts and the prunes and the wine came on, cigars were lit and the mayor rose to propose the toast of the king. His Honor expressed his entire sat-isfaction with His Majesty's reign. Indeed, he expressed a very high opinion of His Majesty and thought that he was as good a king as they could possibly get for the money. (Hear, hear.) He did not think the time yet ripe for the British Empire to be ruled by a commission. They had tried it in Calgary and it was found to be a fail-ure. He was quite agreeable that the king should remain on the throne till the end of his term. (Loud cheers.)

The toast of the Army, Navy and Reserve Forces was ably responded to by Major Charles Fisher, speaker of the Alberta House. In graphic language he sketched the careers of great soldiers from Julius Caesar down to Major Walker, outlined the strategy of Napoleon and pointed out his tactical blunders, criticized in caustic language Nelson's clumsy handling of his ships at the battle of Trafalgar, showed up to the merciless light of day the deficiencies in the military training of Von Moltke, and wound up with a glowing eulogy of the Alberta Light Horse and a fervid appeal for an open canteen. The major resumed his seat amidst thunderous applause.

Mr. R. J. Hutchings, in replying to the toast of the Great West, said: "Mr. Chairman, I presume this toast has spe-cial reference to the firm with which I have been connected more or less along these lines for the past number of years. I must say, Mr. Chairman, that we have endeavored to the best of our capacity to show what is in us and we hope to keep our-our-our shoulder to the wheel along

A man is never ridiculous for what he is, but for assuming to be what he isn't.[2]

those lines. (Hear, hear.) The country around us is developing fast. I might almost say that it is developing at a great rate. (Loud applause.) The government at Edmonton is constructing long distance telephone lines throughout the province and we hope—we trust—nay, we propose, to develop our business along those lines. (Cheers.) I am proud to say that the guest of the evening is a most remarkable man and endowed with a marvellous sense of discrimination. Even in the moment of abstraction, when he took the horse, he selected one of our magnificent sets of single harness from the owner's stable and, having secured the lines, removed the animal along those lines. (Cheers.) I earnestly trust that Mr. McGonigle, whose pallid countenance and general appearance show the effects of his residence in Edmonton, will soon fatten up and be able to resume his chosen avocation along those lines. (Hear, hear.) Before sitting down, Mr. Chairman, I might perhaps be permitted to say that if, as has been suggested, a company is to be formed to harness Kananaskis Falls,—er—might I suggest that they look in on our firm before going elsewhere?" (Loud and prolonged cheering.)

Mr. C. W. Bowley, in response to loud cries, obliged with his great song, "Ye

P. J. responding to an invitation to have a drink

Banks and Brays," and was loudly applauded.

The chairman, Mayor Emerson, on rising to propose the toast of Our Guest, was greeted with vociferous applause.

"Gentlemen, I am 'eartily pleased to be with you this evening to endeavor, if possible, to liven things up a bit. ('Ear, 'ear! and cries of 'Put him out!') My duties as mayor of this great city are sometimes difficult. As is my custom, I 'ad intended to read a little address to our guest, but Gillies refused to write one for me. 'Owever, 'ere goes for a few extempore remarks. ('Stay with it!' 'Put him out!' 'Shut up!') Although not as a rule a believer in a third term, yet, since learning that I am to be succeeded by either Mr. Clifford Jones or Mr. R. J. Stuart, my views on the subject have very materially changed.

"I have frequently, in the dear old mother country which we all love so well (loud and prolonged cheers), as well as in the North-West, shaken 'ands with royalty, but, gentlemen, I 'ave never forgotten the kindly words of friendliness which was spoken to me by 'Is Royal 'Ighness, Prince Harthur of Connaught, when he grasped my 'and at the station and said, 'John, you are the limit.' (Cheers.) Only the hother day at the magnificent reception which me and Gillies got up for

The man who takes himself seriously may be considered a joke by others.[3]

Early Grey, although I tried to look as mild as possible, I overheard 'Is Excellency remark to 'is missus that I was pretty fierce. (Roars of laughter.) It is simple marks of condescension such as these that endear us common folk to royalty. ('Have another prune, John!' 'Shut up!' 'Give him a show!' 'Rats!')

"As you are all aware, our guest has for some time past been most hospitably entertained by His Majesty at his Edmonton shooting box, where he had the honor of meeting our talented and popular fellow-townsman, Mr. Callahan, who is sought after everywhere, and young Mr. Wilson, the Macleod chicken fancier. This district is splendidly adapted for gentlemen of Mr. McGonigle's pursuits, and owing to the persistent reduction of the police force he can conduct his business without serious molestation. A the poet says:

I knew by the smoke that so gracefully curled,
From out the green coulee that a rustler was near,
And I said, if there's peace to be found in this world,
The 'eart that is 'umble may 'ope for it 'ere."

(Tremendous cheers.)

Mr. McGonigle's rising was the signal for a loud and vociferous outburst of applause. It was fully ten minutes before the guest of the evening, who was visibly affected by the warmth of his reception,

was allowed to proceed. On quiet being restored, Mr. McGonigle proceeded to thank those present for their cordial greeting, and said that owing to the many kindnesses which had been shown him that afternoon he felt entirely too full to express his appreciation of the honor done him. ("Good boy!" "Stay with it!") He was willing to let the dead past bury its dead. The horse in question had died shortly after he was parted from it. As a matter of fact, he had been working for a dead horse for a number of years. (Applause.) Had it not been for the ignorance of his lawyer he might have been acquitted, for the horse he stole was not a horse at all, but a mare. This point was entirely overlooked at the trial. It was a horse on him, anyhow.

The speaker paid a high tribute to the hospitality of his Edmonton host, Mr. McCauley, whom he was proud to see there that evening, though he lamented that in spite of the number of bars on his premises there was nothing of an enlivening nature to drink. They were sorry to lose Mr. Callahan from their pleasant little house party. His suite of rooms, however, were being prepared for the long-expected visit of Mr. Philipp Wagner, the distinguished Galician financier.

Mr. McGonigle could not close without making a pathetic reference to the gross partiality of the trial judge, who absolutely ignored his proposition to return the horse and say no more about it. He would ask the company to charge

A man could learn a great many things if he didn't imagine that he already knew them.[4]

their glasses and drink a silent toast to the memory of the dead horse. (Prolonged cheering.)

Mr. Matt McCauley of Edmonton, being called upon for a song, obliged the company with "Abide with Me," which he rendered with deep feeling in a rich staccato voice, which would be none the worse of a little sandpapering. Mr. Frank Wrigley played the accompaniment.

Mr. C. W. Rowley, manager of the Canadian Bank of Commerce and president of the board of trade, in replying to the toast of Frenzied Finance said: "Mr. Chairman and gentlemen, in my capacity as manager of the Canadian Bank of Commerce and president of the board of trade I have developed great faith in the future of this particular district. Yet, Mr. Chairman and gentlemen, I must admit that had Mr. H. Byron Walker, my chief in the Canadian Bank of Commerce, seen fit to send me to conduct a branch of the Canadian Bank of Commerce at Jackfish Bay on the bleak north shore, I should naturally have shown the same faith in the agricultural possibilities of that as yet undeveloped district. (Loud cheers.) I have also great faith in the Canadian Bank of Commerce and its manager, and I would caution the public against doing business anywhere else than with us.

"As president of the board of trade I devote a large portion of my time to drawing the attention of the eastern provinces and the northern states to the C.P.R. irrigation ditch, thus creating the healthy impression that nothing can grow here except on land irrigated from this ditch. (Hear, hear.) It is eminently desirable that people from abroad should be made to believe that this country is as dry as a bone, because so many newcomers dislike a damp climate and the sale of the C.P.R. lands adjacent to the ditch is of paramount importance to the company. (Loud cheers.) Every visitor to Calgary is driven out to the ditch. No visitor has escaped yet. The board of trade has made a specialty of showing off this ditch to every bunch of eastern and American newspaper men that come along, in order that the main feature of their published descriptions of the Calgary district may be set forth in large type as "The Arid Lands of Alberta Saved by a Benevolent C.P.R. Irrigation System." (Vociferous cheering.) Our rate of interest in the Canadian Bank of Commerce will compare favorably with that of any other financial institution in the city and the clearing house returns furnish ample evidence of our increasing popularity. To our great president, the illustrious philanthropist George A. Cox, as well as myself, may be attributed the astonishing success of the Canadian Bank of Commerce.

"As regards the guest of the evening, whom we are assembled 'to have the pleasure to meet' tonight, I can only say that I shall have him driven out to have a look at the ditch in the morning." (Prolonged cheering.)

The chairman here called upon Messrs. Hiebert and Robertson, the sweet warblers, for a song. They cheerfully

Every man has an idea, or has had, that he is either clever or good-looking.[5]

complied with the well-known duet, "Oh, That We Two Were Haying," after which Mr. Robertson in response to the encore, sang "Okotoks, The Gem of the Ocean."

Alderman Stuart, in replying to the toast of the City Police, said that he had become a prominent citizen mainly through the efforts of Lougheed and Bennett in securing his election to the city council. It had been said that honesty was the best policy, but he believed that the twenty-year payment policy issued by his company was by far and away the best. As chairman of the police committee he had deemed it his duty to convince the members of the police force of the necessity of insuring with him, and he had already succeeded in frightening several of the newer and greener members into taking out policies. (Cheers.) He had also scared the life out of the two young lady typewriters at the city hall who were afraid of losing their $40 jobs by incurring his aldermanic displeasure, and had bulldozed them into taking out policies in his company. (Hear, hear, and laughter.) He flattered himself that he had succeeded in insuring all who could not afford to quarrel with him.

This city hall graft was invaluable to a man in his line, and he was going to have himself elected to another term in order to help along his insurance business. Indeed, he hoped to be their next mayor. (Roars of laughter.) He thought that office would give him a wider field for butting in.

In conclusion, Alderman Stuart stated that he had much pleasure in announcing that the guest of the evening had decided to take out an accident policy in his company in case at any future time he might again be placed horse de combat. (Applause.)

A song, "If I Were Only Long Enough, A Sodjer I Would Be," by Joseph Hicks of Macleod, elicited great enthusiasm and he was forced to give his great Shakespearian recitation, "Anthony's address to a Macleod jury."

The proceedings were thereafter brought to a close with "God Save the King" and three cheers for Peter McGonigle, the guest of the evening. (October 6, 1906)

A pretty wedding took place last night at the home of the bride's parents, the contracting parties being Peter J. McGonigle and Miss Iphilenin B. Johnson. The ceremony took place in the drawing-room which was decorated with chrysanthemums and ferns. The bride looked sweet and graceful in her wedding gown of white chantilly lace and open work hosiery. The veil was arranged over a coronet of orange blossoms, and she carried a bouquet of white roses. The groom was attired in an elegant jag and reacted roars of laughter at the dejenuer. (November 10, 1906)

Mrs. Peter McGonigle, wife of Peter McGonigle, had the misfortune to tread

You can't reform a man by telling him that he ought to be as good as you are.[6]

on an axe with her bare foot while hanging clothes on a line, and she will have to hobble more or less for a month. Dr. Welch, of Okotoks, who was sent for, says that if she had fallen she might have cut her throat. (August 25, 1906)

Editor McGonigle, of the *Midnapore Gazette*, took a run up to town last week to have his horoscope taken by McEwen, the magico hypnotic expert. Mr. McGonigle is very superstitious, for a drinking man. McEwen took the horoscope all right, but made a lot of excuses about delaying the delivery thereof until after he had left town. Since McGonigle has returned to Midnapore and McEwen gone to Edmonton, we have received a copy of the horoscope. McGonigle has not seen it yet.

When McGonigle sees this he will be very wrathy, but it is a true horoscope,

nevertheless. Science talks. McEwen returns east by the C.N.R. (January 26, 1907)

Peter J. McGonigle's feelings have been ruffled. He drove out into the country last week to gin up some of his delinquent subscribers. The first house he struck was told by the old woman that Bill was not to be disturbed on any account, as he was busy reading something of the greatest importance.

"Ha, ha!" cried Peter, genially, "the *Midnapore Gazette*, I suppose."

"No, no such rot as that. He's reading his new farmer's almanac from the signs of the zodiac to the sarsaparilla ad on the last page."

"23 for mine," sighed Peter, as he turned homeward. (February 23, 1907)

The editor of the *Midnapore Gazette* ran out of type last week and wired Sam Hodgson of the *Okotoks Times* to borrow a few W's and T's. Sam, who has had dealings with Mr. McGonigle, replied: "You can have a whole case. So long as you don't want to borrow any X's or V's everything is all right. Have a drink on the *Times*." (March 23, 1907)

The Editor of the *Midnapore Gazette* is mourning because the royal and ancient borough of Midnapore is so darned small that he cannot build up a great newspaper as it is his fond ambition to do. He is seriously thinking of moving his plant to

If a man is ignorant he may learn, but if he knows too much there is no hope for him.[7]

Calgary. Cheer up, little box car; you may be a freight shed some day. (June 15, 1907)

The editor of the *Midnapore Gazette*, of whom we have not heard for some time, is back at the old stand and as perky as ever. He denies that he broke jail. The story, he says, was manufactured out of whole cloth. As a matter of fact he got six weeks knocked off for good conduct and has papers to prove it. Mr. McGonigle states in his newspaper that he is out for the stuff from now on and won't accept subscriptions to the *Gazette* in drinks and cigars any more. His new motto is "In Rhino Veritas." We extend congratulations to our contemporary on his release and predict for him a bright future. (July 13, 1907)

P. J. McGonigle, editor of the *Midnapore Gazette*, who has just returned from attending the Presbyterian Synod at Chicago, has handed me the card of a prominent saloon-keeper of that city which makes rather good reading:

Long Winded Telephone, 4-11-44 Main
Remember the Main.
HEINEGABUBELER'S
Hot Air Kaffay
Intoxicating Liquors, Holesail and Retail.
348 State Street, Chicago

Importing agents for:
Delirium Tremens
Bug Juice
Tanglefoot
Rot Gut
Kill Me Quick
Jersey Lightning
Etc., etc.

Bank references:
Sand Bank, Sandusky, Ohio
Faro Bank, Cripple Creek, and
The Banks of the Wabash.

Our motto: "If drinking interferes with your business, quit your business." (October 4, 1907)

Peter Jonah McGonigle, B.A., the brilliant editor of the *Midnapore Gazette*, was born in the county of Huron, Ontario. His parents were very Irish. He was educated at Toronto University, where, under the careful eye of Professor McConkey, he achieved brilliant results and finally took his degree of B.A. (Boozological Artist). Mr. McGonigle decided to come west and finally settled down in Winnipeg where he was shown much attention in police circles. From Winnipeg he moved to Stoney Mountain, where he resided continuously for seven years, after which he came further west to engage in journalism. Midnapore looked good to McGonigle and here he established the famous *Midnapore Gazette*. This publication is a weekly and enjoys a large circulation. (December 7, 1907)

Mr. Peter J. McGonigle is being groomed down at Midnapore for his big campaign at the forthcoming dominion elections.

He who thinks only of himself has very little to think about.[8]

He has made arrangements with Mr. J. Young Byers, of Calgary, to run the *Gazette* during his speaking tour through the riding. Mr. McGonigle has cut out the booze and is getting down to business. His friends think he will make a strong run.

In view of the prominence which Mr. McGonigle has suddenly attained through his determination to run as an independent Conservative in the Calgary district, it may interest the public to read some extracts from last week's issue of his stirring weekly, the *Midnapore Gazette*.

"Mr. John Googlund, our wide awake real estate man, while driving a prospective settler over the country east of town Tuesday, fell out of the rig and was brought back to the city unconscious. The stranger whom he was driving is authority for the statement that Mr. Googlund was very drunk. The many friends of Mr. Googlund will be distressed to learn of this untoward incident,

P. J. singing "Because I Love You" at a Church Social

but hope he will soon be up and around.

"Our talented young friend, Al Hopkins, has accepted a position tending bar in Calgary. The *Gazette* predicts a bright future for Al.

"Mrs. Jeraboam Q. Slopmagulcher, the acknowledged leader of Midnapore's haut ton, gave a pink tea Thursday after-

noon. It was a delightful affair. Old Slopmagulcher, however, who had been playing freeze-out for the drinks over at the hotel all day, rolled home a couple of hours too early and lurched right into the recherche parlor, kicking over the tea table and throwing bric-a-brac at the guests. He was put to bed with difficulty and Mrs. Slop laughingly apologized to her guests, who told her not to mention it as it was of no consequence." (February 15, 1908)

P. J. McGonigle, the Midnapore journalist, is the most unfortunate of men. It appears that during the despondent stage following hard upon his last drunk Mr. McGonigle got religion and joined the church. Having a voice far louder and more raucous than any of Mr. Brodeur's St. Lawrence River foghorns, they put him into the choir and he distinguished himself the very first Sunday by nearly shattering the "Rock of Ages" into a thousand fragments. The trustees asked him to draw it mild, but as he has since been fired out of the church altogether, this makes no material difference.

There happened to be a rather pretty widow who sang contralto in the choir and Peter warmed up to her in great shape. They sang out of the same hymn

More people would go to church if it wasn't exactly the proper thing to do.[9]

book and all that sort of thing. The other fellows naturally grew a bit jealous, though they did not seriously think that an ornery-looking slob like McGonigle would have much chance with the merry widow. However, the hot running made by the celebrated editor made them not a little uneasy.

Now it must be explained that on Mondays, Tuesdays and Wednesdays, when he didn't have to write stuff for the *Gazette*, Mr. McGonigle turned an honest penny by selling sewing machines. He bethought him one evening that to try and sell a sewing machine to the widow would be an excellent excuse for calling. So between eight and nine o'clock, accompanied by his faithful dog, he knocked at the front door of the lady's residence, and, on being admitted, ordered the little dog to lie down on the porch outside and wait for him.

While he was inside doing the polite, the dog sprang down from the porch to run after a passing rig, and during the five minutes that the dog was absent Mr. McGonigle rose to say goodbye. He meandered down to the hotel to get a drink before the bar closed and then went home to bed, wondering lazily what had become of the dog.

It seems that the dog, after chasing the rig for quite a distance down the road, returned to the porch of the widow's cottage and lay down to wait for his master. He was a very faithful animal. Between five and six o'clock the next morning some Midnaporeites who had

to get up early to do their chores espied McGonigle's dog lying asleep at the widow's front door and drew their own conclusions.

Before ten o'clock it was the scandal of the town. In vain did McGonigle try to explain. In vain did the poor widow try to make the womenfolk believe in her innocence. The minister called at the *Gazette* office and cancelled the editor's membership in his church. McGonigle threatened to write the whole lot of them up, but inadvertently got drunk instead. In point of fact, there was no issue last week and it is not likely there will be another for a month, as this drunk looks as if it was going to be a prolonged one. The widow has "gone east to visit friends," and the confounded little dog may be seen at any hour of the day lying outside the bar-room door of the Nevermore Hotel waiting for his master. Mr. McGonigle threatens to move his plant to Okotoks. (May 2, 1908)

All things conspire to the glory of Alberta. The Hon. Peter J. McGonigle of Midnapore has consented to act as judge of the baby show at the dominion fair. If Mr. McGonigle proves as excellent a judge of babies as he is of whiskey, the mothers of this great land will have no kick coming. (May 16, 1908)

"What are your views on currency," asked a stranger of McGonigle, the sage of Midnapore.

Don't boast of your credit. No man's credit is as good as his money.[10]

"Mostly sad and reminiscent," was the reply, "but if it's a drink you're after, I've got a shillin'." (May 16, 1908)

We are indebted to the pen of our dear old college chum and journalistic confrere, Peter J. McGonigle of the *Midnapore Gazette*, for the following account of the grand opening of the boozorium:

My Dear Bob—

You often told me I would wind up in the bughouse if I kept on drinking Midnapore whiskey, and I guess you're right. I was kidnapped last Saturday night after a high old time with the boys, and carted over the hills and far away until I reached this place, which, from what I can gather, is the kind of place you used to talk about, except that they call it a boozorium. The morning after the day I arrived the formal opening of the institution took place, and it certainly was a daisy. In honor of the occasion all restrictions were removed and booze was flowing far more copiously than water does through the C.P.R. ditch. We had Scotch, rye, brandy, Tom gin, square gin, beer and lots of other stuff, and although I sampled them all I found nothing to compare with the good old Midnapore Killmequick, with its benzine and fishhooks.

The opening was a grand affair. Lieutenant-Governor Bulyea came down from Edmonton to preside over the function. He drank comparatively little for a man in his position. The speech he delivered was the same speech that he opened the bull show with last spring, but none of the patients seemed to mind it. He was shown around the boozorium and seemed highly pleased with what he saw. The museum occupied most of his attention, His Honor being particularly struck with snakery. One of the patients who accompanied him invited him into the room where he said he had several other varieties on view, but although the governor went with him he said he could not see them. This is the first day since I came here that I have been able to use a pen, but am tapering off nicely, being down to forty whiskies a day, with a little lager beer for a chaser. Tomorrow I hope to be put into the bromide class and if I have any kind of luck I ought to be promoted into the calomel department early next week.

Several of the patients have endeavored to get leave to go downtown for the mail, as they expect some important letters, but they have been refused permission. Another patient received a telegram, which he unfortunately lost, saying that his mother was dead in Ontario and he had to go east at once. He, too, was turned down, on the ground that the old lady had just telephoned up from town to know how he was getting on. Another patient was most anxious to consult a firm of lawyers downtown about a big land deal he was swinging, but was informed that this same firm had left instructions that he was on no account to be set at large before October 1. All the other fellows are doing nicely

The badness in the best of us and the goodness in the worst of us should restrain any of us from throwing mud at the rest of us.[11]

and we are all perfectly contented and well satisfied. Yours as ever,

Peter J. McGonigle

P.S. If by any chance you could manage to fetch me up a couple of bottles of Scotch without letting these people here get on to it, you would be doing a service which I shall never forget. Come as soon as you can. Don't delay. I need it. (September 19, 1908)

Sport: You lose, P. J. McGonigle's father died peacefully in his bed. He had been suffering from tumors in his stomach, the complaint being aggravated by his inordinate love of Burke's beer, the rosin of which helped along the disease. The old gentleman passed away full of years and tumors in '98, leaving a large family, of which Peter J. is the eldest, to mourn his loss. His further family history may be found in Burke's Beerage. It was probably the grandfather you were thinking of. He was hanged at Fort Walsh in '85. (September 19, 1908)

Peter J. McGonigle, editor of the popular *Midnapore Gazette*, has not had an issue of his paper out for several weeks. He has been down to High River on a business trip. As is well known, a business trip to High River involves considerable drinking, and it will be distressing to many of Mr. McGonigle's friends to learn that he forgot his pledge and, as the local preacher put it, went the whole hog. He was so near the willies that they shut down on

giving him any more booze, and he became a perfect nuisance round the St. George Hotel, where he was stopping. Finally he approached Phil Weinard, the presiding genius of the gurgling bottle, and made a fervid appeal for just one jolt.

"Not on your life, Pete," said Phil, wiping off the bar with great deliberation.

"Then," cried McGonigle in an excess of despair, "I'll be desperate. I'll get a rope and hang myself to the telephone pole in front of the hotel."

"How many times have I got to tell you that I don't want you hanging around here?" shouted Phil.

But Phil, realizing that he had got off something good, relented and passed up the bottle. A valuable life was thus saved and much credit is due Mr. Weinard for his noble magnanimity on this occasion. Jack Binns could have done no more. The next number of the *Midnapore Gazette* will appear shortly if not sooner. (March 6, 1909)

From late advices from Calgary we learn that Peter J. McGonigle and his best girl have become reconciled. This is most gratifying news. We also learn that a most untoward accident happened to Peter J. in Calgary last Tuesday afternoon. He is always having accidents.

Peter was up-town with the lady, who was doing some shopping, and proposed a buggy ride round the suburbs to pass away the balance of the afternoon. The lady was willing and told him to go down to Scott's stables and have the buggy ready and she would follow down in about five minutes. When he reached the stable he found a great hubbub going on. Charlie Roedick, the proprietor, had just caught five rats in a trap and his little black dog Bingo was about to pass sentence. The cage and its occupants were being taken to the street in front of the stable.

Bingo disposed of the first four rats in short order. The fifth rat was a spry rat and with the dog a close second made a bolt for Mr. McGonigle.

Like a rocket the rat scooted up Mr. McGonigle's trousers' leg. Peter J. brought his hand down with a slap on his left back pocket and with the dog trying to kill the rat by nipping the slack of his pants, ran into the stable.

Hastily undoing his pants, but still clutching the rat underneath, he hastily pulled them off and started to get rid of the rat.

As this moment Mr. McGonigle's fiancée entered and the first thing she saw was her future husband standing on the floor of the livery stable, half clad and shaking rats out of his pants. He was a comical-looking sight, and his language was awful. His back was to her and he kept right on flapping the pants in the air.

The fair fiancée tottered hysterically into Mr. Roedick's private office and laughed herself silly for about half an hour. There was no buggy ride. When last heard from, Mr. McGonigle was lapping up booze at a great rate at the Queen's, and looking very morose. (December 4, 1909)

The father of the Calgary girl whom Peter J. McGonigle, of the *Midnapore Gazette*, contemplates marrying in the spring, seems to have soured on his future son-in-law. At least, he ordered him peremptorily from the house the other night. It appears that Peter was slightly under the influence of bugjuice. Not much, but just enough to be cheeky. The old man was on the prod, and said: "There's no use talking, McGonigle, my daughter can never be yours."

"Of course she can't be my daughter," replied Peter, with offensive gaiety. "Who said she could be my daughter? But she's going to be my wife, and the sooner you get the idea out of your head that she isn't, the sooner you'll have room under your lid for another idea. How's that, old cockie?"

Then the old gentleman rose from his seat. (January 1, 1910)

The late J. J. McGonigle, Esq.

There has been so much interest displayed by the reading public in the McGonigle family that we have decided to present the portraits of the late Mr. J. McGonigle, Sr. and of his son Mr. Peter J. McGonigle, editor of the *Midnapore Gazette*. The above is a picture of the elder McGonigle on his death-bed. It will be observed there is no mattress. Mr. McGonigle died very suddenly a number of years ago, in Choteau county, Montana, between Choteau and Ponderay. His grave may still be seen, though it is off the beaten track. There being no flowers in this desolate country, his friends have kept his grave green with that which he loved so well in life, kegs and bottles. This is how he himself would have wished to have it. The band of mares, which was the immediate cause of his taking off, were duly returned to their rightful owners.

Peter J. McGonigle, Esq.

Reading from left to right we have Peter J. McGonigle, the eminent journalist, and Jimmy, the bartender of the Nevermore House. The latter gave us his surname, but as we have reason to believe that it was not the right one, we decline to print it. Accuracy is the main hold of this paper. The gentleman on the porch is merely a stray guest of the house and appears to have been drinking.

Mr. McGonigle is the editor and sole proprietor of the *Midnapore Gazette*, one of the most popular family journals in Western Canada. Its circulation within the past few years has bounded up from 375 to over 600, and is still on the rise. The *Gazette* is independent in politics, the editor favoring the side that "comes through." Owing to the close proximity of the Nevermore House there are occasions when the paper fails to appear but Mr. McGonigle invariably manages to pacify his infuriated subscribers by getting out an extra good number the next time he prints. Mr. McGonigle is well-known in Calgary, and is a great favorite with the Sisters of the Holy Cross hospital, which he never fails to visit when in town, usually with the D.T.'s He is a bachelor, but expects shortly to marry a charming lady in Calgary.

The cross in the foreground indicates the spot where an inebriate from the Nevermore House cut his throat from ear to ear. He was never identified and is buried in the little garden back of the *Gazette* office. The other crosses in the background mark the spots where somewhat similar unfortunate incidents took place, these being regarded by Jimmy, the bartender, as prima facie evidence of his strict attention to business.

The social life of Midnapore fluctuates considerably. It is only nine miles from Calgary, and frequently when there is a musical comedy playing at one of the

*After a man has one foot in the grave it doesn't take
him long to get there with both feet.*[14]

theatres, the local sports will give the chorus girls a flying trip down to the little burg, in automobiles. On these occasions Mr. McGonigle is routed out of bed, and he and Jimmy see that the visitors have a good time. They can kick up all the row they like, for the cattle on the range don't mind and the coyotes rather seem to enjoy it. We predict a great future for Midnapore. (February 19, 1910)

The engagement of Miss Phoebe Delaney of Calgary to Mr. Peter J. McGonigle of Midnapore is at last announced. The wedding has been set for March 17, to be followed by an extended honeymoon to Macleod via Okotoks, High River, Nanton, Staveley and Granum. The happy couple will thereafter take up residence in Midnapore, where Mr. McGonigle has extensive business interests. Midnapore society is all agog over this delightful society event and many balls, routs, dinner parties, pink teas and receptions will be gotten up in their honor.

Mr. McGonigle gave a charming pink whiskey to his male friends last Monday afternoon in the spacious parlors of the Nevermore Hotel, when he formally announced his approaching marriage. A pleasant time was had. The function, which was quite a recherche affair, is still in progress, according to a despatch received at this office before going to press. The guests are engaged in a delightful game of progressive poker, the

prizes being round and flat objects d'art of various hues, white, red, blue and yellow. A little bird has whispered that Mr. John M. Delaney will settle $500 on his daughter, which should enable Mr. McGonigle to get in a new Gordon press for job printing, the old one having been smashed in a fracas last election. In the meantime a ward is being held in readiness for Mr. McGonigle at the Holy Cross Hospital in Calgary, where he will recuperate from his very successful pink whiskey under the care of the family physician and a trained snake charmer. There will be no issue of the *Gazette* next week. (March 5, 1910)

A pretty anecdote is related in connection with the recent McGonigle nuptials at Midnapore. At the wedding breakfast it appears that Mr. McGonigle, in the exuberance of the moment, seized a bottle of whiskey and applied it to his mouth, drinking with great long gulps.

"My dear sir," interposed the minister, "be careful, be careful! I once knew a man who drank from a bottle with such haste and avidity that he dropped dead before he finished it."

"You don't say!" said the happy bridegroom, pausing with a look of unfeigned interest. "And what did they do with the rest of the bottle?" (April 9, 1910)

The wedding of Mr. Peter J. McGonigle of Midnapore and Miss Phoebe Delaney of Calgary was duly solemnized on March

17. The happy couple left immediately after the ceremony for Edmonton, where they travelled by stage into the north country. Mr. McGonigle proposes to study the habits of the Indians up there, and with this purpose in view both he and Mrs. McGonigle have taken up their abode in their midst, adopting their dress and so forth. During Mr. McGonigle's absence the *Midnapore Gazette* is being conducted by the Hon. Thomas Mewburn of Calgary. (April 9, 1910)

Mr. and Mrs. Peter J. McGonigle returned a couple of weeks ago from their honeymoon and have taken up residence in the charming flat above the printing office. Two new chairs and a family Bible have been installed, also a clock. Mrs. McGonigle will receive for the first time next Wednesday afternoon. Mr. McGonigle has only had one mild toot since his wedding, and that was at Edmonton on the trip down from the far north. He would appear to have met the Hon. Joseph Adair. Mr. McGonigle has so far nobly kept his promise to his bride to never again enter the Nevermore Hotel. Jimmy, the faithful bartender, has to slip over every once in a while with a bottle while the happy couple are billing and cooing along the violet-strewn banks of Fish Creek and cache it away in the hell box.

The first tiff of the happy couple came from the family Bible aforesaid, for which Mrs. McGonigle had paid $1.60 in Calgary. On looking over the good book and idly turning over the pages she discovered that her Peter had been using the leaves for cigarette papers, probably because they were so thin. On close scrutiny she found that her husband, whom she thought so noble, so high-minded, so god-like, had smoked up all the gospels and about half of Ezekiel. There was also a suspicious gap in the Psalms. However, Peter J., who is pretty smooth, fixed it up somehow and the goose is now hanging at frightful altitude.

Mr. McGonigle was highly pleased at the manner in which Mr. Thomas Mewburn conducted the *Gazette* during his absence, and by way of remuneration, waved his hand airily and said he "would make it all right with him." McGonigle has a great heart. (June 4, 1910)

Mr. McGonigle of Midnapore had to tear himself away from his bride last week and run up to Calgary on some business connected with the *Gazette*. Of course he had to drop in to have a chat with Fred Adams at the Victoria, and then he had to call around and congratulate Jack Moseley on getting hold of the Imperial, and then he had to see if the same old barkeeps were on deck at the Yale, and then he had to investigate Bart's Beautiful Budge at the Grand Central, and then— he got spiflicated, this making his second fall from grace since his marriage. He was extremely dubious about returning home on the evening train.

A good man who goes wrong is just a bad man who has been found out.[16]

Passing Terrill's florist emporium he was struck with a brilliant idea of taking home a floral peace offering to Mrs. McGonigle. He pointed out some flowers that he thought would do the trick, and the florist made up a dozen for him. As he was leaving he turned to inquire the name of the flowers.

"Wash you call these flowrsh?"

The florist told him they were chrysanthemums, whereupon Mr. McGonigle shook his head sadly.

"Mush have shumthing easier than that," he said, "lemme have shumthing I can say—gimme a dozen pinks." (June 18, 1910)

--···--

The Pan-Boozological Congress of Demented Bartenders was held in Winnipeg this year and met in session last week at the Royal Alexandra. Delegates from all the provinces, with the exception of Quebec, were present. The Quebec delegates had been detained by the Eucharistic Congress in Montreal and could not get here for the opening session. However, a pleasant time was had as the *Free Press* would say.

Mr. Peter J. McGonigle, the distinguished journalist of Midnapore, who was on his way home after taking the jag cure at Port Arthur, was invited to be present and address the delegates. This he kindly consented to do, and in the course of the morning prepared a thoughtful address on "The Horrors of Square Gin." Being unused to public speaking, Mr.

McGonigle nerved himself for the ordeal by slipping round to the bar before the proceedings commenced and throwing three or four stiff old hookers into himself. He argued that one little flurry of rye would not materially affect the good results of his recent cure.

The Chairman, Mr. J. Collins, in introducing the distinguished guest, said that it was indeed an honor to the Pan-Boozological Congress to have Mr. McGonigle with them on this auspicious occasion. Mr. McGonigle was a man who had probably done more for the cause of booze than any other living man. (Cheers.) He had long been an honor to the bar. It was understood that his onerous labors on behalf of the alcoholic industries of this country had constrained his physicians to order a complete rest, but it was to be hoped that in a few months, if not weeks, he would be sufficiently restored to resume active operations in the field where he had attained such lofty pre-eminence. (Loud applause.)

"I take pleasure," concluded the chairman, "in introducing Mr. Peter McGonigle, the champeen heavyweight booze-fighter of the West."

Mr. McGonigle, on rising, was received with tumultuous applause, the delegates rising to their feet and singing "We Won't Go Home Till Morning" with fine effect. Mr. McGonigle's speech, in part, was as follows:

"Mr. Chairman and gentlemen, I am profoundly touched by the warmth of

Every man does things on the quiet that would make him feel quite small if they were found out.[17]

your reception. There are many faces here of which I have a very distinct recollection, while there are others of which I have only an indistinct recollection, but I am glad to be with you all today. The remarkable reception which you have accorded me will ever live in my memory and will be handed down as a family legend to my children, if I ever have any, and to my children's children, if they ever have any. (Loud and prolonged applause.) Mr. Chairman, I had intended addressing your congress this afternoon on the horrors of square gin, but I think it would be more in accordance with the proprieties of the occasion if I simply offered a few remarks on the complex subject of boozology as a general proposition. (Hear, hear!)

"There may be some here who prefer Square Face to Old Tom and it is far from my intention, I assure you, to wound the susceptibilities of any one by lauding one kind of gin to the detriment of another. When a booze artist of average intelligence regards his past life he has food for thought. Having partaken of that food, he has to take several horns to wash it down, and so the world wags on. (Applause.) We all have our good points, but so has a paper of pins. (Laughter.) As Emerson so aptly remarked, 'Hitch your wagon to Three Star.'

"The main cause of drunkenness, Mr. Chairman, in this Canada of ours, is the pathetic tendency most booze-fighters have to taking six drinks before breakfast instead of two. I should like to see some form of legislation introduced whereby it became a crime to take more than two snifters before breakfast. (Hear, hear!) When a man imbibes, say, three Collinses on an empty stomach he gets laid out too soon, having probably to retire to the hay before ten o'clock. Thus your receipts are curtailed for the day and the boss thinks you are knocking down. (A voice, 'That's so!') On the other hand, let your honest booze-fighter confine himself to a couple of snorts in the early morn, just to get the bugs out of his eyes, and then let him make a beeline for the dining room and stuff himself full of ham. What must be the natural result, my friends, of such wise policy? That man will last all day and well into the night. (Loud and prolonged applause.)

"Such a concerted movement on the part of the vast horde of rotgut guzzlers would make the wheels of your great and noble industry move the faster, would hasten the filling of your cash registers, give employment to more men in the breweries and distilleries, spread happiness amongst the hotelkeepers, add to the prosperity of the medical profession, fill your hospitals with paying patients, promote the interests of the calomel and bromide merchants, increase the welfare of every gravedigger in the land and cause the marts of the world to hum with the sound of popping corks to the end that the eternal gaiety of nations might not be dimmed by the disgraceful efforts of those who too lightly claim that Adam's ale is more conducive to longevi-

When a man offers you something for nothing, don't accept it unless you can afford to pay double what it is worth.[18]

ty than Seagram's rye. (Frantic applause, many of the delegates jumping up and waving their handkerchiefs.)

"The economic value of booze is incalculable. Why, for instance, should you pay six bits to go and see the menagerie attached to a circus, when with the simple aid of three bottles of square gin and two of Scotch you can see a far more various and curious collection of animals, and none of them in cages either! You do not even have to leave your place of abode to view them. They come right up to you. (Cheers.)

"Mr. Chairman, I go west tonight. I shall take with me the message to Midnapore that the Pan-Boozological Congress of Demented Bartenders is solid for the unity of the Empire. (Tremendous applause.) I shall convey to the Midnapore board of trade, which consists of myself, my assistant, the local hardware merchant and four cowpunchers, that your congress has declared itself resolutely in favor of free trade in agricultural implements and reciprocity with the United States. I shall tell them that while favoring free trade, you look with grave disfavor on free drinks. (Hear, hear!) Mr. Chairman, and gentlemen, I thank you for your generous courtesy." (Prolonged cheering, followed by the singing of "He's A Jolly Good Fellow.")

After a few words of thanks to Mr. McGonigle from the chairman for his eloquent address, of which only a portion is here given, Mr. Fred Adams of Calgary rose and delivered a monologue

on the agitation which was going on out west in favor of five drinks for a half. He said it was an outrage. Mr. Adams also complained that Sir Wilfrid Laurier on his tour through the West had not declared himself on the subject of free drinks for customers before breakfast. (Shame, shame!) Nor had R. L. Borden made any pronouncement on the subject. Whither were they drifting? What did they put these fellers into office for? Mr. Adams concluded by betting his sweet life that he would use his influence next dominion election to put Laurier where he belonged.

The meeting thereafter adjourned—to the bar. The delegates were delighted with their visit to Winnipeg and were driven round the city in automobiles by some of the more prominent local members of the fraternity. It was decided to hold the congress next year in Port Arthur, the city which would not publish its police court records for reasons of state. "What state?" cried the infuriated prophet. "State of drunkenness, you slob." (September 27, 1910)

It is with unalloyed grief that we record the untimely death of Mr. Peter J. McGonigle, editor and proprietor of the *Midnapore* (Alta.) *Gazette*. This also means the demise of the *Gazette*. While examining an ivory-handled revolver which the bartender of the Nevermore House had, during the editor's absence in Port Arthur, accepted from a stranger in

Eloquence is ordinary gab with its Sunday clothes on.[19]

lieu of payment for a two-day drunk, the weapon unexpectedly went off and lodged a bullet in Mr. McGonigle's abdomen. A physician was hastily summoned by phone from Calgary. In the meanwhile Jimmy, the bartender, summoned help and had his old friend gently raised from the floor and stretched out on the bar with his head comfortably resting on the slot machine. Mr. McGonigle retained consciousness, but complained of great pain. A tumbler of brandy eased his sufferings somewhat, but he whispered to Jimmy that he feared he had been sent for at last. The tender-hearted mixologist thereupon threw another tumbler of brandy into him, after which, as soon as it had percolated through his system, Mr. McGonigle declared himself as feeling much better.

Pending the arrival of the doctor from Calgary, nine miles distant, Jimmy did all he knew to staunch the flow of blood. Ripping open the shirt and locating the spot where the bullet had entered, he took the glass stopper from a Gooderham and Wortz flask and inserted the blunt-pointed end into the hole, keeping it pressed down with his thumb to stop the rush of blood. The contents of the flask he absent-mindedly poured down his own throat from time to time. No one was allowed to enter the bar except a few specially favored friends, one of whom was despatched over to the *Gazette* office to ease Mrs. McGonigle's mind with regard to her husband's absence. This friend admirably per-formed his errand, informing the lady that if she didn't see her husband for a few days she was not to worry or feel the least bit anxious, as he was only off on a little bit of a whizzer. Mrs. McGonigle thereupon indulged in some sarcastic remarks about the Port Arthur Jagcureatorium where P. J. had recently blown in a couple of hundred dollars, but finally wound up by asking the messenger to try and prevail on Mr. McGonigle to make it a three-day jag this time instead of a two-week one as heretofore.

On being informed of the success of his messenger the great editor smiled and said he thought they ought to have a drink on the strength of it. One of the men thereupon took Jimmy's place holding down the glass stopper, while that worthy prepared the round. No one took a cigar. At some one's suggestion, the slot machine was taken from under the wounded man's head, as being too uncomfortable, and the cash register substituted. In lowering Mr. McGonigle's head on to the keyboard they rang up $14.65, but P. J. said it was a great improvement on the slot machine and added that he hoped the doc wouldn't be long, as he felt himself getting awful weak.

An auto suddenly jumped up in front of the Nevermore House and out jumped the long-looked-for doctor, carrying a small black case.

"What room is the man in who was shot?" he curtly inquired of the men gathered in the office.

"He's in the bar," was the response.

A man may not know who his friends are but he usually has his enemies spotted.[20]

242

"In the bar?" ejaculated the doctor, wondering if he had been the victim of a hoax.

A head was poked through the barroom door, revealing the weather-beaten countenance of Jimmy, the mixocographer.

"Step this way, Doc."

"How is he?" whispered the doctor before going in.

"I'm afraid he's a goner, but I've been throwing the booze into him to keep up his nerve till you came."

"Quite right, quite right."

Mr. McGonigle, on the approach of the doctor, turned his head, ringing up $1.40 in the effort, and greeted the doctor with great cordiality, insisting upon his having a drink before making his examination. Then everybody but Jimmy was ordered to "get out and stay out."

As the doctor bent down to examine the wound he could not keep back a smile when he ran on to the glass-stopper stuck in the bullet hole. Jimmy gave a pathetic little grin and explained that it would have taken too long to whittle a cork into shape. Then the doctor's face grew grave.

"The bullet must be located and extracted," said he, "and he will have to be taken to the hospital in Calgary by the first train. You can stretch him out comfortably in the baggage car and I'll be at the depot with the ambulance when the train pulls in."

"I'd better go along, eh, Doc?"

"I should certainly like you to accompany him to Calgary, if you can possibly get away."

"Oh, that part of it will be all right. I can get one of the boys to run the joint."

"Have you any one here you can trust."

Mr. McGonigle stirred slightly and rang up 15 cents.

"We can trust 'em all round here. Can't we, Jimmy?"

"Sure we can," said Jimmy, "but not for drinks."

"No, not for drinks," acquiesced McGonigle.

"Then that is settled," said the doctor. "I will hurry back in my car and arrange for a ward in the Holy Cross. Then—ha ha!—we'll do the chloroform stunt, Mr. McGonigle, cut you open, dive into your poor old gust, slosh around among your bowels for the bullet and then—ha ha ha!—sew you up again and send you back here as right as a trivet."

The doctor threw a peculiar glance over to Jimmy, and Jimmy understood.

"Ha ha ha!" croaked that worthy, with a lump in his throat. "As right as a trivet, as right as a trivet, ha ha ha!"

McGonigle, whose eyes were fixed on the ceiling, said feebly, "Doc, you better have another drink before you go. Have one yourself, Jimmy. You two mutts can't fool me with your 'ha ha ha.' This will be the last time I shall ever set 'em up to anybody on this earth. I'll have one, too, Jimmy."

Two days later word arrived at Midnapore that Peter J. had breathed his

A man who has no enemies is seldom good for anything.
We derive much comfort from this reflection. [21]

last on the operating table. The operation itself was declared to have been entirely successful, but it seems that Mr. McGonigle's heart, storm-beaten as it was by many a howling gale of booze, had failed to rise to the occasion when the supreme call was made upon it. The physicians in attendance were unanimously of the opinion that the rather unfortunate and awkward circumstance of his heart stopping beating had not a little to do with his death. In fact, on calm reflection, they were sure of it.

Before being taken to the operating room, Mr. McGonigle, on the advice of the sister in attendance, executed a will. He directed that the printing plant of the *Gazette*, on which he had made only two payments, should, in the event of his death, be shipped back to the Toronto Type Foundry. The bunch of mares, which only last year he was tried for stealing from the Bar U (being triumphantly acquitted on a technicality), he directed to be sold for the benefit of his wife, who also was left the house and lot in Midnapore. Some minor bequests followed. The will, which was quite brief, Mr. McGonigle not having much to leave, ended with the earnest and expressed wish that, should the worst happen, Jimmy would marry his widow, Mrs. McGonigle, after a decent interval of mourning. Say, a week.

Thus passed away a great spirit. The body was shipped back to Midnapore and interred in the little garden back of the printing office. The defunct *Midnapore Gazette* gave comfort, pleasure and instruction to many in its day, its contents being always of an edifying and uplifting nature. McGonigle now belongs to history and the *Gazette* is a thing of the past. Beware of spurious imitations. (October 15, 1910)

Word comes from Calgary that Mrs. P. J. McGonigle, widow of the late editor of the well-known Midnapore publication, has appealed to the authorities for leave to exhume the body of her husband. Mrs. McGonigle claims that he was buried while in a trance and that within the last week he has recovered consciousness and been trying to communicate with her by telepathic means. The poor distracted widow is so earnest in the matter that it is expected the necessary permission will be granted and the exhumation proceeded with without delay. If P. J. can do the Lazarus act after this lapse of time, he is a dandy. (February 11, 1911)

Mrs. Peter J. McGonigle of Midnapore, relic of the distinguished journalist who passed away six months ago, has given birth to a son with two heads. The youngster is quite lively and healthy and will no doubt prove a source of revenue to the sorrowing widow in years to come. This remarkable curiosity will be on exhibition at the Calgary exhibition in July. (May 6, 1911)

An extraordinary scene was witnessed at

Some men borrow trouble because they have heard that it drives men to drink.[22]

Midnapore last Tuesday when the body of Mr. Peter J. McGonigle, for many years editor of the *Midnapore Gazette*, was exhumed and finally resuscitated. It reads almost like fiction. Ever since the funeral some months ago the sorrowing widow has entertained grave doubts as to her husband being really dead, and had so

The Recrudescence of Peter J. McGonigle

expressed herself to friends. Mrs. McGonigle, for a squaw, was a widely read woman, having educated herself by constant and faithful perusal of the lurid columns of the *Gazette*. She had more than once read stories of people being buried alive when in a state of catalepsy, which, in its outward manifestations, closely resembles death. She finally got it into her head that Mr. McGonigle had been buried alive and might even yet, after the lapse of months, be alive. The suspicion gradually grew on her, and became an obsession.

Obtaining an order from a judge of the Supreme Court, Mrs. McGonigle communicated with several well-known doctors and made arrangements for the coffin to be dug up from the vegetable patch in the little back garden behind the old printing office. Some cabbage and lettuce had been planted over the grave, but the bereft woman was ready for any kind of a sacrifice to have her dear departed back.

The weird scene around the lonely grave would have been more impressive had the sad work been performed in the dead of night, with the moon appearing fitfully from behind the flying clouds, but truth compels us to record that it was pulled off about three o'clock in the afternoon, the hour when the village of Midnapore is beginning to bowl up for the day. Two sturdy yeomen with spades went to work and soon had the dirt flying in all directions. Mrs. McGonigle, ever thoughtful of the comfort of others, had ordered Jimmy, the bartender at the Nevermore Hotel, to have a keg of beer on tap in a corner of the garden. Which, in a manner, accounted for the large crowd present.

It took fully an hour before the spades struck the lid of the coffin. Then excitement ran high. Mrs. McGonigle had to be restrained by physical force from jumping into the grave. At her earnest request one of the diggers rapped loudly on the coffin and cried, "Pete, ho Pete! Are you there?"

There being no response, the heartbroken widow burst into tears and wrung her hands. A sympathetic boozologist offered her a glass of beer, but she waved it aside. The physicians implored her to return to the house, but Mrs. McGonigle was obdurate, insisting on remaining to the end to watch the efforts at resuscitation. In a few minutes the coffin was gen-

In order to enjoy life a man must be a little miserable occasionally.[23]

tly raised to the surface and reverently borne into the old home. Jimmy, the grizzled bar veteran, held the crowd back and prevented all but the physicians from entering the house. Whereupon followed a general stampede back to the garden, there still being about half of the keg left.

The coffin having been placed on the kitchen table, it was the work of only a few minutes to pry open the lid. There, cold and pallid, lay the great editor.

Mrs. McGonigle peered into the face of her beloved Peter and allowed a tear to fall on his rugged features.

"He looks so natural," she sobbed. "He hasn't changed a bit. I'll bet a cookie he's alive and in a trance."

"We'll soon see," said one of the doctors, as he removed his coat and turned up his sleeves as if about to dress a hog. Bending over the coffin, he took hold of the corpse's nose between his thumb and finger and gave it a violent twist.

"Ah," said he, with an air of profound sagacity, "um-um-ha!"

"Cut that out," cried Mrs. McGonigle sharply. "Go ahead and don't look so wise."

"How very statuesque he looks," continued the doctor. And the other two doctors chimed in, "Don't he though! Just as if he had got off a drunk."

"What do you think about it, Doc?" asked the poor woman anxiously.

"Well, he looks to be as dead as a doornail, but, after all, he may be only in a condition of *flexibilitas cerca*. How long has he been dead?"

"About six months."

"Oh, well, there's no particular hurry. I should like to hold a professional consultation with my fellow physicians over at the Nevermore Hotel. We won't be over ten minutes."

"No, you don't!" shouted Mrs. McG. "You'll go over there and stay all afternoon and come back here soused. You stay right here and work on my man to bring him back to life."

"All right," said the doctor, "just as you say. I think, however, it is only fair to tell you that the *rigor mortis catalepticus*, when due to a lesion of the cerebrum or the medulla spinalis, presents a heterogeneous concatenation of moribund possibilities which, if you haven't got jacks or better, should be passed up. Do you not agree with me, gentlemen?"

"Why, cert'nly!"

"But why don't you do something?" cried the distracted woman.

"Have patience, my good woman. You remember what Horace says, 'Patientia virtus est.' Now, if you fill that tub with cold water we will give your deceased husband a shock that will bring him to in a jiffy if he's alive."

Poor Peter was thereupon undressed by the assistants and rudely dumped into a tub of cold water. He looked an odd figure sprawling in the tub, with his inanimate head dangling on his breast.

"Dead as a doornail," pronounced the doctor.

"Doornail," echoed the other two.

The body was taken out of the tub and

Occasionally a man lies by keeping his mouth shut.[24]

dried, the assistants with some difficulty dressing it again in the nice new suit in which it had been interred. Then it was returned to the coffin and the doctors, remarking that nothing more could be done, were about to proceed to their consultation at the Nevermore Hotel.

"Oh, do try something else. Don't go yet!" cried the frantic woman, laying a detaining hand on the doctor's arm. "You haven't tried sticking a pin in him yet."

"By George, that's so!" said the doctor. "Gimme a pin."

The pin produced, Peter was jabbed indiscriminately all over his anatomy.

"Now, ma'am, you see," observed the doctor, as he stuck the pin clear through Mr. McGonigle's nose, "if he were alive the motor centres would be excited by the reflex action. I have no hesitation in pronouncing your husband a gone coon."

The physicians then put on their hats and hied over to the Nevermore Hotel for the consultation, promising to call in before returning to town in their motor. They were soon engaged in the engrossing and popular pastime of throwing the bones to see who would pay for the first round.

Mrs. McGonigle sat by her dead. She studied the well-remembered features of Peter with searching scrutiny. Her head dropped in the attitude of thought, and she looked into nothingness for a long while. Suddenly she arose and went to the door. Giving a peculiar whistle she remained standing on the threshold looking towards the Nevermore Hotel. In

a minute Jimmy, the bartender, issued from his den and looked across. A few high signs passed between the two, and Jimmy disappeared inside. A couple of minutes later he walked into Mrs. McGonigle's house and handed her a bottle of rye whiskey, returning quickly to the hotel.

"Those docs are lapping up the booze in great style," said he. "They're sports all right. I wish they'd stay a week. Old Peter still dead, eh?"

Left alone once more, Mrs. McGonigle looked curiously into her husband's face and then began hunting for a corkscrew. This found, she quickly opened the bottle and sat down beside the coffin. With great deliberation she filled a tumbler to the brim and held it beneath the nostrils of her Peter. Nothing happened for several minutes, while the woman could hear her own heart thumping. Then a faint, almost imperceptible flicker of the eyelids appeared. The glass almost slipped from the devoted woman's hand. The next perceptible movement was of the lips, which seemed to twitch slightly. Then the mouth slowly opened. Mrs. McGonigle inverted the glass, allowing half of it to trickle down his throat. A slight shudder and a faint exclamation which sounded not unlike "Wow!" and Mr. Peter J. McGonigle opened wide his eyes.

Mrs. McGonigle, being only a poor squaw, did not faint. On the contrary, she was instantly full of life and fire, and lost no time in tipping the remainder of the

Too many men salt away money in the brine of other people's tears.[25]

whiskey down her husband's dry gullet.

"Where am I?" asked Peter, staring in a dazed way up at the ceiling.

"Never mind where you are, Pete. You're all right, at home with me. I've got a whole bottle of whiskey here for you and I'm going to give you another drink right now."

"But, say, look here—my, but I feel weak—I thought you hated to see me drink whiskey."

"Well, Pete, this is your birthday, and I want you to drink it."

"All right, my dear, let's have the hooker. Say, great Scott! What in thunder am I doing lying in a box? Has somebody been putting up a job? I wonder how I feel so weak. I never felt so queer before."

"Here, Pete, after you down this I'll tell you all about it."

Peter downed it and lay back to listen to the tale. Instead of being awed by his narrow escape from a frightful death, struggling for life in a coffin six feet underground, the great editor grinned broadly.

"You can't keep a good man down," said he. "And how is Jimmy?"

"Oh, Jimmy's fine. It was he who brought over the whiskey."

"Good old Jimmy! Let's have another horn."

When Mrs. McGonigle, however, started to relate the efforts of the doctors to bring him back to life, Peter got very hostile. He leapt from the coffin and shoved it off the table, kicking it all over the room.

"They stuck a pin through my nose, eh? The only nose I've got! And chucked me into a tub of water! By gum, wait till I see them!"

"They're over at the Nevermore Hotel, but don't do anything violent, Peter. They did their best and were very kind."

"Oh well, I'm glad to hear that. I'll go right over and thank them, but you better give me another drink—I feel pretty weak."

The three physicians were standing at the bar of the Nevermore Hotel, gaily flopping the dice. One of them had just thrown a pair of deuces and was being urbanely told by Jimmy not to despise them because they were small, when the door opened and in walked the late P. J. McGonigle.

"Have a drink, gentlemen," said he, walking calmly up to the bar.

"Pete—it's Pete—damned if it ain't Pete!" gasped Jimmy, upsetting several bottles on the shelf behind him and wagging his head stupidly from side to side.

The doctors wheeled around and gave Peter one look, just one. Then they jumped for the door, looking back fearfully over their shoulders as they darted through it. A loud honk proclaimed that they were off with a rush for the city, flying like so many Tam O'Shanters from a ghost.

"Jimmy, I want you to come over and have tea tonight with me and the missus."

"All right, Pete, I'll come," said Jimmy faintly, "anything you say, Pete."

"And in case the missus runs out of tea

Never trust a man whose dog has gone back on him.[26]

you better fetch over a case of extra-special."

"Extra-special goes," whispered Jimmy hoarsely, blinking his eyes and coughing nervously. "Is it really you, Pete, or am I only drunk and imagining it's you?"

"It's really me, Jimmy, returned from the grave. Let us both have a drink for old times' sake."

"I guess it's you, all right," said Jimmy, greatly relieved, as he placed the bottle and glasses on the bar. "I was afraid I had 'em again, that's all. Drink hearty!" (May 20, 1911)

The carryings on at Midnapore one day last week were little short of disgraceful. We do not as a rule write unpleasant things about neighboring burgs, but in the interests of common decency and propriety this particular case cannot very well be overlooked. It is hard to understand why the mounted police have not made an investigation into the circumstances.

It appears that last Saturday a week ago, while a group of Midnapore citizens were quietly gathered round the bar of the local hotel discussing the pros and cons of the prohibition bill, a man named Crawley blew in and proceeded to set 'em up. This Crawley is a comparative stranger in the village and claims to hail from Lethbridge. Which is possibly true, seeing that the penitentiary is there. After setting 'em up, Crawley joined in the general discussion and showed no little vehemence in his denunciation of the prohibition bill. So earnest and excited did he become that he inadvertently set 'em up again, forgetting that he had already done so. Crawley may have his faults, but he appears to be no piker.

Mr. Bilkey, one of Midnapore's most prominent businessmen and a leader in church circles, took exception to Crawley's arguments and offered the statement that his books were full of outstanding accounts owed him by men who blew in all their money on whiskey and pin pool. He claimed that the elimination of hard liquor would revolutionize the social and business life of Midnapore, making for the higher life and bringing about a much-needed uplift, and was going on to expatiate about the beautiful, the true and the good, when Crawley hauled off and pasted him in the eye. A roughhouse followed.

When things had quieted down and harmony restored, the proprietor set 'em up and the discussion was resumed along more peaceful lines. It so happened that Al, the barkeeper, butted in with a touching reference to the late Peter J. McGonigle, editor of the once famous *Gazette*, adding his opinion that the bill would assuredly have met with Mr. McGonigle's most vigorous disapproval. This started the conversation on another tack.

Crawley, who claimed to have been an old side-kicker of McGonigle's in the early days when horse stealing was rife,

One kind of hypocrite is the man who, after thanking the Lord for his dinner, proceeds to find fault with the cook.[27]

thoroughly agreed with Al's remark and said that he was willing to bet fifty dollars that, owing to threatened prohibition, McGonigle's body, if exhumed, would be found to have turned over in its grave. Mr. Bilkey promptly took the bet and the money was put up with the proprietor.

This was harmless enough if the proceedings had stopped right there, but everybody seemed anxious to see the thing through. Two local bums were quickly requisitioned, loaded up with five or six drinks apiece and despatched with spades to the little garden behind the old newspaper office where Peter J. was buried.

Quite a number of wagers appear to have been made on the side, and before the diggers had half completed their work the whole male population of Midnapore had gathered round the grave. When the spades hit the lid of the coffin Crawley offered to double his wager with Mr. Bilkey, to which that gentleman was quite agreeable. A slight delay ensued until some one had procured a cold chisel with which to pry open the box, the interval being employed to register a few fresh bets at even money.

It did not take over two minutes to open the lid and there, sure enough, stretched out inside the casket was the illustrious editor *lying flat on his stomach.* It was obvious that he had turned over. Mr. Bilkey looked a trifle surprised, but expressed himself as satisfied, after which the crowd wended its way slowly back to the hotel. The paying over of the bets

involved a great deal of drinking and long before supper time the village was in an uproar which lasted far into the night. This episode will be an eternal disgrace to the village of Midnapore.

It seems extraordinary that the authorities have not taken official cognizance of this unauthorized exhumation. How often, pray, is the body of McGonigle to be dug up to settle drunken wagers? The whole proceedings were illegal. Permission to exhume a corpse has first to be obtained from the attorney general's department at Edmonton, without which it becomes nothing better than a wanton act of gruesome ghouls. This man Crawley was the instigator and should be arrested forthwith. Where are our police? (April 3, 1915)

Mrs. Peter J. McGonigle, of Midnapore, who is to be one of the specially honored guests at the Old-Lady-Timers' Luncheon tendered by the Calgary Kiwanis Club, has gone into training for the event. Last week she assembled all the old dames in sight and gave them a blow-out at her home, delivering the speech she is to deliver at the Calgary luncheon and singing her chosen song, "The Land o' the Leal." It was a case of trying it out on the dog, but both speech and song went off so well that Mrs. McGonigle need have no nervous qualms with respect to the main event on the fourteenth. Her song should prove a howling success, anyhow.

For the information of those who

If you want work done well, select a busy man; the other kind has no time.[28]

Mrs. Peter J. McGonigle

Expectant Guest of Honor at the Old Lady-Timers' Blowout on the Fourteenth, Rehearsing Her Song before Midnapore Friends

Mrs. McGonigle, who was deeply attached to her late husband, will give some tender reminiscences at the luncheon, telling of the exciting times when the *Gazette* was going strong and recounting anecdotes of the doings at the bar of the Nevermore Hotel. It is understood that Mr. Inverarity, of the Kiwanis Club, took a run down to Midnapore last Tuesday morning to try and prevail upon Mrs. McGonigle not to sing, but it appears that she insists upon doing so. Otherwise she says she won't come at all, which would make the luncheon look like the play of *Hamlet* with the role of Uncle Tom left out. By all means let her sing! (February 5, 1921)

have not resided in Calgary very long, we should mention that Mrs. McGonigle is the widow of the late Peter J. McGonigle, the drunken editor of the notorious *Midnapore Gazette* which flourished some eight or ten years ago and kept the countryside to the south of Calgary in a constant uproar. Whenever anybody sued McGonigle for libel he would load up with bad whiskey and go forth and beat the man up. Latterly he had very few libel suits. Curiously enough, the late Peter J. had a host of warm friends who deeply mourned his loss when he passed away at a Calgary hospital in a blaze of delirium tremens.

The great man of Canada is made up of one part achievement and nine parts printers' ink.[29]

HINDWORD

May I be permitted on the last page to express a hope that you have derived a few moments' amusement from perusing this Annual?

Thanks, old top!

In collecting material supplementary to my own dope, I have tried to steer clear of the chestnut belt. A few yarns which you have heard before may possibly have crept in while I was out rustling a prescription, but this cannot be helped. A good story circulates with such alarming rapidity that it quickly becomes a chestnut to the boys. If you come across too many, just roast the chestnuts, but spare the book.

Prohibition is responsible for putting a crimp in the funny-yarn business. Everybody is too darned gloomy. No one is funny any more. These are indeed terrible days. However, the foregoing pages may peradventure have relieved the gloom for a brief hour.

As Keats observes:
"A thing of boozy
Is a joy forever." [1]

R C Edwards

---

[1] *Bob Edwards' Summer Annual,* 1920

DRAMATIS PERSONAE

A brief guide to select persons mentioned within this volume, offered in anticipation of boosting the discerning reader's enjoyment of the libel & scuttlebutt & tomfoolery presented herewith. (Not included are persons who at any point held the office of Prime Minster of Canada. Really, you should know those.)

Adams, Fred—Bartender at Bob Edwards's unofficial "office" (the Alberta Hotel). Later proprietor of the Hotel Alexandra.

Boyce, Jerry—Proprietor and barkeep of Wetaskiwin's Walker House Hotel.

Brett, Dr. Robert George—Physician, founder of Banff Sanitarium (a popular dry-out spot for Alberta boozehounds), and Lieutenant-Governor of Alberta (1915–25).

Cushing, William Henry—Calgary alderman (1910–11) and Alberta's Minster of Public Works (1905).

Davidson, W. M.—Editor of the *Albertan* newspaper, and confidante to Bob Edwards.

Davis, Edward P.—Calgary lawyer for the C.P.R. Served as prosecutor at murder trial of club impresario/murderer Jumbo Fisk in 1889. Later King's Council.

Emerson, John—Grocer turned politician. Calgary alderman (1901–02, 1903–05) and mayor (1905–07).

Genge, Colin—Contractor, sandstone quarryman, mayor of Fort Macleod (1904–08), and Alberta M.L.A. (1909–10).

Georgeson, William—Calgary grocer. Later president of the Security Trust Company.

Gillis, Hugh Evan—Calgary City Clerk, early 1900s.

Grady, Alfred Francis—Fort Macleod pioneer. Owned a tinshop. Later elected mayor.

Herron, John—Constable during early days of the R.C.M.P. Possible Mason. Elected Member of Parliament in 1904.

Hughes, Sam—Canada's Minister of Militia during the Great War. Possibly a hero, possibly crazy as an outhouse rat.

Kerby, Rev. Mr. George W.—First minister (1903–11) of Central Methodist Church.

Mackie, Thomas—Calgary Chief of Police (1909–12). Founded the city's vice squad. Resigned after the Mayor and two alderman were pinched in a brothel raid.

Marshall, Duncan—Alberta Minister of Agriculture (1909–21) and Ontario Minister of Agriculture (1934–37). Appointed to the Senate in 1938.

McGillicuddy, Daniel—Publisher of short-lived Calgary Daily News and longtime Edwards rival. Died on December 11, 1912.

McGillicuddy, Owen Ernest—Son of Daniel. Famously plagiarised an E. Pauline Johnson poem ("The Huskies"), which he retitled "The Train Dogs."

McGonigle, Peter J.—Editor of the *Midnapore Gazette*. Best known for not being a real person.

Motherwell, Hon. W. R.—First Saskatchewan Minister of Agriculture. Later federal Minister of Agriculture (1921–30).

Nolan, Patrick (Paddy) James—Legendary criminal lawyer and Bob Edwards' drinking companion.

Oliver, Hon. Frank—Founder of the *Edmonton Bulletin*. Liberal member of parliament (1896–1917).

Peary, Robert Edwin—Explorer. Led whitey's first successful expedition to the North Pole (1909).

Pidhoney, Mike—see Pidhorney, Mike.

Pidhorney, Mike—Murderer, executed in Winnipeg (1909).

Ross, Jessie McCauley—Calgary nurse. Helped Bob Edwards "dry out" on more than one occasion.

Seagram, Joseph Emm—Canadian whisky tycoon and horse-racing enthusiast.

Shinkleblister, P. Q.—For serious? Oh, come now.

Sifton, Clifford—Minister of the Interior (1896–1905) during the Klondike gold rush. Owner of *Winnipeg Free Press*.

Simpson, John A.—M.L.A. for Alberta (1905).

Smart, James "Cappy"—Calgary Fire Chief (1898–1933). Kept parrots, monkeys, and alligators at the fire hall.

Smith, Crispin E.—Calgary police magistrate (1904). Later founded a stenography business.

Travis, Judge Jeremiah—Calgary's first stipendiary magistrate (1885–86). Best known for his fierce anti-booze campaign, during which he jailed the editor of the *Calgary Daily Herald* and wrongheadedly overturned the 1886 civic election. Eventually turfed from the Bench.

Wellman, Walter—Explorer. Made three attempts to fly to the North Pole in motorized "airships" (1906–09). Didn't work out so hot.

Wood, Henry Wise—President of United Farmers of Alberta (1916–31) and chairman of the Alberta Wheat Pool board (1923–27).

To better your appreciation of this volume

1860:	Born in Edinburgh, Scotland on September 17.
*c.*1865-1878:	Attends Clifton Bank School & St. Andrew's.
c. 1879:	Moves to the Continent. Possibly publishes the short-lived *The Traveller* in Milan.
1881:	Debuts *The Channel* in Boulogne-sur-Mer, France. The weekly paper lasts seventeen months.
1883-1891:	Works briefly for Glasgow Town Clerk. Possibly studies at Edinburgh & Glasgow Universities.
1892:	Moves to Wyoming. Works as ranch hand. Possibly contributes to *Boomerang* newspaper.
1894:	Moves to Wetaskiwin, Alberta.
1897:	Debuts *Wetaskiwin Free Lance*. In exchange for printing services, *Calgary Daily Herald* runs excerpts as "Free Lance Sayings" and "Jabs with the Lance."
1898:	Publishes final *Wetaskiwin Free Lance*.
1899:	Moves to Winnipeg to work in *Free Press* newsroom (April), then to Calgary (September).
1900:	Debuts short-lived *Alberta Sun* in Leduc.
1901:	Publishes short-lived *Wetaskiwin Breeze*.
1902:	Debuts *Eye Opener* in High River.
1903:	Government temporarily bans *Eye Opener* from post, ostensibly because erratic publishing schedule disqualifies it as a "weekly."

1904:	Moves *Eye Opener* to Calgary.
1905:	Unsuccessfully sued for libel by J. S. Dennis on behalf of C.P.R.
1906:	Debuts the character of Peter J. McGonigle, editor of the fictional *Midnapore Gazette*, in *Eye Opener*.
1908:	Sues Daniel McGillicuddy for libelous letter printed in *Calgary Daily News*. Wins suit, but loses face.
1909:	Relocates *Eye Opener* to Port Arthur, Ontario. Licks wounds.
1910:	Moves *Eye Opener* to Winnipeg (February). Unsuccessfully sued for literary indecency by Lord's Day Alliance (March). Responds to unauthorized edition of *Midnapore Gazette* by killing off McGonigle character (October).
1911:	Returns *Eye Opener* to Calgary.
1912:	Sued for libel by E. P. Davis. Publicly apologizes; lawsuit dropped.
1915:	Supports Prohibition movement. Bill passes, slobsters weep.
1917:	Marries Kate Penman on June 30.
1920:	Rehashes old material with first *Bob Edwards Summer Annual*.
1921:	Elected independent member of the Alberta Legislature (July). Releases second *Bob Edwards Summer Annual*.
1922:	Makes maiden/only speech to Legislature (March). Releases third *Annual*. Publishes his last *Eye Opener* (July). Dies in Calgary on November 14. Widow publishes memorial *Eye Opener* eleven days later.
1923:	Fourth and final *Annual* published.

END NOTES

CHAPTER ONE
1 November 19, 1904
2 April 19, 1919
3 March 20, 1920
4 September 21, 1918
5 October 19, 1912
6 July 20, 1918
7 August 21, 1921
8 September 16, 1911
9 May 6, 1916
10 March 14, 1914
11 November 16, 1912
12 October 8, 1921
13 December 20, 1919
14 December 2, 1916
15 September 1, 1917
16 *Summer Annual*, 1920
17 *Summer Annual*, 1922
18 July 18, 1908
19 *Summer Annual*, 1920
20 *Summer Annual*, 1920
21 September 21, 1918
22 April 3, 1915
23 April 3, 1915
24 December 11, 1915
25 November 16, 1912
26 *Summer Annual*, 1922
27 August 28, 1920
27 September 1, 1917
29 January 11, 1919
30 August 20, 1921
31 November 11, 1916

CHAPTER TWO
1 July 25, 1903
2 *Summer Annual*, 1922
3 *Summer Annual*, 1924
4 *Summer Annual*, 1924
5 October 28, 1911
6 January 27, 1912
7 February 13, 1904
8 March 15, 1919
9 *Summer Annual*, 1920
10 March 15, 1919

11 June 27, 1908
12 June 27, 1908
13 *Summer Annual*, 1923
14 June 29, 1918
15 April 30, 1921
16 May 22, 1915
17 December 12, 1914

CHAPTER THREE
1 November 21, 1914
2 December 30, 1911
3 May 31, 1919
4 May 31, 1919
5 June 5, 1920
6 January 27, 1917
7 May 31, 1919
8 March 20, 1915
9 March 20, 1920
10 September 16, 1911
11 May 31, 1919
12 May 27, 1916
13 October 23, 1920
14 October 19, 1912
15 *Summer Annual*, 1921
16 March 14, 1914
17 September 7, 1912
18 November 3, 1917
19 December 25, 1920
20 February 5, 1921
21 October 23, 1920
22 May 11, 1918
23 December 6, 1919
24 September 22, 1917
25 September 7, 1912
26 June 17, 1916

CHAPTER FOUR
1 August 12, 1911
2 January 13, 1912
3 January 13, 1912
4 January 28, 1905
5 August 25, 1906
6 May 22, 1915
7 September 11, 1920

8 March 15, 1919
9 *Summer Annual*, 1920
10 November 13, 1909
11 March 23, 1912
12 June 27, 1914
13 May 22, 1915
14 March 9, 1918
15 *Summer Annual*, 1920
16 *Summer Annual*, 1922
17 *Summer Annual*, 1922
18 *Summer Annual*, 1923
19 February 19, 1910
20 August 23, 1919
21 January 22, 1921
22 December 25, 1920
23 June 12, 1915
24 May 17, 1913
25 August 2, 1913
26 July 8, 1916
27 May 22, 1915
28 August 2, 1913
29 January 1, 1910
30 *Summer Annual*, 1921
31 November 11, 1916

CHAPTER FIVE
1 December 21, 1912
2 November 2, 1912
3 *Summer Annual*, 1923
4 January 22, 1921
5 October 5, 1912
6 June 29, 1918
7 October 2, 1920
8 November 3, 1917
9 September 20, 1918
10 September 11, 1920
11 April 25, 1914
12 August 20, 1921
13 October 11, 1919
14 September 1, 1917
15 December 21, 1912
16 December 8, 1917
17 January 25, 1919
18 March 30, 1917

CHAPTER SIX
1 March 11, 1905
2 October 23, 1915
3 November 10, 1906
4 November 20, 1915
5 April 19, 1919
6 May 22, 1915
7 July 26, 1919
8 April 25, 1914
9 July 29, 1922
10 June 11, 1921
11 January 27, 1917
12 May 8, 1915
13 February 19, 1921
14 February 5, 1921
15 December 12, 1914
16 October 23, 1920
17 May 23, 1914
18 February 5, 1921

CHAPTER SEVEN
1 *Wetaskiwin Breeze*, March 13, 1901
2 *Wetaskiwin Breeze*, January 25, 1900
3 December 7, 1918
4 July 8, 1916
5 June 18, 1910
6 January 28, 1905
7 June 3, 1911
8 November 2, 1912
9 August 8, 1903
10 April 4, 1915
11 July 20, 1918
12 August 23, 1919

CHAPTER EIGHT
1 November 8, 1913
2 June 12, 1915
3 *Summer Annual*, 1923
4 *EO*, April 20, 1918
5 *Summer Annual*, 1921
6 *EO*, August 28, 1915
7 *EO*, August 2, 1913
8 *EO*, October 23, 1920
9 *EO*, January 25, 1919
10 *EO*, June 5, 1920

11 *EO*, April 25, 1914
12 December 20, 1919
13 January 27, 1912
14 August 23, 1919
15 May 11, 1918
16 August 23, 1919
17 November 20, 1915
18 March 30, 1918
19 December 20, 1913
20 March 20, 1915

CHAPTER NINE
1 December 21, 1913
2 December 7, 1913
3 July 30, 1911
4 January 28, 1912
5 March 23, 1912
6 March 15, 1919
7 March 15, 1919
8 March 15, 1919
9 May 5, 1919
10 February 26, 1916
11 May 5, 1917
12 April 4, 1915
13 April 3, 1915
14 April 3, 1915
15 January 6, 1917
16 November 19, 1921
17 July 26, 1919

CHAPTER TEN
1 February 19, 1921
2 September 1, 1920
3 May 22, 1915
4 July 20, 1918
5 August 3, 1912
6 April 8, 1916
7 February 5, 1921
8 May 6, 1916
9 *Summer Annual*, 1923
10 March 14, 1914
11 September 1, 1917
12 March 30, 1917
13 March 14, 1914
14 April 30, 1921
15 March 20, 1915
16 September 22, 1917

17 February 8, 1919
18 May 6, 1916
19 March 14, 1914
20 December 8, 1917
21 May 22, 1915
22 March 20, 1915
23 August 9, 1919
24 April 10, 1920
25 March 30, 1917
26 February 19, 1910
27 October 5, 1916
28 *Summer Annual*, 1922
29 February 19, 1910

LIST OF ILLUSTRATIONS

Unless otherwise noted, images are from the *Eye Opener*, and were scanned from original issues in the MacEwan/Foran collection, or from microfilm in various collections including the Glenbow in Calgary and the McLennan Library at McGill University. Quality may vary accordingly.

p. 4: Glenbow Archives NA-450-1; p. 13: May 2 1908; p. 15; April 21 1906; p. 18: February 19, 1910; p. 22: November 24 1906; p. 23: September 19 1908; p. 26: January 9 1904 (by the way, this appears to be the first cartoon published in the Eye Opener); p. 49: October 15 1910; p. 52: March 9 1907; p. 57: June 27 1914; p. 59: June 5 1920; p. 63: February 13 1904; p. 67: November 22 1919; p. 71: July 1 1913; p. 72: September 27 1913; p. 76: December 6 1913; p. 83: whoops, forgot to write down the date of this one. We had been doing so well, too; p. 91: February 7 1919; p. 92: July 29 1922; p. 95: November 8 1913; p. 111: original Peruna ad nabbed from the internet; p. 122: same issue as image on pages 83; p. 124: October 7 1905; p. 125: December 18 1905; p. 126: February 24 1906; p. 128: October 7 1905; p. 130: June 27 1914; p. 138: November 24 1906; p. 139: May 20 1911; p. 142: November 21 1908; p. 162: September 8 1906; p. 165: December 12 1908; p. 172: March 23 1907; p. 178: September 1 1917; this is awfully dry reading, isn't it? Have a drink; p. 196: June 22 1915; p. 197: March 31 1911; p. 200: February 20 1904; p. 205, 210, 211, 216: June 17 1905; p. 224: July 17 1920; p. 228: January 26 1907; p. 230: July 17 1920; p. 234, 235: February 19 1910; p. 244: May 20 1911; p. 250: February 5 1921; p. 256: June 27 1908. That'll do, dear reader, that'll do.

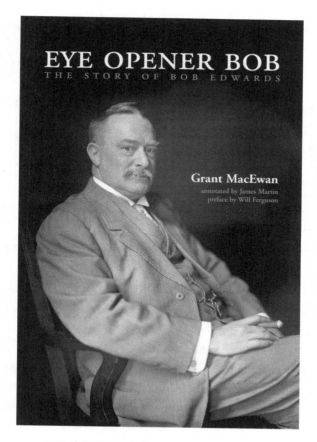

EYE OPENER BOB
THE STORY OF BOB EDWARDS

Grant MacEwan
annotated by James Martin
preface by Will Ferguson

REDISCOVER A CANADIAN ORIGINAL

The man who rewrote the rules of journalism with his bawdy, irreverent turn-of-the-century newspapers comes back to life in this new annotated edition of *Eye Opener Bob*.

In his infamous *Eye Opener*, Robert Chambers "Bob" Edwards skewered corrupt politicians, deflated the pretensions of socialites, created merry havoc with invented news stories, and chronicled—with more than a hint of Fear and Loathing-style manic fatalism—his descent into the maelstrom of alcoholism.

Long out of print, and widely considered to be Grant MacEwan's finest book, *Eye Opener Bob* stands as an entertaining and illuminating portrait of this singular man and his moonshine sketches of the early-twentieth-century Canadian West.

> "[Bob Edwards was] the finest journalist Canada
> has ever had the pleasure of reading"
> —Allan Fotheringham

WWW.BRINDLEANDGLASS.COM

Between 1997 and 2002, J A M E S M A R T I N wrote 283 "Mr. Smutty" columns for *Fast Forward Weekly*, being called everything from a "fine, articulate observer of the social scene" (*Calgary Sun*) to "punctuationally challenged" (again with the *Sun*, but different article). Martin is the co-writer of the moving-picture feature *waydowntown* (2000), and winner of an Alberta Motion Picture Industries Association award for Best Scriptwriter (dramatic) and the Vancouver International Film Festival award for Best Screenplay (Canadian). He is the author of *Calgary: The Unknown City* (2002) and his writing appears in a host of publications, including *enRoute, cinema scope, Saturday Night,* and the *Leg Moustache Advisor*. Martin has been fired from bookstores, scrap-metal yards, and rock'n'roll magazines. He lives in Montréal.